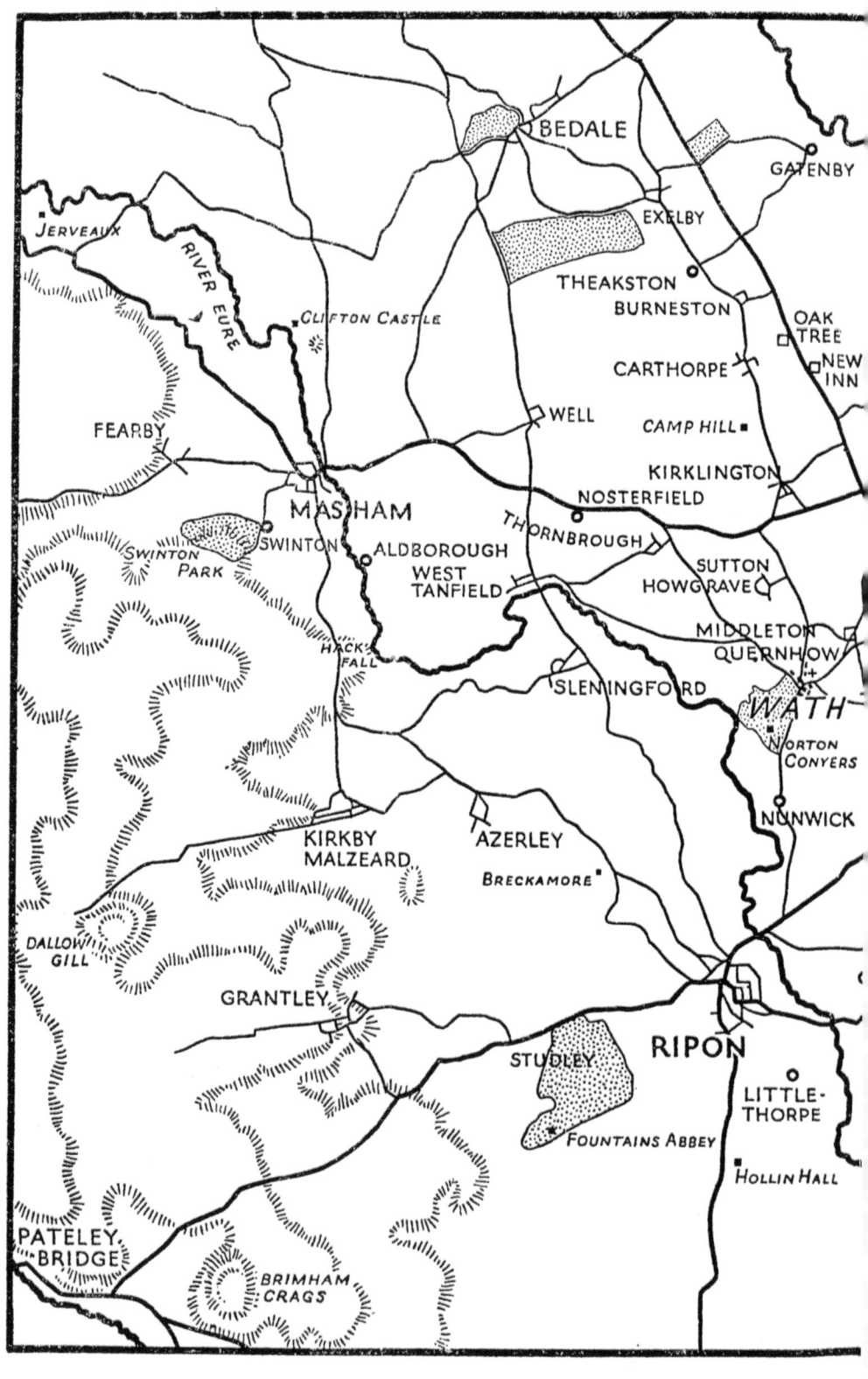

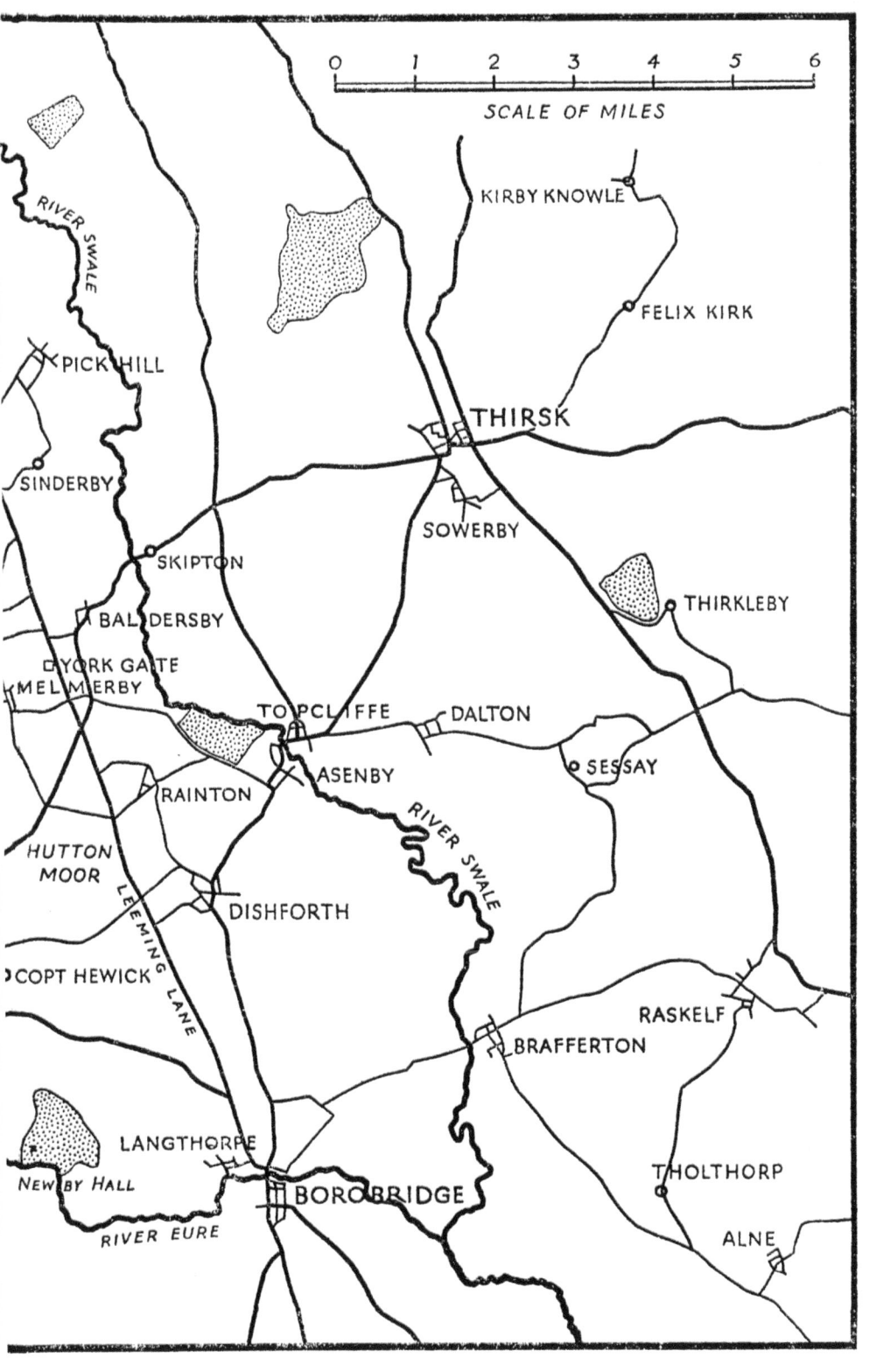

The *Diary* of
BENJAMIN NEWTON

BENJAMIN NEWTON

at the time of his marriage

The *Diary* of
BENJAMIN NEWTON

Rector of Wath

1816–1818

Edited by
C. P. FENDALL
and
E. A. CRUTCHLEY

CAMBRIDGE
AT THE UNIVERSITY PRESS
1933

CAMBRIDGE UNIVERSITY PRESS
Cambridge, New York, Melbourne, Madrid, Cape Town,
Singapore, São Paulo, Delhi, Mexico City

Cambridge University Press
The Edinburgh Building, Cambridge CB2 8RU, UK

Published in the United States of America by Cambridge University Press, New York

www.cambridge.org
Information on this title: www.cambridge.org/9781107683389

First published 1933
First paperback edition 2013

A catalogue record for this publication is available from the British Library

ISBN 978-1-107-68338-9 Paperback

CONTENTS

ILLUSTRATIONS

INTRODUCTION

The Rev. Benjamin Newton's career is briefly described in a manuscript book kept at the Rectory at Wath:

"18 October 1814. Benjamin Newton was instituted at the death of Thomas Brand, on the presentation of Charles Brudenell Bruce, second Earl of Ailesbury of the second creation. Mr Newton, son of the Rev. Benjamin Newton, Vicar of Sandhurst, Glos., was admitted a Pensioner of Jesus College, Cambridge, 17 May 1779. He took his degree of B.A. as tenth senior Optime and junior Chancellor's Medallist in 1783, and was elected a Fellow of his College 17 December 1785, M.A. 1786. His first preferment was the Vicarage of Devynnock, Co. Brecon. He then became Vicar of Little Bedwyn, Co. Wilts, in 1799 and in 1800 of Norton St Philip, Co. Somerset, which two benefices he held together until he was preferred to Wath. He was also Chaplain to the Duke of Portland and a Magistrate for the North Riding of Yorkshire. Mr Newton married 23 April 1788 Mary, daughter of J. Fendall, M.D., of Great Portland Street, by whom he had surviving issue, 1. Mary, married at Wath 14 October 1824 to Charles Loder Stephens, Esq. 2. Anne Frances, married at Wath 16 September 1824 to the Rev. Thomas Commeline: they had a daughter who died young: and with this exception both these ladies died without issue. 3. The Rev. John Farmer Newton, born at Devynnock in 1791, was admitted of Jesus College, Cambridge, 19 October 1807. He married at Little Bedwyn 2 April 1812 Elizabeth, daughter and heir of William Kent, Esq., of that place, by whom (who died in 1850) he has an only son John Fendall Newton, born 6 January 1813, also of Jesus College and married. 4. Caroline Eleanor, married at Wath 10 November 1821 to William Fendall, Esq., now, 1856, a Lt. Col. in the Army and late of the 4th Light Dragoons. They have issue. The Rev. Benjamin Newton had been the early tutor of his patron Lord Ailesbury, when the latter was quite young and thought to be so weak and delicate that he would sink early, as his elder brother had done. Great esteem and friendship subsisted between them down to the time of Mr Newton's death, which event took place at Cheltenham on the 15th of July 1830 at the age of 69. He was buried at St John's Church, Gloucester, in which city he had many friends and relations."[1]

It was during the last period of his career that Newton began a daily record of his activities, filling a succession of note-books with a detailed account of his life and revealing observations on people and events. The village of Wath lies some four miles to the north of Ripon, on the edge of the North Riding of Yorkshire. Here, for sixteen years, Newton combined the duties of Rector with the interests and occupations of a moderately well-to-do country gentleman. He hunted with all the neighbouring packs, he shot over the manors of which he held the deputation of sporting rights and occasionally over the moors of Lord Ailesbury and other friends; he fished, kept greyhounds and went out coursing,

[1] In this account no mention is made of Biddisham, of which Newton held the perpetual curacy. There is also an error in the order of his children: John Newton was born before Anne Frances.

attended the race meetings at Richmond and Catterick, farmed on a considerable scale his glebe and some rented land in addition, bred horses, sat on the County Bench (and was very regular in his attendance), visited and entertained his friends in a constant round of hospitality. On Sundays, as he carefully records, he did duty in the parish church, christening, marrying, visiting, burying, even vaccinating his parishioners as occasion called.

From the pages of his diary a cultured, vivacious, liberal-minded character emerges, full of humour and good nature, punctilious without being pedantic and practically concerned in everybody's interests though he carefully avoided any trace of the busybody. He had a shrewd wit and strong opinions which he conceded to no one. He read much, and in the diary he set out what he found especially interesting in the books of the day, books which are for the most part forgotten now. By his criticisms of their opinions and doctrines, and others of day-to-day occurrences, he clearly shows his attitude to the thought and personalities of his time.

The diary was written when railways were little advanced and there was no telegraph, no cheap postage; though Newton's correspondence does not seem to have been very voluminous his post bill was between thirty and forty pounds a year. The social circle in which a family like his, living in the country at that time, moved was restricted in area to what could be covered with a carriage and pair, and the roads were not too good; and in the social sense to the neighbouring clergy, the country gentlemen living on their estates and some of the professional men of the nearby towns. Periodically the family made tours, as a general rule to the counties of Gloucester, Wilts and Somerset to visit relations and friends.

Laura Commeline, one of Newton's nieces, has left a record of such expeditions. "I remember", she wrote, "that from 1815 to 1830 my maternal uncle who was Rector of one of Lord A's best livings in the North, every second year made a progress to visit his numerous friends in the South and great were the preparations to receive an old family coach and pair of horses, coachman, footman, lady's maid, uncle, aunt and three daughters, who spent a fortnight much to their own contentment and ours. My uncle was a distinguished scholar and a very good preacher. The daughters were clever and well educated, the youngest a good Latin scholar, all gifted with great conversational powers. My aunt was a quiet body and amused herself with making garments, especially babylinen, for the poor, but of material so coarse and stitches so long that my eldest sister was wont to say that if a baby who had worn them died in such a manner as to call for a coroner's inquest, the verdict would surely be 'Mrs Newton's herringbone'."

During the period covered by this volume the three daughters of Mr and Mrs Newton were still unmarried and living at home. Their son John had fallen into financial straits since his marriage some years earlier to Eliza Kent, a wealthy heiress who had taken refuge with the Newtons from an unprincipled step-father. John was still at college when he fell in love with her, eventually outpacing the other suitors for her hand. Their extravagance, however, made serious inroads upon her estate and her trustees intervened to prevent further prodigality. The result was a financial embarrassment which led to an estrangement between Benjamin Newton and his son, happily overcome in time.

Thanks are due to several people for help they have given in the editing of this diary; to the present Rector of Wath for the loan of the pencil sketch of the Rectory and Church; and to Sir Guy Graham of Norton Conyers for permission to reproduce the picture of Sir Bellingham Graham from a painting in his possession.

Benjamin Newton's note-books had descended through his daughter Caroline to his great-grandson Brigadier-General C. P. Fendall, C.B., C.M.G., D.S.O., who first proposed their publication. The task of editing them and correcting proofs was nearly done, when General Fendall died suddenly, and it was left to me to finish the work in which we had been collaborating.

E. A. C.

NEWTON

Names in italics occur in the Diary

Benjamin Newton
Rector of St John's, Gloucester,
and Vicar of Sandhurst, Glos. = Anne Farmer
b. 1718, d. 1787

Mary = *Benjamin Newton*
dau. of John Fendall | Rector of Wath
(see FENDALL) | b. 1762, d. 1830

Anne Farmer = James
Commeline
Vicar of Redmarley

Mary
m. (1824) Charles
Loder Stephens
d. s. p.

*John Farmer
Newton*
b. 1791, m. (1812)
Eliza
dau. of William Kent

Anne Frances
m. (1824) Thomas
Commeline
no surviving
issue

*Caroline
Eleanor*
m. (1821) her cousin,
William Fendall
(see FENDALL)
and had issue

1. *James Commeline*
2. *Anne Rachel (Kit)*
3. *Charlotte*, m. *Rev. J. Chesshyre*
4. *Maria Newton*
5. *Laura Horde*

*John Fendall
Newton*
b. 1813
m. (1848) his cousin, Harriet
Fendall (see FENDALL)

FENDALL

Names in italics occur in the Diary

John Fendall = Sarah Bolder
b. 1729, d. 1793

William Fendall d. 1813
1. Jane Benson
2. *Jane Lydford* = (née Lodge)

John Fendall b. 1793, d. 1862 m. and had a dau. Harriet who m. *John Fendall Newton* (see NEWTON)

Henry Fendall b. 1795 d. 1880 m. and had issue

Mary m. (1819) *Charles Bathurst*

John Fendall = *Mary Farquharson* of Java and Bengal d. 1824

Harriet m. *George Moultrie* Vicar of Cleobury
1. Edward Moultrie
2. *Emily*

Mary m. *Benjamin Newton* (see NEWTON)

John Fendall b. 1792 d. s. p. 1815

William Fendall b. 1793 d. 1888 m. *Caroline Newton* (see NEWTON)

Mary b. 1793 m. Sir John D'Oyley

Harriet b. 1797 m. George Powney Thompson

Louisa b. 1799 m. John Lowis

James Fendall b. 1801 m. thrice

Henry Fendall b. 1802 m. twice

Frances Ann b. 1809 d. unm.

John Fendall of Java and Bengal married secondly Harriet Halcot and by her had two sons, Thomas (b. 1822) and John (b. 1824)

As *I mean this diary to be in some sort a register of my life, studies and opinions and as I have a great respect for that heathen precept, Know thyself, I shall make an attempt to describe myself or in other words to delineate my body and mind. The former (tho' I have spent as little time as most men either in the admiration of it or in cultivating or adorning it) I take to have no particular claim to be thought beautiful but I bless God that it is in general healthy and more active and vigorous than the bodies of persons of my age in general. I think however it requires considerable attention to keep it in order and in health, and that especially without considerable exercise it would soon get unwieldy and consequently inactive and unhealthy. My height is 5 ft 9¾ high, my weight about 12 stone, my complexion dark, my head bald, my eyes hazel, and as they tell me quick and bright, not to say sometimes fierce, my nose trusee, turned up, my mouth wide and my teeth which once were good very much impaired, my chin round, my neck rather short, my arms and legs rather slender, my gait upright, my body slightly inclined to corpulency, my health good, my sleep generally divided into two naps, the first of five hours the second of two. The only bodily inconvenience I labour under is a great tendency to flatulency which sometimes disorders my whole system for a time but is generally of short duration. My mind is generally actively tho' often I fear not profitably employed. I am naturally very irritable*

but I trust I have in a considerable degree subdued that propensity. My vanity is considerable and I am ashamed of not having made the same conquest of my vanity that I have of my anger. I have in general good spirits which are seldom depressed except from a sense of my own sins. I have been singularly fortunate and happy thro' life and I think it a duty I owe to God to bear all the little inconveniences I meet with in patience and gratitude. I have considerable power of application but am nevertheless desultory in my employments. I go shooting for health and hunting for society which I like to meet better in the field than at any dinner where I must drink more wine than I like. Of all luxuries I delight most in tea. My appetite is so good I have few predelictions. I prefer venison and mutton to all other meat. I like reading, am a great enemy to Tyranny, and greater still to Anarchy. Pitt was too monarchical and Fox too democratical especially during the French Revolution and the Irish Rebellion. My opinion of the Regent I cannot express, his ministers are wicked in nourishing his extravagance. My inclination often leads me to be sarcastic and I am sometimes thought to say a witty thing tho' I did not intend it. I fear I feel too much pleasure in epigram and satyr for a Christian and a Clergyman. I salve my conscience by a conviction that I have no malice. I hate nothing but affectation except outright villainy and sin. I trust I am sufficiently indulgent to my family and servants and too much so to my dogs. I am still charmed with female beauty but rather fastidious in my taste. I am naturally shy but have conquered my shyness by great effort from seeing very early the disadvantage of it. I am not a great talker except I think it civil to join or lead the conversation, and I think I can acquit myself of having ever started a subject with the idea of shewing myself off though a sudden impulse often makes me shoot a bolt. I seldom or ever tell stories, even short ones. My friends seem fond of my society, rate me much too high. I have studied much to find out my own fort. I think it is a sort of power of eliciting fun and wit from the conversation of others rather than from anything of my own 'exers ipse secundo'. My religious opinions I display at least once a week to my parishioners and therefore have no occasion to record them here. I dread controversy which makes shipwreck of charity and I see no good in publishing my opinions which are not articles of the Apostles' Creed. As for Bible Societies, Christian Knowledge Societies etc, I think it better to pray for one fold under one shepherd leaving the time and the means to the good Shepherd himself to accomplish.

July 12th.   Lansdown Grove, Bath. In the house Mrs Wilmot, Mr Blomfield, Mrs Newton, Mary and myself. Settled accounts of Biddisham[1] till Christmas last. Called at Tugwell's, Mrs Wheeler's, Parfitt told story of Williams my Philip's Norton successor borrowing gig, paying his own horse penny at turnpike and left remainder to be paid by owner of gig. Mr Keate at dinner, went with him, Mr Blomfield, Mrs Newton, Mary and Anne to see Kean in Sir G. Overreach and Abel Drugger; much delighted.

13th.   Mrs Wilmot told me she would leave me the reversion of an estate at Desford in Leicestershire to which she believed herself entitled after the deaths of Mr and Mrs Radcliffe by the will of Mr Ward, the father of Mrs R, who left it to Mrs R for her life, after to Mr R for his life, and in case of

---

[1] Newton held the perpetual curacy of Biddisham, a small village in Somersetshire.

their dying without issue to Mrs W, who believes the estate to be worth £3 or 400 per ann.[1] Parfitt promised to remit produce of Biddisham annually in January. Lord Erskine on having a case sent him involving points of Common and Chancery Law about a week before he was made Chancellor answered the points of Common Law but added, "Of the Chancery Law I know nothing". Heard Emily Moultrie[2] was in love with Mr G and caused her illness and it was suggested that her father wished her to attract the notice of Mr G's pupil.

14th.   Went to Church, heard a sermon on the Death of the Righteous. Received an offer from Mr Thacklethwaite offering £2900 for 69 acres, the timber amounting to at least £800. Answered it by a refusal. Mrs Wilmot carried Miss Linwood to Corsham to see the picture of our Saviour and the Sacramental Elements. She worked the one at Burleigh and pronounced the Corsham one to be a repeated picture and not a copy, as there was such a deviation in many points that no copyist would have ventured upon. For Miss L's worked picture the Russian Ambassador offered £2000 and increased to £7000 for the Empress Catherine and Mrs W heard Miss L refuse and declare she never would sell any capital piece of her work. Mrs W first suggested the work to Miss L who sitting by Mrs W etching was told by her she might work with greater effect with a needle.

15th.   Left L. Grove with great regret and increased attachment to my dear Mrs W. Arrived at Easton Grey, found Mr and Mrs Smith in high health and spirits, Smith having

---

[1] Mrs Wilmot and Mrs Radcliffe were second cousins to Newton.
[2] Daughter of Mrs Newton's sister, Harriet Moultrie. See p. xiii.

received a letter from Mr Hobhouse[1] with an account of Princess of Wales having been brought to bed of a fine boy in the harem of the Dey of Tunis. Mr Binda, an Italian, with Mr Warburton who acts his travelling mentor, both belonging to Lady Holley's[2] coterie. Binda young sensible well-informed, speaking English. Warburton very sensible but as yet *n'a pas grands attraits pour moi*.

16th.   Mr Warburton says Zabzeiger cheese is made by putting in the entire plant and a very great quantity of salt.

17th.   Went at 6 to breakfast at Eastington, met Mr Austin, went to meet the Bullo Pill Co.[3] Mr Cambridge and Mr Watson not arriving owing to the illness of the latter, the meeting was adjourned till tomorrow. Dined at L. Dean with Mr Kempson who seemed depressed.

18th.   Met Mr Watson, Mr Cambridge, Mr Philpotts, Mr Thompson, J. Fendall,[4] Sir J. Jelf and Mr Js Jones. All business went on with good humour and the accounts taken into consideration, some preliminary byelaws made to which the Company seal was affixed, it was determined to adjourn till Monday to receive the report of Mr Woodhouse, a person sent for out of Derbyshire to inspect the colliery and give his advice as to the best mode of opening the High Delf and the management of the colliery. It appears Sir J. Jelf has done

---

[1] John Cam Hobhouse, afterwards Lord Broughton, a Whig politician and friend of Byron.

[2] Lady Holland, the hostess of Holland House.

[3] The Bullo Pill Company owned a coal-mine and small railway in the Forest of Dean. The Fendall family had an interest in it and Newton acted for his brother-in-law, John Fendall, while the latter was abroad.

[4] John Fendall the younger, son of Newton's brother-in-law, William Fendall, who had died in 1813. See p. xiii. John Fendall was a frequent visitor to Wath.

some good in lowering the tonnage 3d per ton and also the royalty on the Belson colliery. Set out with J. F. for E. Grey at 4 o'clock and arrived at ½ past 7, the mare having reared and fallen backwards at Hunter's Hill on attempting to harness her for the gig. Played a drawn game and won one at chess of Mr Binda. Had nothing to eat from 8 to 8. Heard that Sir J. J. had been so mobbed at Blakeney as to be obliged to leave his house and hire another,[1] that H. Fendall[2] was engaged to Thompson's son and L. Fendall refused an offer previous to her arrival at Java, that Js Fendall is to be bred a lawyer and sent to College, that the Governor of Java's state is equal to that of Governor of Bengal. Mr Warburton had left E. Grey.

19th. Mr Howes, Mr Wheeler and Miss George dined here, played chess, Italian literature, music. Began a letter to J. F. at Java.

20th. A letter from Hattersley about Methodist meeting at Melmerby.[3]

21st. A most tremendous storm in the last night of thunder and lightening. An express sent from Newnham by Archdeacon Cambridge to require my attendance Monday at their meeting. Received a letter yesterday from a man named William Warren telling me he could procure me some money if I would pay him a percentage on it, one from J. F. N.[4]

---

[1] A bank with which Sir James Jelf was associated had failed.

[2] Harriet, Louisa and James, children of the elder John Fendall. See p. xiii. John Fendall was at this time in Java, where he was the last British Governor. He was transferred to Bengal, as a member of the Supreme Council, in 1817.

[3] Melmerby, with Norton, Middleton and Wath, formed one parish. The Rev. Thomas Hattersley had been master of the school at Wath since 1774.   [4] Newton's son. See p. xii.

announcing his intention of going into Devon for the winter with Eliza. Dined at Mr Paul's with H. Hickes. Wrote to Joshua,[1] William Warren, Henry[2] and J. F. N.

22nd.   70 lb of eels caught last night at the mill. Wrote to Ward enclosing a draft for £66 for Mr Wentworth, to Lord Ailesbury,[3] to J. F. at Java. Went to Badminton, pictures 2 Claudes, indifferent, St John Guido, Virgin, Jesus and St John Julio Romano, Old men and infant Rubens, the three best, several Salvator, Guido, Holbein. A very good Vandyke, a beautiful Mosaic Cabinet, a sarcophagus of white marble *alto relievo*, a cartoon being the bottom of Raphael's Transfiguration is in the Chapel in a very bad light, much mutilated. Susanna and Elders by Domiessichino. There are pictures said to be by Raphael in the drawing room. Portrait of Salvator Rosa by himself, Annibal Carrachi by himself, Guido by himself, Erasmus, Sir T. Mar. Portraits of the house of Somerset in the males from John of Gaunt to the present Duke, 5th Duke of Beaufort. A fine whole length of Lord Granville, the present Duchess's brother, by Lawrence, the Duchess Dowager by Sir J. Reynolds. Many landscapes and hunting pieces by Wotton. Mr Binda a great bibliosophist, especially in Italian printed books; he beat me at chess but by no means to convince me he is my superior having twice given back his queen and lost the last game by an oversight. J. Fendall returned this morning to Little Dean.

[1] Joshua Hutchinson, Newton's broker and man of business in London.

[2] Henry Fendall, younger son of William. See p. xiii.

[3] The Earl (afterwards Marquis) of Ailesbury, patron of the living of Wath. See Introduction.

23rd. When Napoleon landed from Elba Jerome was at
Trieste, Talleyrand proposed that every member of the
Buonaparte family that could be laid hold on should be
arrested. Winzengende the Wurtemberg minister sent to
apprize Jerome, who got into a boat in which he was used
to sail backwards and forwards to a country house he had in
Istria with four or five boatmen and sailed for the Kingdom
of Naples but being overtaken by a storm was obliged to put
back and the Austrian Government having given orders for
his arrest a party of twelve were sent, whom he beat back
with his crew, seized their provisions which he was in great
want of, set sail again, arrived in the Bay of Naples with most
of his money and his portfolio but no cloths and the vessel
being obliged to perform quarantine Mr Binda was dispatched
by Murat to bring him on shore. He had only the cloths on
his back and Binda supplied him with cloths to come on
shore out of his portmanteau. Jerome remained 25 days in
Naples and then escaping the English cruisers arrived in
France. Binda spoke highly of his courage and added it was
a delightful life when every two hours produced some new
catastrophe. A letter from Howard, beat Mr Binda at chess
two games on the balance. The Pauls at dinner. The Morning
Chronicle says the troops are to be withdrawn from France.
Mr Wyatt dined here.

24th. Letters from H. and L. Fendall, J. Fendall with an
account of the Bullo Pill and the necessity of £3000 more
money to complete, from Mr Warren saying 5 dividends on
5 per cents are due to me from 1809. Called at Shipton, at
Mr Wheeler's, after the utmost difficulty to make the horse
proceed who lay down in the road and was loosened and put

in again and made to go at last. Dr Baron arrived. L. Fendall says they are in great dread of losing their situation at Java which they much prefer to Calcutta. Binda beat me one game and two after dinner. Binda gave us a satyrical character of the Duke of Wellington said to be written by B. Constant, " Un héros froid et médiocre que la nature a fait pour montrer que la science militaire peut exister sans autre talent et l'intégrité pécuniaire sans autre vertu". I am quite sick of Hobhouse's book, his abuse of the Bourbons is not worth answering; if it were true its unaltered violence defeats its own malignity. The publication of the Bodleian and Ashmolean letters are very amusing in three volumes.

25th. The following written by Dr Worthington appeared in the Morning Chronicle.

> Epistle from Tom Cribb to Big Ben concerning some
> foul play in a late transaction.[1]
>
> What, Ben, my big hero! Is this thy renown?
> Is this the new go? Kick a man when he's down!
> When the foe has knocked under to tread on him then!
> By the fist of my father I blush for thee, Ben.
> "Foul! Foul!" all the lads of the fancy exclaim,
> Charley Shock is electrified, Belcher spits flame
> And Molyneux, ay even Blackey, cries "Shame!"
> Time was when John Bull little difference spied
> 'Twixt the foe at his feet and the friend at his side,
> When he found such his humour in fighting and eating
> The foe, like his beefsteak, the sweeter for beating.
> But this comes, Master Ben, of your cursed foreign notions,
> Your trinkets, wigs, thingumbobs, gold lace and lotions,
> Your Noyaus, Curacoas and the Devil knows what.
> One swig of Blue Ruin is worth the whole lot.

[1] Tom Cribb and Big Ben, and the other men named in the poem were well-known prize-fighters.

Your great and small crosses, my eyes, what a brood!
A cross buttock from me would do them some good.
Which have spoilt you till hardly a drop, my old porpoise,
Of pure English claret is left in your corpus,
And, as Jim says, the only one trick good or bad
Of the fancy you're up to is Fibbing, my lad.
Hence it comes, Boxiana, disgrace to thy page,
Having floored by good luck the first swell of your age,
Having conquered the Prime one that milled us all round,
You kick him, old Ben, as he gasped on the ground,
Ay, just at the time to show spunk if you had any,
You kicked him and jawed him and lag'd him to Botany.
Oh Shade of the Cheesemonger, you who, alas,
Doubled up by the dozens those Mounseers in brass
On that great day of milling when blood lay in lakes,
When Kings held the bottle and Europe the stakes,
Look down upon Ben, see him dunghill all o'er
Insult the fall'n foe that can harm him no more.
Out, cowardly, spoony, again and again,
By the fist of my father I blush for thee, Ben.
To show the white feather is many men's doom
But what of one feather? Ben shews a whole plume.

N.B. *Blue Ruin*. Gin.

Cheesemonger. Shaw the Life Guardsman, one of
the fancy killed after distinguishing himself in the late set-to.[1]

Mr and Mrs Ricardo[2] called here. Discussion on the moral
right of deception in some cases. Mr Ricardo's opinion that
the depression and commercial difficulties are only temporary.
A letter from J. F. N. announced his setting out this day for
Sidmouth on account of his wife's health, there to winter,

[1] Waterloo, where Shaw's courageous behaviour drew a panegyric
from Sir Walter Scott.
[2] David Ricardo, the economist.

offers his gig and harness for £20. Called at Mr Paul's and Mr Wheeler's who came here.

27th.   Went fishing to Estcourt. A letter from Joshua saying the dividends due and unclaimed amount to £103. £3 was given to the clerk who helped Joshua to it. Mr and Mrs Ricardo and son and daughter, Mr and Mr S. Paul, Mr Filkin, Mr E. Estcourt at dinner.

28th.   Letter from Mrs Fendall saying £2000 more would be required for the Bullo Pill. Preached at E. Grey.

29th.   Drove to Malmsbury, saw the Abbey.

30th.   Left Easton Grey, arrived at Gloucester where we saw the Duke of Wellington arrive to receive the freedom of the City. Dined at Mrs Pitt's on turtle, Champagne, Barsac, etc, with Mr and Mrs Goodrich, Mr and Mrs Phelps, Mr T. Davies, all the Commelines[1] and came to Redmarley at night. Saw Duke of Beaufort, Sir W. Guise, S. Commeline, P. Jones, Mrs Chandler, Capt Drummond, J. and W. Fendall, Mr Hyett, two Hickes's, Mr Hallifax, Mr Clifton. Found Maria much grown, Laura looking very thin, Kit as usual, Jim very well, Mrs C very fat, Commeline as he was. Very fine crops of wheat, clover, Swedish turnips on C's farm. Wrote to Ward and Howard, to the first about Fulmer,[2] to the last about estate in Leicestershire and arresting Wm Miller at Biddisham. A very fine haymaking day, being the first this month.

[1] Newton's sister had named the Rev. James Commeline, Vicar of Redmarley, Worcs. See p. xii. S. Commeline was his brother, Samuel.

[2] Newton's son, John, had taken a house at Fulmer, Bucks, soon after his marriage (see Introduction, p. x). The establishment ran him into debt and he was obliged to give it up.

August 1st. Mr Biscoe, Mr P. Jones at dinner. The Duke went in the Bishop's carriage to drink tea and returned to Cheltenham.

2nd. Drew Commeline's pond, at least 100 carp and tench at a draft. Drove out near Ledbury. Mr Hill and Brown Jones at dinner. Mr and Mrs Chesshyre came in the evening.

3rd. Drove out to Ledbury with Commeline, Anne, C, and M. N. junior.[1] Horses went worse than ever I knew them. Having read Kitt's Flowers of Wit I pronounce them to be mere daisies. Everywhere there are anachronisms and tales so silly that it is surprising a man of any literary repute would set his name to them.

4th. Went a party of twelve to Malvern and drank tea at Mr Biscoe's at Underdown. Met Tomesson on the road.

6th. Ledbury Fair. Mr Ferret, Mr Kearney, Mr Jenkins, Turberville, J. C. junior came from cricket. Anne C refused to teach Laura anything. In consequence of A. C.'s refusing to teach Laura any longer because her mother took her to church I wrote the following, as the child is considerably advanced in arithmetic.

A SONG FOR LAURA

I'm the poor child that was taken to church
And then by my governess left in the lurch.
I'm the poor child that, when taught to read,
Am forbidden to look at the Lord's Prayer or Creed.
I'm the poor child too that, tho' taught to add,
Am forbidden to learn what's good from what's bad.
I'm the poor child that, tho' taught to subtract,
To God or to Man must not learn how to act.

[1] Anne Frances, Caroline Eleanor and Mary, Newton's three daughters.

In division I've had too a practical lecture
And Kitty's queer practice exceeds all conjecture,
And I really am fearful lest Kit's rule of three
Should sever herself from my mother and me.
To catechize children the whole world's now taught
But all men's opinions to Kitty are naught.
Her mode of instruction's a glorious plan
To keep me an atheist as long as she can,
And she thinks that I shan't care a pin for a rod
When I hear there exists such a being as God.

7th. To Little Dean, found Mrs F, J and H and Jas and Henry and Fan.[1] Went to Newnham, bought J. F.'s horse. Recommended J. F. to write to Mr Watson to say that he could not go on with the payments and as a *dernier resort* to give up his share of the lease to Mr Cambridge. N.B. Mr Chesshyre read the service very well last Sunday.

8th. Mr and Mrs Pyrke dined here. Mr P said the father of a soldier consulted him how to get his son's pay who was dead and on Mr P's asking him whether his son died or was killed in action the man said he had forgotten whether in the last letter he had from his son he had said that he died or was killed in action. We found H. and Jas Fendall so much grown that I did not know Henry. The Bishop of Gloucester in his sermon last Sunday on the Sabbath asked the audience if they never had taken a walk with an agreeable associate. Have you, he continued, never written a letter on Sunday? Have you never made any temporal provision for the morrow? J. Commeline told me that without any notice to Mr Jones

---

[1] Mrs Fendall, widow of William Fendall, and her two sons, John and Henry. James, Henry and Fan (Frances Ann) were the younger children of John Fendall of Java, who remained in England during their parents' absence abroad.

who had been Chaplain to the Gloucester Infirmary for upwards of 20 years the Bishop as President discharged him by
merely leaving word at the Infirmary that in future the
Chaplain's office at that hospital would be executed by his
own Chaplain. Mr Kempthorne Drinkwater the horse doctor,
a very large man, being sent for in his business to Hay Hill
and it growing late, Mr E. Jones told him the house was so
full that he could not by any means give him a bed, on which
Drinkwater said he was not particular and did not mind
having a bedfellow, telling him he should not mind sleeping
with him, which Mr E. Jones refusing D said he need not hold
his head so high, for the last man he slept with and that not
so many nights ago was a much greater man than he was, for
he had slept with the Duke of Norfolk at Horn.

10th.   Went to Gloucester, dined Hempstead and returned
to Redmarley. At Hempstead all the Commelines and Mrs
Pitt. Paid J. Fendall for Brawn, John Newton's gig arrived
and I returned in it from Gloucester to Redmarley. Lord
Henry Kerr arrived at Little Dean Wednesday. Mrs Commeline would not make her appearance though she had not
seen Mr and Mrs Chesshyre since their marriage. Bought a
little mare of J. Fendall for J. N.'s gig, brought us here very
well. Received a draft from Deighton[1] at Cambridge for
£6. 1. 0. for my Cambridge list at two months, tho' he had
the books ever since 1808.

12th.   Went to the Boyce, heard someone had stolen a
miniature of Mrs Drummond out of the drawing room, suspect she knew the thief.

[1] A bookshop, now Deighton, Bell and Co.

13th. Went to Ledbury to the Upper Hall; saw the pictures, Jupiter and Leda, a girl by Rembrandt, a Venus by Rubens, Titian's Last Supper, from thence to Hope End, saw a most beautiful woman Mrs Butler, sister to Mrs Barret, I put her down about No 4 for face and about No 2 for shape. Mrs Hallard is the next pretty woman I have seen since I left home. The house at Hope End very eccentric, the furniture most costly. An Irishman who belonged to the 3rd or 4th Dragoons was condemned about three years since at Gloucester for robbing the landlord of the Crown on the lawn and afterwards firing at him. As soon as he was condemned he applied to his Captain, then in Court, and hoped they would give him his pay and discharge. Chesshyre the most unceasing flirter I ever beheld but very polite and attentive to all the girls.

16th. Left Redmarley for Hereford, the road but indifferent. For about five miles between Ledbury and the Hay road was at least half unstoned, on account of Shent's restiveness the last six miles did not reach Hay till near 9, the road the most beautiful that can be imagined approaching to the grand. The church at Hay so dark that I should think it impossible to have read the service this day. The view of the Wye and the bridge and the railway very delightful. From the round hill close to the Swan and the deep excavation down to the Wye I have little doubt that the present site of the Hay church is an old British fortification and that the pathway to the church from the town was the way to a drawbridge. Had a terrible journey owing to the restiveness of the horse to Aberconlais where we found all our friends well and the Canon returned from Brecon having sold his wheat for £1 per bushel and told us that barley brought nine shillings. We found he had 700 acre of land in his hand. Reech at Penpont saw a laburnum one limb of which was in full bloom. Saw Mr and Mrs Yeats and Mr and Mrs Williams at Chapel, all very near stationary. N.B. Scarce any appearance of alteration in Miss W and Miss S of Aberconlais tho' it is ten years since I saw them. The girls extremely delighted with the country all the way from Hay. Meat about 6½d per lb here, lime 12/- for 30 b's at the pit. Coal 12/- per ton at Brecon, oats 4/9 10 gallons. The bannisters of this house are made of box. The two heads of these families are exactly Pompey and Caesar.

22nd.   At Major Price's Mr and Mrs Griffith, Mr and Mrs Rynd and the Aberconlais party. J. Meredith, Mrs T. Bold called at Penpont and went to Devynnock. D. Morgan's complaint of the Archdeacon was that he had sold his father's stock out at 60. Morgan Morgans wanted to see me about mortgage. Archdeacon Davies still lying in bed reading novels. All his relations agree that he is better in bed for that when he is up he does so many extravagant things that he will certainly ruin himself. In the case of North the wag-goner's bankruptcy he went to London to make North an honest man and afterwards called him a great scoundrel, yet desired that the bank at Brecon would pay North's notes and place them to his credit, supposed this frolic will cost him five hundred pounds.

23rd.   Mr and Mrs Rynd, Rainal Davies and Rob Wynter at dinner. R. D. intimate with Mrs Ed Carter of Theakston, talked incessantly about Lords and Ladies and never said anything. R. Wynter a little like his father. Went to Devyn-nock, called on Mr and Mrs Williams the curate, saw Miss

Morgan all dirt and rags. N.B. Never saw the poorest parishioner of Wath half so untidy tho' she is very handsome and has £6000, about 21 years of age. If an instance was wanting to shew how very little advantage money is unless properly directed it is impossible to adduce a stronger than that of Phil Morgan's family, all of them make beasts of themselves with the £40,000 he left behind him, some by drink and the rest by dirt. The whole of this week it has rained more or less, tho' I apprehend the rain has only extended to the parts under the influence of the Welsh mountains and that the damp sort of weather has been preparatory to dry weather of some considerable continuance.

24th.   This day begins the first of sunshine.

25th.   Sunshine continues. Dined yesterday at Penpont with Bolds and the Prices. Young Hugh Bold is very amusing, he is exactly the size that is proper for a coxcomb. I never saw a very short person of the male sex that was not one. I rather think that tall women are more given to vanity than short ones, they think height gives them a sort of commanding superiority. This day all the discussions and conversation was on points and topics that no one understood and of course the debate was unusually warm. Mrs Wms of Penpont looks quite as young as when she was married and not at all too old for her husband. Davies continues abed and won't see me. Mr Pendrell, Mr Rd Williams and Mr Frederick Williams dined at Aberconlais and Mrs Williams, curate's wife of Devynnock. Preached at Penpont. Heard D. Lewis having had a dispute with his wife about sowing a field he had prepared for turnips, she insisting on its being sown with wheat and he with turnips, she put the turnip seed

in the oven and baked it and then enjoyed his disappointment
when he had sowed the seed and none of it came up. Having
waited for a day or two for £40 which I had desired Joshua
to send me I am again disappointed today (28th) at not receiving it.

26th.   The Bolds and Griffiths dined here. Mrs Bold not of
the party having been terribly alarmed by a drunken driver
returning from Penpont Saturday night. In going down
the hill about two miles from Brecon the driver nearly ran
the carriage over a precipice and pulling up very abruptly
the pole of Major Price's carriage which was following close
struck the sword case of Bold's carriage and drove it in so
violently as to send the door of the sword case with such
violence against Mrs Bold and her son as to send their heads
through the window, the glass of which luckily was down.
The Griffiths slept at Aberconlais and we dined there yesterday with the Prices and the Rynds and afterwards went to
a ball kicked up by the Canon for our girls and mustered
about nine couple. Danced with great glee till one and got
home to Aberconlais at two.

28th.   Went in the morning to Pennoyre which consists of
a very handsome ground floor of four rooms, one of which
has a circular end and another is a complete circle. The
situation is by far the finest I have seen in Breconshire, having
the fine feature of Vennyfach wood in the foreground and
the Van as the distance. The palky plantations about eight
yards square and the excessive slovenliness of all the lands
from the lodge to the house injure the beautiful effect which
the situation naturally possesses in a very great degree. Mrs W
and her daughters were very polite, the second handsome in

person but not beautiful to the degree in which the Breconians estimate her. Saw Sir C. Morgan at Davies's, looks well and acknowledged me as his old acquaintance. Dined at Bold's. I have kept off melancholy reflections since I entered the Principality but it is impossible not to be in some degree affected with the recollection that there is not a single gentleman's house in the town or county of Brecon inhabited by the same master as when I came into the county and very few have not changed their owners since I left it. Bullock, Lloyds, Walter Jeffreys, Williams, Wilkens, Mr Griffith, Wm Wynter, Tho Williams, John Powell, Pennoyre Watkins, Tho Jones, Canon Davies, Robert Williams, William Morgan, Harry Davies, Mrs Hughes, John Wilkins, T. Williams of Aberbran, Hugh Jones, Robert Wynter, old Mr Wynter, Mr Gunter, Mr Prichard, Mr James, Aberconlais, Penpont, Llangoed, the Lodge, Dwyncynten, Skethiog, Llangattock, Dany Gray, Buckland and Williams of Wheatsheet form the only exceptions, unless you add Mr Meredith. Many or most of those who are gone as young or younger than myself. Mrs T. Bold is sister to Mrs T. Parfitt in Somersetshire. Major Price got drunk as usual. B. Griffith gave Hock and Bold Barsac, Penry Williams Sauterne. A letter from John F. N. to Anne saying his wife is much improved.

30th. Left our good friends and Mr Rob Williams at Aberconlais. We breakfasted with Major Price and had a very gay set out. I changed my note and set out with post horses to the Hay. Received an angry letter from Mr Western and one from Mr Ward and two letters from India. Arrived at 1 at the Hay and set out again for Leominster thro' a most beautiful country and a much better road than I expected.

Leominster partly very old, particularly near the Market Place, which is a fine antique. The turnpikes amounted to more than 2d a mile for the carriage and 1d for the gig. Shent performed capitally. N.B. In the 43 miles from Aberconlais to Leominster we met no carriage or a single horse till we met the people returning from Leominster market. Saw wheat cut about half way between Brecon and the Hay and one field between Hay and Leominster. All the wheat had the appearance of being more or less blighted. Set out from Leominster after having seen the Church, the original windows of which are very handsome but two have been repaired and have spoiled the appearance of the Church on the outside by not being repaired on the plan of the old ones, the fret work and rustic being omitted. Nothing in these days can exceed the hilliness of the road from Tenbury to Cleobury or the badness of it from Leominster for the first six miles towards Tenbury, the country was so beautiful as to force itself upon our observation tho' we had just left Wales and it rained hard the whole way. Tenbury is a very neat town and not badly represented in miniature by Wath.

September 1st. Preached and administered the Sacrament and read Evening Prayer at Cleobury, G. M.[1] having an attack of asthma, saw the whole family of Compsons, wrote to Mrs Wilmot, for whom I got Fox to draw up the form of a codicil that she might leave me the reversionary interest she has in an estate at Houghton Leicestershire after Mr and Mrs Radcliffe. Received a letter from J. Fendall consulting me on the propriety of his quitting Cambridge, also from Joshua telling me he sent a Bank Post Bill for £40 on the 21st ult. An

---

[1] The Rev. George Moultrie, Vicar of Cleobury Mortimer, Shropshire, Mrs Newton's brother-in-law. See note on p. 4.

entertaining German dined here who teaches the girls music and plays delightfully and sings well with no voice having been shot through the lung. A Mr Causer having been bit in a drunken frolic by a man of the name of Shipley in the leg last week is obliged to suffer amputation. During an armistice in which the Prussian and French officers were drinking together a son of Blucher gave for a toast the King of Prussia, which a French officer would not drink and soon after when it came to his turn gave Buonaparte which young Blucher would not drink, on which the officer went up to him and without saying anything struck him a smash in the face. Blucher said nothing but went out of the room and returned immediately with a pair of pistols, with one of which without uttering a word he shot the officer dead and then held up the other and said he had that ready for any man who would take up the quarrel. This came to his father's knowledge, who put him under arrest for six weeks. Rode to Bewdley, no corn cut. Write to J. Fendall and received letters from Ward and his son. N.B. Dinner eaten entirely up.

5th. The Botfields at dinner and Rev Wood, who told a story of the Shropshire roads very much in point, of a person who saw a hat lying in the road and on taking it up he saw a head under it which opened his mouth and begged to be drawn out of the slough which was at length effected and the man said he had a horse under him which he would have been obliged to abandon had he not the spur stuck in the long tail and gave him an opportunity of laying hold of a few hairs. Waggoners are sometimes rescued when there is nothing to be seen but the lash of his long whip.

6th. Rode to Hopton where we are to dine. Mr Wood
married a neice of Sir W. Pulteney and has all the deputations
of Lord Darlington's manors in Salop. N.B. does not think
meanly of himself. Invited me to dine and visit the Brown
Clee hill. Called on the Compsons. Dined at Mr Botfield's
at Hopton, met Mr Child, Mr and Mrs W. Child and Lady
Blount. Mr B the best specimen of a man risen to great
opulence from his own industry. His house very magnificent,
Mrs B very obliging. N.B. The road to Ludlow is to be
made entirely of the Clee hill blue stone called by the people
Jew's stone from the supposed hardness of a Jew's heart. Two
very magnificent pillars of Clee hill marble, each of one piece,
in the dining room and a most magnificent specimen of
jasper, red and white, in the drawing room, bought at Lord
Oxford's sale. Mr B gave me two snuff boxes, specimens of
Kentsill coal. Survey'd the Clee hill with Mr Botfield. The
field of coal very small. The top of the hill all basalt to the
depth of 60 yards, then fine micaccius sandstone, then coarse
sandstone full of impressions of vegetables, then schist, the
coal at the greatest depth 140 yards. Cheaper to wind up
than to bring out through the level. Mr Moultrie left Cleobury for Aston. No tidings of my £40. Saw Mr Thomas
of Hopton who went with Mr Moultrie. M. N. junior had a
letter from M. Fendall from St Asaph saying the Bishop of
Norwich and his three daughters, who are accomplished
misses, had been at St Asaph but sent John Luxmoore out
of the room that they might tell dirty stories. I can not leave
this place without noting a thing which I despair of gaining
credit for except with persons well acquainted with the
neighbourhood and that is a gentleman upwards of 60 with
a fortune of near £2000 per ann., who has a family of seven

children all grown up, who is a grandfather, has been seen standing at his door for more than six hours a day for the last fifteen years for the sole purpose of gazing at a house nearly 200 yards from his own which contains a farmer's wife who now and then indulges him by appearing at her window. N.B. The gentleman's wife is still living with him and was one of the handsomest women in the county.

8th. G. M. went to Hopton and I did the duty at Cleobury. Saw horsemanship last night in a field by a troop from Astley's. Agriculture seems to have made no progress in these parts for the last 25 years. Turnips badly managed, all too late sown and left too thick, i.e. from the Hay to Kinlet.

9th. Rained all day so as to prevent Anne and me from setting out, tho' we sent John[1] to Bridgenorth with two of the horses.

10th. Left Cleobury with Anne for Bridgenorth, found the road remarkably hilly but not so bad as the Bewdley road. Had no tidings of my £40 before I left Cleobury. Went from Bridgenorth to the Iron Bridge and Coalbrook Dale, disappointed rather at the view of the Iron Bridge as the prints I had seen of it exaggerated the appearance of the span. The Severn is extremely rapid there and Coalbrook Dale and its smoke and cottages spread on the perpendicular banks in all directions has a very pleasing and romantic effect. Arrived at Shifnal and dined at the Star, a very clean inn, and proceeded to Newport where we found the inn, the Red Lion, very comfortable; supped, drank tea and set out for Eccleshall this morning (12th), found the road very tolerable, breakfasted at an indifferent inn, the best in the place, though

---

[1] John Waters, Newton's coachman.

the approach is through the butchers' shambles which are
kept under the principal rooms, which are supported on
arches. The Church here is particular handsome. The road
all the way from Coalbrook Dale seemed made of the same
materials, gravel or sandstone, and from Eccleshall made of
gravel and larger pebbles of granite, serpentine, etc, got from
the hills to the East. I picked up specimens of jasper. Proceeded by Stone to Newcastle through the magnificent and
princely domain of the Marquis of Stafford. The wood on
the hill to the west of the house the most magnificent and
rich I ever saw. The immense extent is grand beyond anything I ever saw and the verdure and fertility of the land
was highly gratifying. I forgot to mention that soon after
we left Newport we saw the finest piece of water I have ever
seen in England before Aqualate Hall. The town of Newport
very good, Eccleshall middling, Stone pretty good and Newcastle very handsome. The road from thence to Congleton,
tho' apparently quite smooth, the most shaking that can be
imagined owing to the impracticability and indestructability
of the granite and serpentine which mixed with other stones
of less durable nature wear so unequally as to produce the
effect complained of. None of the turnpike keepers or shop-
keepers will take sixpences.[1] Wrote last night to Joshua
and put in the post at Stone. Left Congleton at $\frac{1}{2}$ past 7 and
breakfasted at Wilmslow, dined at Manchester and found
the roads deluged with rain which otherwise would have
been very good to this place (Rochdale), with the exception
of the last mile into Manchester which we ought to have
avoided by another road. Lost Cary out of the gig and

---

[1] A new silver coinage was about to be issued and an alarm had
spread that on its appearance the old coins would be discredited.

bought Patterson,[1] far inferior. Nothing but trade and smoke and dirt at Manchester, nor do I expect anything else till I get out of the manufacturing district, which I shall nearly do, I trust, tomorrow. The finest place on the road was Mr Davenport's and Sir J. Stanley's which join Congleton, a poor town beautifully situated, Wilmslow worse. All the way to Rochdale from Manchester the houses as thick as in the environs of London.

13th.   Rode through a most beautiful country to Otley. The roads in many places for a mile or two scarcely passable, the first four miles from Rochdale excessively bad, two miles in the middle between Halifax and Bradford very bad, a mile down to the bridge over the Aire between Bradford and Otley, these parts are the worst, but it is a matter of great surprize that the whole of the road should be in such indifferent repair and some execrably bad through the whole of this manufacturing district, that the whole and sole cause where the road is not pitched is the not letting the water off or breaking the stones and that the whole distance from Congleton to Otley there were not 20 persons employed in either of these occupations, notwithstanding they tell you half the people are out of employ and every three miles at furthest there is a shilling turnpike for a chaise and pair. The environs of Rochdale, Ripponden, Halifax, Bradford, the bridge over the Aire and Otley are beautiful in the extreme and were it not for the reflection that the greatness of Great Britain depended I may say principally on the defacing of the hand of nature in these parts by the hand of man, which produces not only riches in every way from exportation and

[1] Road-books.

taxation at home and raises in time of war an innumerable population which is seen over the whole district for the armies, one could not help regretting that scenes so romantic and lovely should be impaired and destroyed by the black steam engines, by the yarn, the cloth, the cotton, the morals of the people destroyed by being crowded together and the hammers of the water engines perpetually affrighting quiet and comfort from vallies which at first view one would imagine were placed by nature in the most remote and sequestered situations for the peculiar residence of innocence and peace. The seats or rather the villas of the manufacturers like the citizens in the neighbourhood of London have neatness to recommend them but scarcely any character through the whole district that distinguishes one very much from another.

14th. The descent into Otley down the Chevin is by far the steepest hill for the length I have ever travelled yet and I can scarcely name a sum that would induce me to travel on the top of a coach from Liverpool to Hull by that part of the road which we have passed in our journey. Two persons incurred my high displeasure, the first by suffering me to lose my way after I had enquired my road of him and the other by recommending me to sink the most tremendous hill when I was three parts of the way to the top in order to go down to Guiseley and take a bit of the Chevin, as he called it, by which I might save a $\frac{1}{4}$ of a mile by one mile and $\frac{1}{2}$ of steep hill with my little mare almost tired, however I grew better reconciled by the reflection that this poor manfacturer possibly never used any other mode of conveyance than his own feet. Arrived at Wath after a journey made tedious by the excessive hilliness of the roads and the bleakness of the country after we left Wharfedale till we arrived at Ripley. The brace of the gig broke and let us down twice. Nothing could have been more fortunate than our journey, escaping wet though it rained almost without example during the summer, gaining health for my wife and pleasure for all the party except by prolonging their stay at Cleobury rather after they wished to be at home. *Laus Deo.* Found letters, J. C. junior giving an account of Morris M.P. for Gloucester's death, a bad account of J. Sadler, and Mrs Naylor saying Webb was a candidate and no Blue could be found. My farm in good order and my cattle all looking capitally. Found oats and wheat cut. N.B. Black poplars appear not to like my peaty soil.

15th. Preached at Wath and read prayers in the evening. N.B. A water closet and granary built in my absence, water closet finished. Howard[1] called, advised my tendering money to Williams of Philip's Norton.

16th. Administered Sacrament to Beckwith's wife the carpenter. Letter from Joshua saying payment of £40 was stopped at the bank. The weather seems now to have taken up the thermometer during the last two nights having been near 60 and at this present writing 69 in the shade. Saw Lady Graham[2] and her two eldest boys and girl. She looked delightfully both as to health and beauty and I was sorry to learn that they had determined on shutting up Norton for three years, Sir B having taken a place near Doncaster. The

---

[1] Newton's solicitor.

[2] Wife of Sir Bellingham Graham, 7th baronet, of Norton Conyers, near Wath. He was at this time Master of the Badsworth hounds, leaving them for the Atherstone country in 1817. Subsequently he hunted both the Pytchley and Quorn packs.

Grevilles, she told us, were still in France with Lord Combermere. Rode on to Ripon, saw Dr Whaley, Mrs Danby and Mrs Hardcastle. Farrer told me of Colonel Serjeantson[1] having lost £50 sent in a letter from Camp Hill to Eton, suspects his servant. F said that after 14 days all missent and misdirected letters are returned to the General Post Office, there opened and sent to their proper destination, hence hopes of my £40 soon making its appearance. Wrote to Joshua, desired him to send Mrs N a bank post bill to Cleobury and pay £70 into Esdaile.[2] Mrs Wrigglesworth asked me to apply to Mr Claridge[3] for the farm lately rented by the brother George. Wrote to H. F. a word of advice.

18th. Wrote to Lord Ailesbury. A touch of my gout. N.B. found wheat, oats and barley all cutting on my farm on my return last Saturday. Sent to Appleton who has carried no tithe.

A Case. A a single woman with a bastard child. B and C trustees of the deceased reputed father of the child and pay 4/- per week to the overseers of D for the maintenance of the child and 16/- per ann for a house in which A resides. E marries A and after the marriage for a year or more the rent is received by the overseers of D just as before A married E. In order to get rid of E and A the overseers of D break open the house in the absence of E and A and take all his goods away and fasten up the door. Q. Are the overseers

---

[1] Col. Serjeantson, of Camp Hill, near Bedale, a fellow-magistrate of Newton for the North Riding.

[2] A bank in London, upon which Newton's Ripon bank, Coates and Co., drew.

[3] Agent for Lord Ailesbury's Yorkshire estates. He, his daughter Mary and his son Henry were frequent visitors to Wath. They lived at Jerveaux.

Wath Rectory and Church in Newton's time.

justified in so doing on the score of E's not being the tenant
and how does it appear that he is not the tenant? Is this not
a breach of the peace or is it solely a trespass for which an
action would lie?

21st.   Went to Coates to ask whether Appleton is to pay
me my tithe or I had better take it in kind.

22nd.   Rode to Dishforth to Mr Geo Appleton who promised in presence of Mr Mason of Withernwick to settle for
W. A.'s Middleton tithe. Preached and did evening duty
yesterday at Wath. Dined at Mr Morley's[1] with Mr Redfern,
his wife and Miss Stuart, two agreable Scotch women.
Letters from my wife and J. Commeline. Mr Redfern well
acquainted with J. Fendall in India, came over in the same ship
as poor Indigo and Lynd whose death I saw yesterday in
the papers. Read Shuckford's Connections, Galt's Life of
West. The former is the work of a man of great learning and
little judgment, in the latter is recorded one of the noblest
instances of religious liberality in a Quaker that I ever met
with of any sect, the speech of John Williamson delivered in
a meeting house at Springfield in America where the family
of West were met to consult the Quaker Society on the
propriety and legality of breeding young West a painter.
Painting being one of those worldly arts which the Quakers
prohibit. Pointing to the father of West and his family and
having expatiated on the blameless reputation they had so
long maintained and merited, "They have had", said he, "ten
children whom they have carefully brought up in the fear of
God and in the Christian religion and the youth whose lot

---

[1] The Rev. T. W. Morley, curate of Kirklington, who officiated for
an absentee Rector from 1815 to 1828.

in life we are now convened to consider is Benjamin, their youngest child. It is known to you all that God is pleased from time to time to bestow upon some men extraordinary gifts of mind and you need not be told by how wonderful inspiration their son has been led to cultivate the art of painting. It is true that our tenets deny the utility of this art to mankind. But God has bestowed on the youth a genius for this art and can we believe that Omniscience bestows his gifts but for great purposes? What God has given who shall dare to throw away? Let us not estimate wisdom by our notions, let us not presume to arraign his judgment by our ignorance, but in the evident propensity of that young man be assured we see an impulse of the Divine hand operating towards some high and benificent end". The speech prevailed on the assembly and young West was requested to attend a private meeting of the Society at his father's house. John Williamson resumed the subject and beginning by an observation that things merely ornamental should be excluded as superfluous from the usages and manners in their Society, he proceeded in a strain which at the present juncture I would recommend most earnestly to our Bible Society polemics. "In this proscription we have included the study of the fine arts for we see them applied to embellish pleasures and to gratify the senses at the expense of our immortal claims. But because we have seen painting put to this use and have in consequence prohibited its cultivation among us, are we sure that it is not one of those gracious gifts which God has bestowed on the world not to add to the sensual pleasures of man but to improve him as a moral and social being? The fine arts are called the Emblems and Offspring of Peace. The Christian religion is the doctrine of goodwill to man. Can those things that only prosper in peace be contrary to the Christian religion? Can those arts which call on man to exercise his intellectual powers more than his physical strength be contrary to Christianity and adverse to the benevolence of the Deity? I speak not of the fine arts as the means of amusement, nor the study of them as pastime for vacant hours, but even as such the taste for them deserves to be regarded as a manifestation of the Divine favor, disposing the heart to kind and gentle inclination. I think them ordained by God for some great and holy purpose. The professors of the fine arts are often distinguished by special gifts. The progress of the fine arts often exhibits the immediate interposition of the Deity when He raises up those great characters whose imaginations have an interminable influence on posterity and are elevated above the rest of mankind by the name of men of genius. The Almighty God in this remote wilderness has endowed a youth with the rich gift of talents for an art which was previously thought an unnecessary ministration to the sensual propensities of our nature. May his life and works demonstrate the gift of God has not been bestowed in vain nor the motives which induce us to suspend our particular tenets prove barren of religious effect. From the example of Benjamin West in this world we hope there will arise such a love of the arts of peace as shall draw the ties of affection closer and diffuse over a wider extent the interest and blessing of fraternal love."

28th. Mrs N, M. N. and C. N. arrived in perfect health for which I trust we all are grateful, bringing with them a letter from Smith in Holland who seems highly gratified with his tour. My females were most pleased with the road through

Bridgenorth, Bakewell and to Leeds. Excepting one acre of wheat, wheat, oats and barley were finished this evening.

29th.   Preached and did morning and evening duty at Wath. Jeremy Taylor says in his Holy Living that St John used to amuse himself with playing with a tame partridge. He mentions also that Theophyl, last Patriarch of Constantinople, ran from the Altar of St Sophia to his stable in all his Pontificals to see a colt just dropped by his favourite mare Phertante.

30th.   Went to Jerveaux, met three Colonels, Straubenzie, Dalton and Serjeantson, found myself stupid and contributing nothing to the amusement or information of the company. Got a note from Costabadie[1] announcing his intention of coming with two of his daughters to Wath on Monday, continued at Jerveaux till 2 October on account of incessant rain, got home dry. Read Jeremy Taylor, a good genealogist, Envy married Idleness and the produce was Curiosity. Spoke to Mr Claridge for Wrigglesworth of Middleton who passed off my application without seeming regard. Incessant rain this day prevented my attending Bedale Book club. A letter from J. C. junior announcing the commencement of the Gloucester City Election on the 1st. Col and Mrs Dalton at Wath.

October 6th.   Preached and administered the Sacrament and did morning and evening duty. Received a letter and a haunch of venison from Lord Ailesbury. Very much struck at the unpreachable style of Clarke on the attributes, his

[1] The Rev. Jacob Costabadie, Rector of Wensley-cum-Leyburn, was an old friend of Newton's. They had been contemporaries at Jesus College, Cambridge. Of his seven sons and four daughters, Henry, Mary, Charlotte and Fanny are particularly mentioned in this diary.

logical and metaphysical views, his answers to Lucretius, Hobbes and Spinoza. What a difference times and place create; were I to treat my congregation with the productions of this great writer, in three Sundays I should scarce expect half a dozen hearers, not six swine to devour his pearls.

7th.   Mr Costabadie and two daughters came here.

8th.   Went with the Costabadies to the Ripon Ball. The most numerous but one that I ever attended. Costabadie's two boys came from Ripon.

10th.   Mr and Mrs Serjeantson and Capt Dalton dined here on Lord A's Venison.

11th.   Went to Bedale to the Agricultural meeting and dine with forty fine fellows who talked of beef and ate pudding and drank wine like trueborn Britons. Laycock, mason, arrived to put up Mr Brand's monument.[1] Heard that Webb on the sixth day's poll at Gloucester had a majority of 110. Costabadie left Wath, told me a story of his brother-in-law putting ten weathercocks on one tower because he did not know better how to dispose of the money left for the repair of his church. The Grantham Arms on this side Boro'bridge set wilfully on fire. The incendiaries a party of thirty who travelled with pottery and who threatened the landlady with a hot supper when she refused them more liquor about 7 Thursday evening. Brought before me by Mr Mason, Lord G's steward, and Mr Hostott.

[1] The Rev. Thomas Brand was Newton's predecessor as Rector of Wath, and, like Newton, had once been tutor to Lord Ailesbury. The monument, a marble tablet by Flaxman, was erected by Lord Ailesbury as 'a tribute of regard from a pupil to his preceptor'.

12th.   Dined at the Serjeantsons' with Mr and Mrs Carter, Mr C. Elsley and Mr Newsam junior, heard that Mr Webb was returned for the City of Gloucester.

13th.   Did duty morning and evening at Wath. Mr Hattersley dined here and told us of giving 19/- for a bushel of wheat at Ripon on Thursday.

14th.   Shooting with Capt Dalton.

15th and 16th.   Finished oat, barley and wheat harvest. Mr Brand's monument erected by Lord A in Wath Church.

17th and 18th.   Shooting with Capt Dalton.

20th.   Did duty morning and evening. Letters from Smith and Mrs Commeline, a returned bill from the latter of Deighton's, Cambridge. Wrote to Deighton. In the review of Tweddell's Remains where it is said that out of religious motives he refrained from animal food, it struck me that were this practice to become general instead of benefitting the species it meant to protect it would lead to their total extinction, in a few years we should have neither sheep, swine, oxen, poultry or game any more than wolves in this country, as the cultivators of grain would then look on all these species as spoilers and depredators of their crops. Therefore abstinence from animal food seems contrary to reason and Scripture, but a question arises whether or not human population would be increased by the destruction of the brute species above mentioned. The Hindu countries are very populous, can their populousness be imputed to the want of the animals eaten by Europeans? If it can it is I think very clear that in such a kingdom as England less corn would be raised if the edible species were destroyed than at present and of course fewer human beings would be subsisted.

21st. Ripon Book Club, present the Dean, Williamson, Oxley, Whaley, Bury, Howard and myself. Called at Howard's about Ward's will. It is impossible not to love Howard, at the same time there is something about him that courts quizzing almost irresistibly. I mention putting up our horses at the Unicorn and being charged nothing for them when I asked the ostler what was to pay. The idea of a future judgment seems the strongest argument for social worship. Every man's apprehension for himself must awaken fears for others and Christian charity would lead him to pray for mercy upon all men and they for the same reason would be led to pray for him.

22nd. Dined at Mr Carter's with Messrs Elsley, Newsam junior, E. Carter and wife, Hutton, Mrs Hardcastle. Read part of History of Fiction. Rode with M. N. junior to London-derry. Finished my peas harvest. Cutting beans. Called on Mr Hunton who tells me my Scots sheep will come next week. Mr Hattersley came after his salary and the collectors for assessed taxes.

23rd. Rode with Caroline to Baldersby. Bespoke a pair of string shoes, string boots and corderoy breeches.

24th. Rained whole day. Drafts for assessed taxes and Mr Hattersley's salary.

25th. Mr D'Oyley's sale, bought a straw cutter and horse collars. The poorest review of any book I have yet met in the Edinburgh is that of Goethe.

26th. Justice meeting at York Gate.

27th. Did duty morning and evening. Mr and Miss Claridge at dinner. Called Saturday on Mr Barstow.

28th.   Mr Claridge went. Rode to Laysthorp, called on Mr Newsam. Mr Barstow called. Wrote to Costabadie. Sent the affidavit for Bellerby income tax to tax office. Discussion on the propriety of married women dancing.

29th.   Letter from J. Fendall saying that Jones had turned out a great rogue and was £1000 deficient in his accounts. A pheasant and two partridges from Mr Claridge. Read Wilkins and Visconti on the Elgin Marbles. Wilkins' assertions that Visconti does not think the relievos on the frieze and the metopes to be the work of Phidias not correct and I apprehend his ideas of chariots driving into the temples or up the platforms into the porticoes of the temples by means of temporary inclined planes to be entirely an invention of his own without classical authority. I don't believe that even in a Roman triumph the car of the Victor was driven into the Capitol, and I rather think the Athenians did not use their cars except in war or in their games. I believe there are reliefs that represent ladies riding about to pay visits to their acquaintances. Visconti's memoir and restoration of the Greek Epigrams is very ingenious. I should be very glad to have a reason assigned for the making of the Athenian inscription. I can easily conceive reasons for taking the account of what was wanting to finish the temple but why the necessary repairs should be engraved in marble I know not. I cannot see the use of so permanent a record, if they were not to be done almost directly the record would be useless as other repairs would be wanting (*vide* Wilkins' publication).

30th.   Visited Clarkson's wife who insisted on my reading prayers tho' she could not hear a word and is to have the Sacrament administered tomorrow. Taking up potatoes.

31st. Administered Sacraments to Clarkson's wife who is I fear past hope of recovery. Read Bishop of Gloucester's Charge which I think excellent for its devotion, its liberality, its style and manner and think no harm would accrue to the Church were all the Bishops such Methodists as he appears in his Charge.

November 1st. Went hunting to Thornbrough, found a fox at Norton, had a sharp run for about an hour. Sold my horse Benjamin to Mr G. Lane Fox who I saw next day at Pickhill where they found a fox. He gave me a letter covering a draft expressive of his satisfaction at the horse which he told me he had ridden that morning 19 miles in an hour and quarter, and I have since heard he broke his back at Boro'bridge on his return.

3rd. Did duty morning and evening. Mr Hattersley at dinner.

4th. Went to Wensley, called on Mrs Hardcastle. Found all the Costabadies but Mary.

5th. Mr Wilson dined at Wensley. Middleham Moor Fair with Costabadie.

6th. Ditto. Snow.

7th. Mr Claridge, Miss Claridge and Mr Menzies dined at Wensley.

8th. To Jerveaux. Mr Costabadie and Miss and Charlotte dined there. Deep snow and frost. Thermometer 27.

9th. Returned thro' the snow four inches deep at Tanfield. All the snow gone at Wath.

10th.   Did duty morning and evening. Mrs Maude gave me a few specimens of fluers, etc, would have given me any that she had. Bespoke a cabinet at Leyburn. Charlotte Costabadie grows more and more delightful. A score of Scots wethers came from Mr Hunton in my absence. Severe frost, thermometer 27. A large field of wheat uncut between Wensley and Middleham Moor. Find by Coates that Sir Bellingham Graham had not paid the Lady Day rent of tithe and that my last income tax was paid by Coates in July. Desired Costabadie to order me a pipe of Port from Hull. Price he thinks about £95. Poor Clarkson's wife died in my absence Tuesday and was buried Thursday. The passage made to the water closet but no roof put yet. A new pair of boots brought home.

11th.   Letter from B. Sadler announcing the death of his poor brother Samuel, one of the best men I ever knew. One too from Z. Scaping requiring income tax for Philip's Norton up to the 5th April, tho' Mr Williams was presented in March.

12th.   Dined Col Serjeantson's with Mr and Mrs Redfern, Miss Stuart, Capt Clifton, and Rev Newsam junior.

13th.   Called at Hollin Hall.[1] Dined at Howards with Dr Whaley, Rob Howard, Mr Saunders, Mr Fenton. Got in most of my beans in tolerable order.

14th.   Dined at Mr Morley's with Mr Stanley, Miss Morley, Rev Newsam junior. Letter enclosing receipt for income tax on Receiver General. A most curious epistle from Archdeacon Cambridge on the Bullo Pill contract.

[1] Mr Gilpin's house.

15th. Wrote to B. Sadler, to Archdeacon Cambridge and Mr Thompson. Hard frost yesterday and today with snow. The papers announce the death of the King of Wurtemburg not without hints of his being taken off in consequence of disputes with his people. The Gilpins refuse to dine here because of the cold. Morley agreed to take half the pipe of Port which Costabadie in a letter received says he has ordered. Paid a bill for bricks had in my absence by draft on Coates, £7. 13. 0. Mrs N hired a maid in James' place. Signed a warrant to seize on Close of Mia Bath for highway rates. Heard Mr Fox had broken Benjamin's back in returning Saturday last from Pickhill and that he was lying at Boro'bridge.

17th. Did duty morning and evening. Went into mourning for B. Sadler.

18th. At home. Called on Col Dalbiac and Mrs Hall, heard of Mrs Walker Harrison's having a son. Spoke to Mrs Hall about an old woman aged 105 lately resident at Well. Letter from Joshua enclosing an affidavit to enable me to recover the £40 sent to Aberconlais. Saw the eclipse very well.

20th. Went hunting to Baldersby, found four foxes, two at Baldersby and two at Hutton Moor, ran neither. The largest field I ever saw, about six from Mr Fox's hunt, Lord Darlington and three whippers in, Col Pulleine and Mr Askew, Capt Clifton, L. Serjeantson, Wyvill, Monson,[1] Hall,

---

[1] The Hon. and Rev. Thomas John Monson was the fifth son of the second Lord Monson and Rector of Bedale. His son, the Rev. John Monson, later Chaplain to Queen Victoria, had married in 1813 Elizabeth Anne, daughter of the Rev. Christopher Wyvill of Constable Burton, and her sister Sarah became in 1824 the second wife of the elder Monson.

Milbanke, Hutton, Dawson, Harrison, two Scropes, Treacher, Clough, Sir J. Beresford, Strangeways, Haw, Robb, Ribson, Whitwell, Fall and 20 other farmers, etc.

21st. Rode to Camp Hill, made the affidavit before Col Serjeantson. Mrs N and Caroline at Thirsk. Finished carrying all the beans. Received a letter from Smith giving an account of his seeing a man beating a field of standing barley of 40 acres between Easton Grey and Kingscote with several fields of standing oats and beans near it and that Phillimore had his harvest home only on Friday last. New pair of double milled kerseymere grey small clothes.

22nd. My parishioners very desirous of spinning flax during the winter and Mrs N and Caroline went to Thirsk to get some. Dined at Mr E. Carter's with Col Coore, Mr and Mrs Clark Milbanke, Miss Smith, Mrs Hardcastle, Newsam junior.

23rd. Went to Ripon and hired Wm Houseman at £7 per annum to come on Thursday next.[1] Called on Coates who gave me the name of James Hammet Esq to be joined in the bond with Joshua to get my £40 from the bank. Returned the affidavit to him.

24th. Did duty morning and evening. Christened a girl. Very hard frost, thermometer last night only 23.

25th. Went to Jerveaux, met there Dr Marsham, Capt Stile, R.N., and Mr A. Marsham. Spent three days very pleasantly, went to Bellerby Tuesday, to Thorpe Wednesday, returned to Wath Thursday.

29th. Went to Tanfield, bought a cow.

[1] As plowboy.

30th. Justice meeting at the Oak Tree, committed a man
for stealing hay who in order to get rid of the accusation
went to Col Serjeantson and swore Whitling the Landlord
of the Oak Tree his wife, Joseph Tooes the ostler who saw
him steal the hay, with another young woman robbed him
of three guineas and upwards on the highway. Refused to
join the Colonel in committing a boy who refused to go to
his place under the idea that the Magistrates have not cognizance of servants in husbandry till they have entered on
their service, tho' the old law considers the service to commence by the retainer, the statute only gives cognizance to
the Magistrates in case the servant misbehaves. I conceive
therefore that by accepting a retainer a servant makes himself
liable to an action if he refuses to enter on the service but
that the Magistrate has no cognizance till the servant has gone
to his place. 1st. The Law now does not consider the service
to commence till the servant enters on his place, as the time
previous to the entry does not reckon towards getting a
settlement for the servant. 2nd. There is no reciprocity in
such proceeding, the Magistrate not having power to compel
the master to take the servant he has retained after giving
him a retainer if he refuses. 3rd. It appears absurd in fact to
say that in this case the service had commenced with a new
master when the servant continued in his old place, for by
this supposition the servant is serving two masters in two
different parishes at the same time. The Colonel and Mr
I'Anson the clerk thought this reasoning not conclusive and
the Colonel committed the servant who positively refused to
go to his place, having sent back the retainer before the day
agreed upon for entering on his service. A Mr Raper was
summoned by Col S for not paying a maid servant her wages

on the plea of her having obtained leave to go and see her mother who is ill by a forged letter. This however Raper did not prove and paid his maid who had been hired for £5 per ann after the rate of 2/8 per week whereas he ought to have paid somewhat less than 2/ per week. As he did not settle with the girl before the Justices and had given her considerable trouble and loss of time before she could get her wages, was it incumbent on me to tell the master of his mistake when I could get no compensation for the girl for the trouble and loss of time she had sustained? He paid her 36 weeks at 2/8 amounting to £4. 5.; whereas he strictly ought to have paid only £3. 10. for the 36 weeks. Miss Claridge came to Wath.

December 1st.   Did duty morning and evening. The girls began their Sunday School with 13 of 12 years old and upwards.

2nd.   Went hunting, found a fox at Norton and killed at the Plaister Pits. Found another at Melmerby, ran very hard and lost at Littlethorpe.

3rd.   Ripon Assembly, Mrs N, Mary, Anne and I went. Very thin.

4th.   Bedale Club, only seven present.

5th.   Mr and Mrs Dalton, Mr Morley, Mr Stanley, Miss Compson, Miss M. A. Thorpe dined and two latter slept here.

6th.   Hunting at Newby and Hutton Moor, no sport. Dined with Mrs N, Caroline and Anne at Mrs Harrison's, met Mr and Mrs Oxley, Mr Charnock Dawson.

7th.   Bought R. Barker's turnips on Glebeland at 20 guineas. I was surprised to find my daughter Mary defending the late Lord Barrington's remaining in office as Secretary at War

during the American War tho' the war was against his
opinion and his conscience. His brother the Bishop of
Durham indeed says the answer is complete but the reasons
he assigns only amount to this, that the King told him that
his remaining in office was absolutely necessary for his
service. Surely the Bishop means the answer is complete
politically speaking, not *morally*. The Secretary at War is the
principal instrument in that cut throat work and he that can
hold such a post one moment against his conscience appears
to me to have a greater regard for his earthly Sovereign than
for the King of Kings. Certainly of all the wars that have
occurred in our memory the American War was the one in
which men's minds were most divided as to the moral justice
of it and how a man who disapproved of its principle could
continue to be the principal instrument to give it effect, and
who must think if the principle was unjust that every man
who fell in it was absolutely murdered, is a point of casuistry
much more easily solved by a Machivellian politician than by
a Christian bishop.

8th.   Did morning and evening duty.

12th.   Mr Claridge called yesterday on his return from
London and brought with him half a doe from Lord A.
Bought a great coat and pair of gaiters and a new pair of
shoes. This week I received a letter from J. C. junior to consult me as to what sum he should have for going abroad with
J. Scudamore, to which I replied £100 down and £150 every
half year and I think as he has the character of being stingy
I have not set him too high. J. C. is now of an age and of an
inclination to settle.

15th.   Received letter from Mrs Hickes, answered it, wrote

to Lord A, did duty morning and evening. George Wrigglesworth's wife and G. Tinsley's wife's mother died today. Began to make W. Houseman write. J. Fendall arrived on
Thursday to raise money by Howard. Received my malt
back from the makers, 63½ bushels. Cut the top of my finger
off in shewing off my strawcutter to J. Fendall, sent for Hague
and had it dressed and am quite surprized to find I feel so
little pain from it. Mr Hattersley dined here and seemed very
unwell but grew better.

16th.   Mr Howard came to talk to J. F., seemed to think he
could get him what he wants but on very high terms, 12½ per
cent.

17th.   J. F. recollected he could get by far the greater part of
his brother and sister on much better terms. This being my
tithe day I was well satisfied with the result, the whole except
£96 being paid and of that I received £37, so that now the
arrears are £59. Walked shooting Monday with J. F. and lost
my seals between York Gate and home in the fields.

18th.   Rode to Ripon, carried the money I received yesterday to Coates, £676.

19th.   Received a letter out of the West,[1] the less about
which is said or written the better. I pray God only the
writer may come to a better mind and that quickly.

20th.   Dined at E. Carter's with Miss Costabadie and Charlotte and returned when the thermometer was only 12. The
girls slept at Theakston and returned in the morning.

21st.   Rev Newsam junior called and asked me to dine at
Carthorpe Friday. F. Alman paid me the charity money

---

[1] I.e. from his son, J. F. N., whose financial straits had caused a
family dispute.

(£9. 10.), ten shillings being allowed for income tax. Read Bingley's Useful Knowledge, Jocular Tenures, Pyle; much interrupted by Justice business.

22nd. Preached and sent Joshua a pig and hare and a turkey to the New Inn, carriage paid. My opinion as to J. C. junior's remuneration coincided exactly with R. Raikes's and I fancy will be acceded to. Wrote Thursday to Merriman and Parfitt and sent him measure of Biddisham, wrote also to Mrs Mogg about tithe of Redcliff mead.

23rd. Rode to Theakston and Sleningford, got wet through, obliged to send in the evening to Dr Whaley for Anne who had a bilious attack. Paid Busby for the school £11. 11. 0. and £23 for myself; paid Coates, taylor, £13. 18. 0, paid Gant the sadler £8. 0. 0.

25th. Preached and administered the Sacrament, 29 Communicants. A very large congregation at Church today. Anne better. Weather very mild, thermometer 43.

26th. J. Fendall and I dined with Mr J. Newsam, meeting Tim Hutton, Ed. Carter and Morley. T. H. a famous hand at a goose.

27th. Col, Mrs and G. Serjeantson, Mrs, Miss and J. Harrison, Col Dalbiac and J. Dalton at dinner.

28th. Justice meeting at York Gate, disputes between overseers and labourers.

29th. Thermometer 42, very windy night, broke drawing room windows. Letters from Bellerby tenant and Costabadie.

30th. Mrs Costabadie and Mary and Charlotte came to Wath. Ed. Carter called.

31st. Ripon Ball.

1817

January 1. The Costabadies left us very much pleased with their last night's ball which was a very good one, 19 couples.

2nd. Went to Ripon and paid Farrer and Thompson. Dined at Col Dalton's with the Dalbiacs, Serjeantsons, Newsams and Capt D. Lost my money.

4th. Dined at Mr Howard's with Capt McConochy, a well informed Navy Officer.

5th. Did duty morning and evening and gave away the Charity and Sacrament money. Mr Hattersley at dinner.

7th. Miss Harding came to Wath unexpectedly by arriving before her letter. Received letters from J. Commeline junior telling me that his negociation with J. Scudamore was completed and that it was intended they should start for Geneva via Paris in about a fortnight. News having arrived from Zebedee Scaping and Capt Symonds of the death of my successor at P. Norton I wrote to the Bishop of Bath and Wells to give it to J. F. N. with no very great confidence of success.

9th. J. Fendall left Wath for Bullo Pill under no very pleasant ideas, having had a demand made upon him for the furniture by his uncle Benson, he seems to wish to saddle John with what of right belongs to the executors of his father and certainly should have notified it when the plan for giving his mother £200 per annum was submitted to him and approved by him which certainly was meant and I believe expressed to exonerate J. F. from any other charges than those expressed in the plan. I begin to suspect that people think M. N. junior very often dogmatical and positive and that it may deter the male sex from coming ever nearer than is necessary for a sparring match. Sent a draft to Hull of £105. 10. 6. for a pipe of wine to be delivered in spring, of which a $\frac{1}{4}$ is to be Mr Morley's and $\frac{1}{4}$ Costabadie's who sent a draft for the money.

10th.   Dined at Camp Hill with Daltons, Dalbiacs, Miss Hume, Miss Harding, Newsam.

11th.   A letter from Mr Beadon saying his father had given away the living of Philip's Norton on first hearing of Williams' death. *Credat Judaeus.* Wrote to Parfitt, Bishop of Bath and Wells, Joshua and Gibbs and Co. Letter from Lord A.

12th.   Did duty morning and evening.

13th.   Shooting.

14th.   Quarter Sessions, indited Melmerby Road over Hutton Moor on my own view, returned to dinner, a great show of magistrates many of whom I did not know. Gave away 12 pair of blankets. The butcher refused to cut the pigs but in the increase of the moon.

16th.   Sold 6 quarter of oats at £2 per quarter. Miss Harding contended that the pig-faced lady is Lord Ailesbury's sister and that she spent last winter in a very expensive style at Edinburgh. She told us also that a voyage to Madeira and living there a year cost a friend of hers thirty thousand pounds and that the mutton came from England. An account in the papers of Mrs W. Long being married to Rich the Rope Dancer, old Billy Long was'a fine contrast to him.

17th.   Dined at Capt Dalton's with the Oxleys, Askwiths and Col Dalbiac.

19th.   Did duty morning and evening.

20th.   Ripon Book Club, all the members present except Mr Allanson and Mr Wood.

21st.   Granted a warrant to apprehend wood stealers from Heflet wood (Lord A's).

23rd.   Went hunting with Mr Bell's hounds. Saw Mr Claridge's advertisement for the sale of 11,695 trees of which 5241 were oaks.

24th.   When the Persian Ambassador was in England he was one day very unwell and sent for a physician who prescribed for him and his Excellency gave him to understand that he was engaged to dinner and he must contrive that the operation of the medicine should be over before dinner time which the physician told him would be the case, however it turned out otherwise and he rang his bell and ordered the physician to be instantaneously beheaded. Did duty morning and evening yesterday. Saw today in the paper that Philip's Norton was given to Mr Warner. Paid Henry and Heslop's wine bill.

28th.   Ripon Ball. Capt Elliot refused Mrs N having a card table in the Ball Room for which both she and I trim'd him.

29th.   The Bedale Club, 13 members present, Monson, Elsley, Serjeantson, Clarke, two Robsons, Glaister, Newsam,

Morley, Scrope, Newton, determined to have no more auctions but that each member should pay ½ a guinea and take the books he ordered at ¼ price and that if any book should be enquired for and not found in the room on a club day a bottle of wine should be forfeited to the club and charged to the person in whose possession it is found.

February 1st. Dined at Camp Hill with two Miss and Major Elsley.

2nd. Did duty morning and evening, christened and churched. Wrote to Lord A and Mrs Vilet.

3rd. The Mayor's dinner at Ripon, dined there, company a hundred, Carter the watchmaker Mayor. I don't intend to dine there again. Miss Harding went in the evening by mail to London. This lady is as well pleased with herself as anyone else can be. Her head is very loosely put on but turns to all parts of the company with great ease and some degree of elegance. Of 2000 stories she told in the month she was at Wath 1999 have most probably escaped the memories of all in the house, they were just interesting enough to keep the narrator awake. One or two incredible stories may be an exception to the general run. Met with the word scrumbling, the rubbing over a picture with a liquid to glaze and harmonize the colours.

5th. Dined at Mr Barstow's with Messrs Crompton, Ewanson, Butterwick, Cayley, Ward, Barton and Dent. More wine than wit flowed.

6th. This day Mrs Hardcastle left us being driven to Theakston by Mrs Newton. I have changed my ink from black to red to do honor to the gaiety, the sentimentality, the curiosity, the romanticness of this lady, who is so alive at the age of near threescore to all tender impressions, has such lively recollections of feelings which ladies 40 years younger than herself suppose to have vanished long since, that it would be unsafe to trust her by her own account in the love inviting scenes of Hackfall without a friend of her own sex to calm the rising perturbations of her heart and conduct her in safety and virtue past the fishing house which she knows to have been a spot on which with very little importunity many ladies have surrendered themselves for life to their aspiring swains. Went hunting with Mr Bell's hounds, had tolerable sport, these hounds please me much as they are attended by gentlemen only, no farmers. Saw Mr Scott who told me that by a frolic of Geo Fox's who bought Benjamin he got the mare of him he was then riding for £20 tho' she cost Fox £440. He was going to kill her for refusing a leap when Scott told him to take £20 for her to which he acceded. To a common observer the mare might appear worth about £50 or 60. At Appleton's sale at Middleton I bought a drill, a bull and a mare for £13.

8th.   This evening is the most remarkable I ever saw, tho' the moon is now in the last Quarter it has not been darker than a moonlight near the full and the sky when free from clouds has been illuminated by a fleeting lambent light like a slight reflection from distant fire upon a wall, the meteor constantly appearing so white and filmy as that the stars are seen quite clearly thro' it, the light almost vertical seemed incessantly agitated as if by a light wind or like a flame moving very quickly, there seems a permanent light in the North and this fleeting light reaches across the welkin to the East and into the South East, it lasted from sunset till near ten when it grew as dark as it usually is in an evening at this time of year without moon or stars, the wind continued during the whole appearance very high from West or S West. The thermometer stood at 45 and Fahrenheit's barometer was 29 7/10 between changeable and fair and appeared to be rising. On going out at ten though it rained a little the night was not dark and there was still a light appearance in the N East. The moon entered her last quarter at 8 this evening. Read Kidd's Geological Essay and an account of 10 years residence in Tripoli. Kidd's a very bad embarrassed style. Account of Tripoli amusing enough. I read Wood's Isle of Man because I knew nothing of it and he has said little from there being very little to say. Dallaway on Sculpture is very slovenly from the little pains he takes to be clear. It is very difficult to know what antecedent word he refers to. His book suggests two things, the power there is in England of making a grand gallery of sculpture by the bringing together all the undoubted antique sculptures we possess and the facility of seeing some very fine works on almost every tour that we can make. I intend to begin with Lord Grantham's, Lord Carlisle's and Mr Duncomb's which I trust I shall see the ensuing summer, and I will endeavour to make out a statuary tour and insert it in my journal.

9th. Did duty morning and evening. Mr Hattersley at dinner as absurd as usual in rejecting those he is bound to teach, have a mind to begin a new edition of Bede, my present residence having thrown me into the neighbourhood in which he lived.

12th. Went to Northallerton, it being the fair, and called with Mrs Newton and Anne on Mr and Mrs Macfarlane. Read Warden's account of Buonaparte. Whether or not W wrote this account with a view to influence his readers in favor of Buonaparte I know not but I think there are few people who will not think rather better of Napoleon after reading it than before. It has infinitely more effect than a studied apology or defence of him could have had. I conceive the account of the Ex-Emperor's tranquillity and submission to his fate to be the point which calls forth our admiration of his present conduct not to say our approbation. The biographer himself seems to have been in some degree seduced into a better opinion of him as he grew more and more acquainted with him and he has at least influenced his readers as much or more as any decided apologist, viz: Johnson in his life of Savage or Boswell in his life of Johnson. This is a proof of how much better pleased men in general are by thinking for themselves in reading biography than in the writer's thinking for them. Many who certainly never were nor can be Buonapartists must allow the influence of Warden's book tho' it would be injurious to his interest to state that the motive of the publication was to raise the fallen Emperor in the eyes of his conquerors.

13th. Wood's account of the Isle of Man details some laws for the regulation of servants in that Isle which prevailed till 1777, so absurd as scarcely to be credible if they had not been inscribed in their statute book. Read Lord Chesterfield's Letters to his Godson in which I see nothing to admire but the gentlemany style but his lax morality is shocking to every serious thinking man.

14th. Attended the meeting to enroll the Militia. Little Militia but some Justice business done and we were told of a girl at Burneston who would have been brought to filiate a child she was big with by her own father but her being brought to bed that morning prevented it; the name Nattress. Sold Shent at Northallerton fair.

15th. Went coursing to Norton with Mr Morley where at least 200 people were assembled and 8 brace of hares killed. The thoughts of the misunderstanding with the Gentleman in the West[1] are a grievous weight.

16th. On a spinster of 55 who was always talking of old maids and oldmaidishness as if she did not belong to the sisterhood:

> She talks of old maids as if she was a mother;
> She knows she's not one and perhaps not the other.

This lady who is young in her body and old in her shape appears like an antique statue of bronze where the trunk has been new soldered and draped with a marble head that has not been retouched or restored. Did duty morning and evening. Ward of Middleton came here and offered me a guinea as a funeral fee for Miss Allanson. I refused on the plea of not thinking it right to accept anything from the family of my predecessor Rector of Wath.[2] The fee if it had been anything should have been such as would have been demanded by me from a person desiring to make a vault in the chancel who was not a parishioner, which would have been from twenty to fifty guineas. Mrs Brand had no more

---

[1] J. F. N.

[2] The Rev. Cuthbert Allanson, Chaplain to the House of Commons, had been Rector of Wath from 1756 till his death in 1780.

right to assign the use of the vault which Mr Brand made in the vestry to Mr Allanson's family than Mrs Newton would have a right to assign the use of the water closet which I have built to Mr Allanson's family after my decease. My opinion is that the demand for a vault within the church ought to amount nearly to a prohibition especially to a non parishioner, but I mean this as no reflection on Mr Allanson from whom I get quite enough as Rector of Wath and if he thought it right to interchange the civility of a request to Mrs Brand and she of acceding to it I have no reason to object to it. I merely enter this record that the right was in me and the civility of ceding the vault was mine because I might have said I shall retain the vault for the use of my own family and will not suffer another to be made within the walls to accommodate any person who is not a parishioner.

17th. Wrote to J. Fendall, called on Mr Allanson and the Howards. Accounts in paper of persons sent to Tower for High Treason.[1] M. N. junior heard from Miss Harding that the Duke of Marlborough had left her sister £5000 besides a small annuity.

18th. Went hunting with Mr Bell's hounds. On Saturday a man (Whitlet who keeps the Oak Tree) rode against a tree coursing and when he got up fancied he had been ridden over and that the horse had trod on his head both with his hind feet and fore. Letter from W. Fendall[2] saying he can't get

---

[1] The distressed state of the country after the Napoleonic wars had led to serious disturbances. Following a riotous meeting at Spa Fields four ringleaders were arrested and charged with high treason, but after a long trial were acquitted.

[2] William Fendall (see p. xiii) held a commission in the 4th Light Dragoons and was now stationed in Ireland.

leave because of a Court Martial. Continue under great concern at C. E. N.'s not eating and dread lest during the approaching Lent she may starve herself so as to make her recovery of her strength and spirits very doubtful. A life like hers cannot require such abstinence as will endanger her health. Can we be expected to destroy health as a duty, to reject the best blessing of Heaven or make ourselves less able to perform acts that require vigour of body as well as benevolence?

19th. Ash Wednesday. In blossom in the garden daisy, snowdrop, hepatica, mezereon, primrose, aconite, yellow and green, Christmas rose.

20th. Attended a meeting at Richmond to take into consideration the clauses of the Bill to be brought in for the regulation of the clergy which give a power to the Bishops to impose a curate on a clergyman doing his own duty whenever they think proper and to prevent their taking more than 20 acres to farm without the leave of the Bishop. Mr Headlam was in the chair and read a petition of his own drawing up to the Bishop of Chester, in which after a complimentary preamble much too long he respectfully represented the hardship such a clause might be to the clergy, tho' he acknowledged that the permission to farm 20 acres was an alleviation of the act of the 43rd of Geo 3rd and that they must accept as a boon. On which I desired an addition might be made to say that we considered that if the clergy were left as regard to farming as the Statute of Henry VIIIth left them it would answer every purpose and be much more agreable to the clergy. Mr Headlam had also a long objection founded on the hardship which might accrue to a clergyman who might have an estate of his own thrown on his hands, as the Bill prohibited his buying or selling any stock for land which was not glebe or held by the leave of the Bishop. The persons at the meeting were the Rev Wilkinson, Tate, Costabadie, Wharton, Headlam, Redshaw, Morley, Newton, Monson, Atkinson, Dr Dodsworth, Collins, Thornhill. Returned as far as Catterick, dined and slept at Mrs Morley's.

21st. Came home through a considerable fall of snow which reached only to Londonderry.

22nd. Spent the whole morning at York. Had letters from Warner, Smith and Dr Meyrick.

23rd. Did duty morning and evening. Read the report of the secret Committee setting forth the treasonable attempts to overthrow the Government and divide all the property.[1] Had a conversation with C. E. N. on fasting, being under the most serious apprehension that she would have reduced herself past recovery had she persisted through the present Lent as she did through the last.

24th. Went with the Howards to Lord Grantham's, saw the pictures and statues. The pictures are very few and not very excellent and are detailed in the Ripon Guide. The statue of the Venus is by far the finest I ever saw tho' the head of the statue which Dallaway says is the head of a Pudicitia I should say belonged to a slighter grown figure, it is however in itself exquisitely beautiful and the veil is said to have been worked by Paulli to the resemblance of hair. The Minerva is a fine statue but has a head not belonging to

[1] The Committee produced an alarmist report, as a result of which special powers were granted to the authorities for dealing with seditious outbursts and propaganda.

the original statue and I have an infinitely less relish for draped statues than for nudities. On this account I should esteem the Silenus and the Brutus, as it is called, the second and third in the collection. The Silenus exhibits the antique mode of keeping wine in goatskins very satisfactorily, the legs being cut off and the skin being stripped off without any incision down the belly makes a seam in the skin unnecessary, the part where the legs were cut off being merely tied round with a small cord or thong. Now I am going to say what may perhaps be called presumption with regard to the statue called the Brutus as I am confident it is not a statue of Brutus but of some gladiator. It has indeed a Brutus's head but even that I should rather say belonged to the spare Cassius. The only reason I can divine why it is called Brutus is that it has a dagger in the right hand. The head is too small to have belonged to the statue and too old to have been the head of Brutus at the time of Caesar's assassination, and indeed the whole statue is the statue of a man past the bloom of youth, if not the vigour of manhood, which as he was esteemed the son of Julius Caesar who was slain at fifty-six Brutus could scarcely have been. There is a small sitting figure of a Senator that has great dignity. The sarcophagus is very large and curious but having no relievo is not very interesting. The idea that it is a bath I cannot well entertain, as I should conceive it very inconvenient to remove the lid of several cwt every time it was to be used. There is an admirable small modern group in alabaster (I suppose by Canova) of three figures, a man carrying off a woman, I don't exactly know what the third figure is, as a third figure can have nothing to do in the rape of Proserpine. If it be Susanna and the two elders one of the old gentlemen seems very quiescent while the other is triumphantly bearing off the lady. I forgot to add that the statue called the Brutus is much in the attitude of one of the athletes in the Villa Borghese (Plate 18, Dallaway) and that I do not think the Roman Senators were often represented nudities in the early times, i.e. before the time of Nero, when decency and everything else that was praiseworthy forsook them.

26th.   Bedale Club, only four present. In the night a violent storm of thunder and lightening.

27th.   In the morning saw two apricots in blossom. Attended the Agricultural Committee in Ripon. Read Clarke, the first volume, and Burder's illustration of Scripture, one volume.

28th.   Average height of thermometer this month was 41 9/28.

March 1st.   Wrote to Dr Meyrick and sent the answers to queries about Biddisham to Bishop of Bath and Wells.

2nd.   Did duty morning and evening. Heard that J. Commeline and his pupil Scudamore left Redmarley for the Continent. Had rather a favourable report from J. Fendall of the Colliery. Finished second volume of Burder. Began Gibbon's account of his own life; I think he is but a bad biographer, having given very little amiability to his own character, which is not increased by his noble commentator. My old friend Mr Hoare thought his character more remarkable than pleasing and used to speak of him as a disagreable prodigy when a lad.

4th.   I have now finished the *morceau* so highly recommended by my nephew, the Account of Gibbon's life and writings by himself and confess myself greatly disappointed, not indeed in the style which is like himself in the History, but I am disappointed at not being able to discover one single amiable trait in the picture he has drawn. He is more selfish and more Epicurean than Hume. He appears to have indeed a regard for truth but that alone does not entitle a man to the character of an amiable man. His regard for his Father who indulged him in idleness at an expense he could ill afford and caused him embarrassments which embittered by Gibbon's own account all the latter part of his life and brought him to his grave has never called forth one ray of gratitude or one expression of acknowledgment. His political conduct is of no better sort than his filial piety. His friend and apologist says he defended and supported the American War but he does not venture to say he was satisfied with it. He appears to have entered Parliament to get a place and to have abandoned his country at the very moment and for no other reason than that he lost it, and it should not escape the recollection of every Christian that the friend and apologist of Gibbon was a defender of the Slave Trade. The testimony which Gibbon bears to Mr Fox in three lines is worth all the notes of the Right Honourable Lord Sheffield (which is repeated till one is sick at the head of almost all his letters) in defence or apology for the life and writings of his friend. Fox was of opposite principles and party and Gibbon after having received a three days' visit from him at Lausanne, "In his tour in Switzerland (Sept 1788) Mr Fox gave me two days of free and private society. He seemed to feel and even to envy the happiness of my situation, while I admired the powers of a superior man as they are blended in his attractive character with the softness and simplicity of a child. Perhaps no human being was ever more perfectly exempt from the taint of malevolence, vanity or falsehood".

5th.   The E. Carters, Messrs Newsam, Barstow and young Costabadies at dinner. It has occurred to me that one of the strongest parts of our Constitution, at least one which is the greatest security against revolutions, is that which merges all the younger sons of Nobles into the mass of the people, by which the Nobles and Commoners are linked in the strongest possible manner together, and the marriage of the clergy not allowed in Catholic countries cements that body to the laity and in the present times to the most powerful and respectable part of the laity, the great merchants or the country gentlemen from whose families the clergy and their wives (with very few exceptions) are now almost universally taken.

6th.   An account of a Bill having past for the suspension of the Habeas Corpus Act in consequence of seditious meetings, practices and combinations in various parts of the country and petitions from all parts for an alteration and reform of abuses and the duration of Parliaments and I cannot refrain from quoting from one of Gibbon's letters to Lord Sheffield in 1792 "If you allow them to perplex Government, if you trifle with this solemn business, if you do not resist the spirit of innovation in the first attempt, if you admit the smallest and most specious change in our Parliamentary system, you are lost. You will be driven from one step to another, from principles just in theory to consequences most pernicious in practice; and your first concessions will be productive of every subsequent mischief for which you will be answerable to your Country and Posterity. Do not suffer yourself to be lulled into a false security, remember the proud fabric of the

French Monarchy; not four years ago it stood founded as it might seem on the rock of time, force and opinion, supported by the triple Aristocracy of the Church, the Nobility and the Parliaments. They are crumbled into dust, they are vanished from the earth. If this tremendous warning has no effect on the men of property in England, if it does not open every eye and raise every arm you will deserve your fate". Date May 30. In November he writes "Next winter may be the crisis of our fate, and if you begin to improve the constitution you may be driven step by step from the disfranchisement of Old Sarum to the King in Newgate, the Lords voted useless, the Bishops abolished and a House of Commons without articles (*sans culottes*)".

7th.   The Costabadies left us and we had a large party at dinner, Mrs and Misses, Mr J. and Mrs Dalton, Col Dalbiac, Col and Miss Serjeantson, Mr and Mrs Carter and Mrs Hardcastle.

8th.   I trust I may be able to follow the maxim I here lay down as I am convinced of its prudence and propriety and that it is highly conducive to happiness. Never impart a secret to any person but for the purpose of obtaining his assistance or advice on the point of secrecy. The greatest part of what are called secrets are imparted merely because the imparter cannot contain them any longer, possibly a slight gratification may be intended for the hearer but the delivery of himself is the grand object of the labour. In reading Franklin's correspondence it is impossible not to be entertained by his lively style and I think not to be convinced that he did all in his power to prevent the rupture between Great Britain and the Colonies, but I am astonished that the printer of it and the publisher have not been prosecuted for a libel. I have no doubt but that if Belsham had said one half in his Reign of George 3rd of what the Editor has published as a letter of his grandfather's to Hutton the Moravian, he would have been prosecuted, fined and imprisoned to the end of his days. According to modern doctrines that publications are not less libellous for being true, I conceive also that they are not less liable to prosecution for having been written by those who are dead, otherwise men might publish any libel under pretext of it being a letter or forge it or not produce anything genuine. If Dr F is what a strict moralist would blame I think it appears most in the different mode in which he speaks of the tumults and divisions which were said to take place in the Colonies soon after they recovered their independence. He absolutely denies them to his English correspondents but so far admits them to his French correspondent that it is sufficiently apparent to the subject of what nation he is writing on this subject whenever it occurs without looking at the direction of the letter. His religious creed he says was a doubt of the Divinity of our Saviour, but thinks the belief of the doctrine may have a good consequence in making his doctrines more respected and more observed.

9th.   Did duty morning and evening. Wrote to Mrs Wilmot in reply to a letter of February 22 in which she says Mr Ward's will was proved in Doctors' Commons by Mrs Ward August 3 1798, in which the reversion of the Houghton Estate is given to Mrs Wilmot, her heirs and assigns in case she survives Mrs Radcliffe and her husband and in case Mrs Wilmot dies in the lifetime of either of them the reversion is given to Mr Radcliffe. Wrote to Sir B. Graham.

10th.   The Howards, Miss Compson and Miss Beale till Friday.

11th.   Read Clarke and Madame La Roche Jaqueline.

12th.   Went hunting. Mr Strangeways rode my mare and dined here.

13th.   Mr Barstow dined here.

14th.   Went to a sale at Little Thorpe.

15th.   Mr Hattersley came to tell me he had turned the boys out of the school whose parents attended the Methodists' meeting. My intention is not to interfere but let him and the parishioners settle the point as they can. Received a letter from James Commeline, execute the conveyance of the Bullo Pill to J. Fendall and the conveyance of India J. Fendall's Littleworth property, witnessed by Mr Howard. Gave Capt Dalton a pointer, Bob.

16th.   Duty morning and evening. Wrote to Mr Smith. Read Buonaparte's Memorial to Sir Hudson Lowe, a poor performance and utterly unworthy his fallen greatness. Lamenting that he did not choose to surrender to the Emperor of Austria his father in law, to the Emperor of Russia his friend whom he assisted in putting out the fire of Moscow, or to the King of Prussia whom he four times suffered to remount his throne, he only showed his want of judgment in selecting to surrender himself to the English. The fact is that he wanted to get to America and his selection was only that the Channel was so full of English ships that it was next to impossible that he should escape them, and the English are not obliged to him for the preference. His complaint if true that he is treated as tho' hatred had more to do in the mode

of his confinement than policy comes badly from a man
whose hatred of the English drove him almost to madness in
the time of his power and manifested itself in the most
dastardly way in detaining the innocent travellers who happened to be in France at the time of the rupture in a long
captivity at Verdun. His crying and whining after his empty
title of Emperor is likewise far beneath him. His treatment
of that amiable being the first Queen of the King of Prussia
must have been a full balance to all the favors he ever bestowed on that Monarch. His attack on Russia was the most
unprovoked that ever was heard of. His escape and conduct
from Elba must politically be deemed a sufficient cause of
caution in those burnt children, the Allied Powers, and the
perpetual imprisonment he is doomed to is only what he
must have expected let him have surrendered to whom he
might and he may think himself well off that he is not in an
iron cage and in an iron mask, tho' Sir Hudson Lowe may
not relax one tittle of his instructions and may enforce them
with all the rigor the letter of his instruction may allow.
I forgot to note the handsome way in which J. Commeline
speaks of his pupil noting his delicacy, his good humour and
freedom from fastidiousness; may this opinion always remain. He mentions too that they were only $2\frac{1}{2}$ hours in
crossing from Dover to Calais.

17th.   Went to Wensley with Mrs N and Anne.

18th.   Mr Anderson dined at Wensley.

20th.   Col and Capt Straubenzie dined at Wensley, attended
a sale at the heirs of poor Tennant who talks of going to
Cheddar to live. Bought a mare and colt at £8. Called on
Mr Baines at Tanfield to enquire whether he sanctioned Mr

Hattersley's turning the boys whose parents attended the Methodists out of the school as Mr H had told me. Mr Baines said that he had never heard a word about the Methodists but that Miss H had called there on her return from Sleningford and told him (what was a lie) that I sent children there that could not tell their letters. The Trustees agreed the proper age was seven. He refused Bradwith's boy at nine and then took him on my remonstrating.

21st.   Dined at Mrs Maude's with Col and Capt Straubenzie, Mr and Miss Anderson and Miss Maude.

22nd.   Returned from Wensley, called going and returning on Mrs Hardcastle. Received a letter from Z. Scaping charging £38 for measuring 500 acres at Biddisham, likewise one from Mr Baines to tell me I was elected a Commissioner of the Masham and Bedale roads and that there was a meeting at the New Inn on the 31st. Read at Wensley Sir J. Reynolds' discourses before the Academy and was highly delighted with many of them, which are almost equal to Horace's Art of Poetry in conveying useful instruction for general purposes in which he conveys his precepts for the art. Lord Bathurst refutes the charges about the treatment of Buonaparte on a motion of Lord Holland's grounded on Montholen's memorial.

24th.   Received a letter from J. Fendall dated Batavia November 19, 1816 enclosing 3 drafts one value £500, one £700, and one value £800, making £2000, which I immediately transmitted per post to Joshua as the bills were drawn at six months sight and are intended for the purpose of purchasing a troop for William with an intention of letting

Mrs F have something in case the Bullo Pill should not furnish a sufficiency.

26th. Went to Bedale Club, present Messrs Monson, Elsley, Paterson, Macfarlane, Redshaw, Newsam, Glaister, B. N. Read Pottinger's travel in Baluchistan, very interesting, Sancho the Proverbialist a lively religious work, if one were inclined to cavil the assumed character seems of no purpose as the author (Mr Cunningham, Vicar of Harrow) has avowed himself. His pretending, I had almost said his asserting himself, to be a Layman is not quite consistent with the pure Christian character he assumes through the book.

27th. Dined with Mr Morley, present Mr J. Newsam, Mr Stanley and a younger brother. I forgot to mention having visited Mr Redfern of Langton Lodge on Tuesday, 16 miles for a morning call. They had called on us while we were at Wensley and I was very anxious to know what the appointment of Sirdar was which we had heard was destined for our dear brother J. Fendall. Mr Redfern said it only meant Chief and that the emolument depended on the district to which he might be appointed. Wrote to Parfitt and to Philpotts.

28th. Received a letter from Joshua acknowledging receipt of the bills for J. Fendall's £2000 and returned him an answer. Wrote to Mr Hattersley enclosing £5 of his stipend and telling him Mr Baines, Mr Monson and Mr Elsley thought he was wrong in rejecting the Methodists' children from the school.

29th. Long letter from Mrs Vilet. Justices meeting at York Gate, not at home till between 5 and 6. Wrote to J. Fendall in India.

30th. The custom of mixing the assessment of the highways with the poor rate is illegal. No distress for such a rate could be granted by the Magistrates. Disputed the necessity of a parent's consent to apprenticing a child whose parents receive parish relief.

31st. Dined at the Turnpike meeting at the New Inn, present Mr Monson, Mr Danby, Col Serjeantson, Col Dalton, Major Elsley, Mr E. Carter, Mr Strangeways, B. N. and Mr Baines. One sailor brought in for picking the pocket of another when in bed of £5, committed by Messrs Monson and Elsley to Northallerton. The letting of tolls of Skipton Bridge Bar and Themborough Bar the only business of the meeting except eating a good dinner. The first bar let for £130, the second for £25.

April 1st. Mr Barstow, Mr and Mrs Allanson called.

2nd. Ride with Mr Barstow to Snape to look at a horse. Mr B at dinner, professed his high opinion of the superiority of barristers or men bred to the Bar to other men. I allow that the eminent men at the Bar are in general men of ability and information, but the herd of fellows who attend Sessions, etc, are a mulish set between attorneys and statesmen with all the quibble and chicanery of the one and some of the knowledge but without any of the enlarged views of the other. With three of these men in company it is not possible for any number of men of another profession or of no profession to have any other topic of conversation than a law question which one of them will start and then all three will run yelping after till the rest of the company are drunk or asleep, except these said barristers should happen to be Yorkshire sportsmen and then the breeding will sometimes come out in spite of the training.

3rd. Read Bonney's Life of Jeremy Taylor which only proves that Bonney knew nothing of Jeremy Taylor but that he was the author of some works which he has garbled and would have spoiled if Taylor's works could be destroyed, all that is worth reading is certainly not what Bonney has written. Had he given the whole of Rust's funeral sermon I would have excused half his own meagre performance but as the Bishop Taylor's works have been so very lately re-published the making a book which consists almost wholly of unconnected quotation from them is a piece of imposition on the public which no one ever practised in such a barefaced manner as bookmaker Bonney. Had looked into Stathallan and was quickly tired and disgusted with the absurdity of it.

4th. Good Friday. Did morning and evening duty, administered the Sacrament to 22, was particularly struck with a passage of Rust in his character of Jeremy Taylor "To sum up all, this great Prelate had the good humour of a Gentleman, the eloquence of an Orator, the fancy of a Poet, the astuteness of a Schoolman, the profoundness of a Philosopher, the wisdom of a Counsellor, the sagacity of a Prophet, the reason of an Angel and the piety of a Saint. He had devotion enough for a cloister, learning enough for a university and wit enough for a college of Virtuosi and had his parts and endowments been parcelled out amongst his clergy that he left behind him it would perhaps have made one of the best dioceses in the world. He is fixed in an Orb of Glory and shines among his brethren stars, that in their several ages gave light to the World and turned many souls into Righteousness and we that are left behind, though we can never reach his perfections, must study to imitate his virtues that we may at last come to sit at his feet in the mansions of glory".

5th. At a sale at Azerley.

6th. Easter Sunday. Did duty morning and evening, administered the Sacrament to 28. Christened a child in the evening. Mr Hattersley at dinner.

7th. Bought a horse for £22. Had all the morning occupied with Justice business. W. Fendall still detained in Ireland by the Regent's not looking over the minutes of the Court Martial.

8th. To Jerveaux, Mr and Miss Collins of Knaresborough there, both agreeable, Mr and Mrs Brere at dinner.

9th. To Catterick races, good sport, saw there Sir B. Graham and all the principal people of this neighbourhood. My new horse performed excellently, told Mr Morley he might have Twopenny which he accepted at the price £12. 12, was inclined to wish he had not taken her as she would have been invaluable to Mr Collins. Mrs N very angry at my keeping my word as a gentleman, and declared she had rather I had sold any horse I had. Now I had much rather have sold Elfin or Mrs Fall or Lady Sarah. No one knows the age of Twopenny, she is of no use on the farm and the new horse will have saved me five guineas at least before we return from Craike where we are to go on Monday.

10th. Saw Sir C. Loraine with Morley at the races, Mr and Mrs Orde Powlett, Costabadies, Mrs Maude, Duke of Leeds, Marquis of Carmarthen, Wyvill, Monson, Monson, Milbanke,

Elsley, Askwith, Jacques, Dr and Mrs Dodsworth, Col Pulleine, Marquis of Queensberry, Mr Graham, Healy, three Booths, Mr Harvey.

11th. Returned from Jerveaux and dined at Mr Morley's with Sir C. Loraine and Col Pulleine.

12th. Mrs N and the girls returned from Jerveaux.

13th. Did duty morning and evening.

14th. Went to Craike, met Mr and Mrs Dixon and Miss Harriet Fenton there. We were very much pleased with our reception and spent two very pleasant days.

15th. Went to Byland Abbey called by Dugdale "Belle Lande", was much struck by the ruins which tho' neither so complete or near so extensive as Fountains or even Jerveaux, is infinitely superior to the latter and rivals the former from the mere circumstance of having been left alone in the way that time and desolation left it, not having met such an improver as Mr Aislabie whose taste seems to have been very duly estimated by the late Mr Gilpin. We then went to Coxwold which is a very beautiful village, I called on my namesake whom I found at home with his two daughters and two other ladies, rather genteel looking women. Two striking monuments are in the Church, one erected to two of the Bellasyzes, one of whom married one of Oliver Cromwell's daughters and was son to the other gentleman. Both are in the Roman costume in armour, one with the *pallium*, the other not quite correctly dressed, but both have the immense peruques of Charles the second's time and are heavier than any head dress that can well be conceived. The other monument is older, erected to a Bellasyze and his wife, the lady kneels the hindmost of the two and I should think there are not less than a 150 quarterings of shields emblazoned on the background of the monument. The Park at Newburgh is a very extensive one ploughed here and there in patches, I find Mr Wynn Belasyse very unpopular for preventing any one riding in the Park and every man is very deservedly so who prevents another's pleasure without any profit to himself. No good reason can be assigned for any man shutting up his grounds from the gentry of the neighbourhood. I can easily conceive that this little gentleman's reason is his pride as every step you take betrays poverty, all the gates, roads, etc, being out of repair and I suppose he is ashamed to let the neighbourhood see how poor he is. The ride up the Dingle is very pretty. The piece of water pretty large, the house large, about the standing of King William. He has just ordered in all the keys from the gentlemen who had permission. We got in from having business with the keeper. Craike Castle appears to have been very old Norman I should think. There is a curious crypt mentioned by Leland used as a cowhouse.

16th.   Stopped today on our return to see the Church at Raskelf which both on the inside and the outside bears greater marks of antiquity than any I ever saw. The tower is nothing but deal boards nailed together and three or four unhewn trees leaning by way of props against it to keep it up to the Church.

17th.   A good sized leveret brought me yesterday by Wm Appleton of Middleton who requests me to recommend him to a place. Saw Mr Cholmondeley at dinner Tuesday at Craike, a very gentlemanlike Roman Catholic. Agricultural

Society meeting at Ripon at which about 45 dined. I entered in a sweepstake with Mr J. Monson and some others to shew a shearling tup at the October meeting. Sat by Mr Stapylton, formerly Martyn Bree the advertising surgeon in Parliament Street. Col Dalton obtained the prize for the best sow, Mr Wyvill for the yearling bull, and Mr R. Booth for the best aged bull.

18th. Paid my assessed taxes and made my return for the current year. Called on Mr and Mrs Ramsden who are to dine here Wednesday.

19th. Mary received a letter from Meliora[1] giving a melancholy account of J. F. N.'s affairs and that he was quite in despair as to relieving them. I cannot but attribute all his misfortunes to his having yielded to his wife's plan of taking him into Devon instead of coming here which would have let me have an opportunity of knowing his affairs to the bottom and of applying the best remedy in my power. The only satisfaction I can draw from the case is a very poor one, namely that the plan was in direct opposition to his mother's advice and persuasions as well as mine and we have not to charge ourselves with being the cause of her miscarriage or of her present distressing condition of health, after having given Devon climate the fullest and the fairest trial it appears she is in as bad or worse condition than she ever was at the end of any former winter. We should have been told, had our advice or John's authority prevailed upon her to winter in Yorkshire, that we had been the cause of her present state of health, tho' she might at one half the expense have had an artificial climate made for her at Wath which has turned out

---

[1] 'Meliora' has not been identified.

so successful with Mrs Smith, Lady Graham, Miss Harvey and is in the opinion of all understanding physicians in such cases of more beneficial tendency than any natural climate can be. Heard that Mr Skey had quarrelled with Lord A because he repaired his pew in Great Bedwyn Church and refused to do duty any more at T. Park[1] without coming to any explanation or discussion whatever. M. N. junior went to Kersley Bridge with Miss Claridge. John Fendall's account of the coal is that they get 50 ton per diem and will get 70 before he writes again. Heard of J. Commeline's arrival at Geneva, wrote to him.

20th.   Did duty morning and evening.

21st.   Heard from Mrs Fendall saying the men had quitted work in the forest, that she had applied to Mr Farquharson to lend her money according to his offer but that he had refused on the score of not having any.

23rd.   I wrote to Mrs F and was obliged to say I could not assist her until I had seen how J. F. N.'s affairs could be arranged. Mr and Mrs Ramsden, Mr and Mrs Allanson and Mr Morley dined with us. We were all delighted with Mrs R and he is far from being a disagreeable man but conversed principally with Dr Whaley. Morley shewed a letter at the card table from the Clerk of the Peace telling him his name had been sent up by the Chairman, Mr Headlam, to the Lord Lieutenant for the Commission of the Peace for the North Riding. I forgot to mention we dined (22nd) with Mr Askwith who told us he had let the Unicorn. Staveley dined there, Major Hall, Mrs Lucas, Miss Hodges, and two female and two male young Harrisons.

---

[1] Tottenham Park, Lord Ailesbury's house in Wiltshire.

24th. I dined with Mr Barstow, met Ewanson, Allanson of Topcliffe, Lascelles, Noble; Mr Cayley a friend of T. Hodgson's on my recognising him told a story of Tom Newton now of Coxwold refusing to drink and on Hodgson's asking why replied with great simplicity because his mother told him not to drink.

25th. Dined at Mr Allanson's with the Howards and Howard's brother.

26th. The Howards and Mr Barstow dined here.

27th. Did duty morning and evening. Had a long conversation yesterday with Mr Monson and Major Elsley whom I met at the Oak Tree being the monthly meeting, about Morley's being on the Commission, and they told me how it happened that he had not been put in the Commission before. Never was a poor unfortunate wight so unpopular. The J. Daltons prevented from dining here on Friday by the death of his grandmother Mrs Prescot.

28th. Received a letter from J. F. N. full of absurd despondency, I replied in a way that I think must bring him to Wath if anything will, in short if he and his wife are not both bent upon ruin. Made Anne copy the letter and send it to Melly. Went to Boro'bridge where there was a fair, principally to speak about my coal and to a job of Justice about Paul Vallet's child.

29th. Spent the whole morning justicing, principally on account of a summons I had issued to the Constable of Cundall which he had made no return to. A man appeared for not threshing Hunton's corn properly. An old woman applied for a summons for an assault by a woman who accused her of poisoning a fowl by administering mercury. The woman killed the fowl to see if it was poisoned and found it full of mercury. Another woman applied for relief against the Tanfield Overseer.

30th. An application was made to me by Col Serjeantson's keeper for advice in consequence of some persons having cut off Miss Serjeantson's dog's tail and I advised printing hand bills with two guineas reward.

May 1st. Sold oats at 45/- per quarter, barley at 44/-.

2nd. Dined at Mr Howards with R. Howard, Mr and Mrs Allanson and Mr Barstow.

3rd. Rode to Camp Hill about dog's tail, saw the amputation close to the body, a very ugly black terrier.

4th. Did duty in the morning at Wath and in the evening at Kirklington, Mr Morley having had a quinsey sore throat. At the Bedale Club on Wednesday I ordered the Oxford and Cambridge Calendars and Meessinger's works. Ten members were present.

5th. Dined at Mr Carter's with Mrs Ardens, Col Coore and Mr and Mrs Ed. Carter. Miss Claridge expressed her opinion of Caroline's stupidity and desired Mary to go to avoid being bored by it. Mr Claridge dined and slept here on Sunday and was off soon after 5 in the morning.

6th. Justicing and giving an affidavit to Lt Alison to enable him to receive his pay. Mr Barstow called, Miss C came here last Thursday and brought M. N. junior from Kersley. Borrowed Bakewell's Geology from Mr Morley. My new cabinet came from Leyburn and I have been occupied in arranging it. To mark Miss Claridge's character it is only necessary to say that with no one thing to do the whole day she retires at ½ past 11 to write her letters to be put under her chamber door to go by the post in the morning tho' there's no chance of the servants being in the way to give it the post boy.

7th.   Letters from Mrs Fendall saying that the one enclosed gave her £600 of the money lately sent from India and £200 for William. This is very different from anything conveyed in letters to me as he there states that the first wish is that the remittance should be applied to the purchase of William's troop and the next to be applied to Mrs Fendall's use in aid of what comes from the Bullo Pill, which is a very different thing to giving £800 out of the £2000 immediately and thereby rendering the primary object of the remittance of no avail as the troop will at the least cost £1700 and therefore there will be £500 short as soon as the money is applied as directed by J. Fendall's letter enclosed to me by Mrs Fendall.

8th.   Long letters from John and Eliza announcing their intentions of setting out for Fulmer on the 12th and remaining there till Michaelmas and mentioning that Western had issued a writ against him for the last year's rent.

9th.   Dined at Mr Hunton's with three Newsams, old Elsley, Redshaw, Thompson, and Simpson from Richmond, at this party was expended more wine than wit.

10th.   Dined with Mr J. Newsam with Mr Anderson and Mr E. Carter.

11th.   Did duty morning and evening at Wath, administered the Sacrament to G. Brockhill who appeared not likely to live 48 hours.

12th.   Wrote to Melly the substance of a letter I had directed to Exmouth after having had conversation with Howard. Dined with Caroline at Mr E. Carter's and agreed to take his piano at £12. 12. for Fanny Fendall. E. C. seemed inclined to buy Lady Sarah and agreed to come over to Wath to ride her.

13th.   Received a note from Mr E. Carter to put off coming to Wath tomorrow. Overwhelmed with justicing. Wrote to Joshua and Mrs Fendall about the India remittance.

14th.   I must here note that for nine weeks, that is from the 3rd of March to the 8th of May, there was not sufficient rain to wet a pocket handkerchief through or to lay the dust in the roads for a single hour. It has rained a very little since the 8th but it is not in the memory of man that so long a series of dry weather has occurred at this season of the year. Today a considerable quantity has fallen beginning with a violent hail storm. A pipe of wine was brought by my horse Miller in a cart from Boro'bridge and safely deposited in the coach house to be divided between me and Mr Morley. Mr J. Newsam dined here and assisted Miss Claridge who arrived this morning in turning my house out of the windows by dancing quadrilles with my girls. Began reading McCulloch on wines which seems very sensible tho' very philosophic. Wrote to Joshua to discount the £500 bill and place it to the disposal of Mrs Fendall. E. Carter did not come today. Mentioned today to Mr Walker of Melmerby that he had incurred a penalty of £20 by permitting a preachment by Methodists in his house that is vacant without having it licensed. Visited and prayed with Brockhill, found him no worse and no better.

15th. Went to the sale of Martin's effects at Bedale, bought a lot of china and ordered four dozen of Cape Madeira of Atkinson who promised me the bottles and rack at Martin's.

16th. Found myself very unwell for the last two or three days with a headache and sore throat, took salts and salines.

17th. My birthday. On the starving system. Heard from J. F. N., holds out the Priory business not being settled as his reason for not coming to Wath. I trust his mother's reply will satisfy him. Howard called with a letter from Western, civil enough.

18th. Mr Hattersley dined here. I did duty morning and evening. Called on Brockhill and found him rather better, a slight remain of my indisposition, wrote to Dr Gaskin for Bibles and Prayer Books. Sowed my mangel worzel and carrots on Friday. It has rained from ½ past 2 to 10.

20th. The Howards dined here.

21st. Mr Claridge called, took Miss C home with him. Dined at Capt Dalton's with Morley and the Sleningford Daltons.

22nd. Dined at Morley's with Mr and Mrs Redfern and Miss Swinton and Capt Dalton. Gave Miss Dalton one of Sprite's puppies and promised one to little John Dalton. Morley to send all the bottles he has, Capt D offered to lend me what I want. Received a letter from Col Wilton saying that he should come to Wath on his way to Allonby leaving Hickley on the 4th June. Finished threshing all my corn amounting to somewhat more than 800 bushels. Both Mr Howard and Mr Claridge firmly of opinion that there will not be the least difficulty in getting rid of Fulmer. A letter

from Melly states that John and Eliza are perfectly willing to
come to Wath so soon as ever they shall have arranged their
affairs. I am very apprehensive from the past that the
arrangement will be nothing decisive but some half measure
that will draw him on so as not to leave him at liberty to go
where he pleases on a curacy and so endeth my suspicion.

25th. Whit Sunday. Did duty morning and evening, administered the Sacrament to 33 Communicants.

27th. Mr Newsam and Miss Claridge came.

28th. Miss Williams arrived at Wath.

30th. Dr Harrison and Mr Newsam came to Wath and took
lessons of Miss Claridge in quadrilles, the Dr bolted as the
clock struck eleven as his horse was brought to the door in
the midst of a quadrille without making his bow or thanking
Miss Claridge for the pains she had taken with him.

31st. The meeting at York Gate improperly called so as no
other Justice met me, tho' the old Dean promised to meet me
the meeting before and the meeting at York Gate was four
miles nearer than the Oak Tree. Luckily there was no great
occasion for a second Justice, but the meeting is not near so
respectable if only one Magistrate attends and does not carry
the same weight in the eyes of the country.

June 1st. Did duty morning and evening.

2nd. Mrs Howard came to Wath.

3rd. Miss Newsam and Morley dined here and danced
quadrilles.

4th. Ripon Ball. Went a large party tho' Miss Claridge rode
off on purpose to avoid going; as soon as she had left Wath

Mr John Tweedy arrived at Wath and dined and next day brought a friend, a young Mr Swan, I suppose for a foil as Tweedy is an agreeable, unaffected, well informed young man and Swan is one of the greatest puppies I have met with a long time. I played four or five rubbers and lost about ten shillings.

6th. Col, Mrs and Miss Wilton and their nephew Mr J. Wilton with a man and maid arrived in a barouche and four.

7th. Went with the party to Studley. Mr Morley drove Mrs Newton, Col Wilton drove Miss Williams, five went in the gig. I rode with Miss Claridge and Mary.

8th. Did duty morning and evening.

9th. Went with the Wiltons and Miss Claridge and the Williams to Hackfall thro' Masham and returned by Sleningford.

10th. The Wiltons left us on their way to Allonby, our servants and Miss Claridge's maid Thompson unanimously complained of the blackguard b——dy conversation of Wilton's man and maid servant and Mrs Newton told Mrs Wilton she could not help mentioning to her what a very improper person they represented her to be for an attendant on her two sweet girls. Caroline went Monday to Howards. Miss Claridge received the following account from her father who is in Cumberland on a survey of the Greenwich Hospital Estates. "On Monday last I explored the great Nentfers level which was begun 35 years ago and has been and is continually making night and day to this hour. It is 100 yards below the bottom of all the mines and is making for the purpose of relieving the whole of them from water. It will take ten or fifteen years more to perfect it, it has already cost £50,000 and will cost £40,000 more to finish it. To prepare for this we dressed in miners' cloths and in a boat went up the level 4864 yards, arriving at the end we found three brothers, fine young men, at work, kept alive by wooden pipes of air from a shaft above at a very considerable distance and as they were at work upon solid rock there was no other means of getting it to pieces than blasting it with gunpowder. When we had viewed this wonderful work we returned in our boat to some distance when the men fired six or seven shots which caused such a concussion in the narrow place in which we were afloat that it blew most of our candles out and the noise almost deafened my old head for the moment. This expedition took us about 3½ hours and is estimated in my mind as one of the greatest labours of art I ever saw or heard of."

11th. Miss Claridge left us for Col Pulleine's, Mary dined at Howards. Received three dozen of Lissa from David Cogan and Co and four dozen of Cape Madeira from Atkinson of Bedale. Caroline went to Mrs Howard's and returned with Anne who went yesterday. Wrote to J. Fendall and recommended him by all means to marry.

14th. Received a letter from Mr Gauntlett and from Mrs Commeline. The former contained a most pressing invitation to Hampton Lacey, the latter gave a tolerably comfortable account of her visit to Little Easton and of her daughter Chesshyre being brought to bed in September. Miss Claridge returned from Col Pulleine's.

15th. Did duty morning and evening. Mr Hattersley to dinner.

16th. Bottled the Port. Mr Morley at dinner. The pipe ran 57 dozen and there will apparently be at least three more dozen. Received a parcel of Bibles and Testaments and Prayer Books from the Society for Christian Knowledge for £3. 9. 0.

18th. Mr R. Howard, Mrs J. Howard, H. Howard, Miss Compson, Mr Barstow, Mr C. Abdy, Mr Newsam at dinner. Went fishing with the cast in the morning. Black mare's (bought at Appleton's sale) filly died.

19th. At three o'clock this day the thermometer was 76 in shade and 106 in the sun and at four it began to thunder and continued almost an hour and half in one continued peal with hailstones near an inch in diameter and such rain as no person in my house had ever seen before. The succession of thunderstorms lasted till near 11 at night.

20th. At 9 o'clock the thermometer in the sun was 111. Caught an eel in the Stell that weighed above a pound. At 4 the thermometer was 107 in the sun, 77 in the shade.

21st. The hot weather still continued. Thermometer between 70 and 80 greatest part of the day.

22nd. Did duty morning and evening.

23rd. Set out at nine o'clock with the thermometer near 80 for Duncombe Park in our own carriage and horses in which were Miss Williams, Miss Sarah, Anne and myself, and in Miss Claridge's were herself and Mary Newton on the barouche and Mrs N and Caroline inside and so we arrived at Mr Barstow's where we were joined by Mr Barstow, Mr C. Abdy, and Mr J. Newsam who mounted the barouche in Mary Newton's place who got inside, and so we proceeded through Thirsk to Whistoncliffe when the post horses in Miss C's carriage refused to take the empty carriage up that tremendous hill for we had all got out at the foot of it notwithstanding the heat which was excessive, this delayed us a great while and the ladies having walked to the top of the hill joined the party in our carriage and held a parley as to what was best to do when we agreed to send John to Hamilton House to try for a pair of plough horses which he succeeded in procuring and we proceeded to Helmsley leaving them to follow when they should have procured them and got ready. When we got to Helmsley we found Mr Barstow and Mr Abdy who had preceded us in a gig had ordered dinner and we waited until Miss C's carriage should arrive before we sat down. Nothing could exceed the richness of the picturesque disposal of the wooded landscape that broke upon us as we descended from the Hamilton Hills which we did thro' a narrow defile or dingle whose perpendicular side was clothed with wood from top to bottom and the winding of the road presented an infinite variety of form of wooded banks and vallies that were only too beautiful not to be sublime, that is had nothing terrific but was luxuriant to excess in foliage and picturesque in form till we get to the bottom of the valley to Chawley Bridge where the beauty of the ride was *au comble* by exhibiting the ruins of Rivaulx Abbey in the most romantically secluded spot that can be conceived, overhung by woody perpendicular banks of an immense height with a beautiful rivulet running at the foot close to the Abbey walls. The natural way in which these ruins appear gives a decided superiority to the taste of the possessor over that of any ruin of this part of the kingdom that I have seen, for though not so perfect as Fountains nor of so florid a style it is of a chaste order and the choir sufficiently perfect for picturesque effect and has not been spoilt by the silly improvement and moderning of the ground which Fountains and many others exhibit, while it is not so rugged and wild as Byland Abbey at no great distance from it, but it is overhung by a modern temple which I think a man of true taste (if he was determined to build one) would have placed out of sight so that it should not abstract the attention of the spectator from the unity, simplicity and grandeur which the Abbey itself must command without the display of a Grecian building which shews more the wealth than the taste of the projector.

24th.   Received letters from the Biddisham tenants giving me notice of their intention to quit the tithes and also a letter from Mr Williams the curate there saying that he had already quitted the curacy and also an application from a gentleman who has the curacy of Bleadon offering to undertake the duty. Called on Mr Barstow and Mr C. Abdy.

25th.   Col Dalton laid an information against a poacher. Bedale Club. The thermometer this day about 9 was $118\frac{1}{2}$. At the club were Mr Monson and his brother, Mr Gale, Mr Wright, Mr Robson, Col Coore junior, Mr Pattison, Mr Elsley and myself. Mr Monson promised to meet me Saturday at the Oak Tree. Barely escaped a thunderstorm which fell with greater violence at Wath than at Bedale. Brought away Display, Watkins' Life of Sheridan, Ionian Isles, Lives of Pocock and Bishop Newton, Remarks on English character.

26th.   Gathered the first ripe strawberries. Wheat in ear and peas fit to gather.

27th.   Went to Pickhill.

28th. Meeting at Oak Tree, met Mr Monson, made three orders of maintenance in consequence of three filiations, convicted Geo. Berry of Howgrave in having snares for hares in his possession.

29th. Did duty morning and evening. Finished the Life of Bishop Newton which consists chiefly of anecdotes of political characters of his time and has little that is interesting of his family, his works or his Bishopric. I always understood that he was a relation of my family which was I believe acknowledged by the Bishop who gave my father almost the only living in his gift. I was disappointed as my pedigree is very deficient. I read also Mrs Carter's remarks on the scriptures from which I received little information except that she was a most amiable and pious woman. One passage I think she has well illustrated, I mean the question of the Disciples of our Saviour about the man who was born blind, which I trust I shall remember to read as I have pointed it below, "And his Disciples asked him saying, Master, Who did sin? this man? or his parents that he was born blind?" I conceive this mode of pointing and accenting does away the difficulty or rather the quirk or reflection on Providence who made a man blind for his sin before he was born, whereas the Disciples might see the man was blind but not know that he was born so, and under the notion that this infliction must be in consequence of sin they ask, Did this man sin and so has received this grievous affliction as a temporal punishment of his wickedness, or did his parents and so this man was born blind according to that threat in the second Commandment that God would visit the sins of the fathers upon the children unto the third and fourth generation.

30th. Received a letter from Mr Abrahall of Badgworth asking for the curacy of Biddisham. Wrote to him, to Parfitt, to Williams, and to Mr Blake and to J. F. N., all about the curacy of Biddisham. Received a letter from J. Commeline junior with two anecdotes well worth transcribing. When the Congress were sitting at Vienna the Genoese expressed a wish that if they were to be given up to the King of Sardinia they might at least be allowed a constitution on which Lord Castlereagh replied *d'un air moqueux* that such an insignificant state couldn't have much of a constitution. The other anecdote was that Mr Lascelles, the grandson of Lord Harewood, said that all public meetings in England ought to be dispersed by grapeshot and that all petitions either to the Lords or Commons ought to be considered treason. A thunderstorm began soon after 11 in the forenoon. Miss Abdy, Barstow and Newsam at dinner.

July 1st. Miss Claridge left Wath to return to Jerveaux. Mrs Bury has just been seized with a violent longing fit to see her mother, no one knew she had a mother and she has never seen her or mentioned her till within a few days tho' she has lived at Ripon and has children grown up and the Riponites are anxious to develop the mystery. Wrote to Mrs Commeline. As the girls were returning from Ripon where they had gone with Miss Claridge they saw a man leaning against a bank near Sir B. Graham's gate who appeared to be dying or dead and as soon as they came home I despatched the boy to see what was the matter with him, this was about ½ after 2, the boy never arrived at home till near 4, it turned out to be Squire Peacock of Carthorpe almost dead drunk, fallen from his horse which had run away and had not arrived so soon as his master who was attended home by Clarkson's apprentice as well as my boy.

2nd.   Called at Col Serjeantson's and Mr Morley's. Received a salmon from Newcastle from Mr Claridge and Anne had a long letter from John announcing that Eliza would be confined in October.

4th.   Received of Sir B. Graham's agent £75 being half a year of the tithe of Norton.

5th.   Dined with Mr Barstow, Mr Monson, and Col Serjeantson. Took off the indictment from Melmerby Road.

6th.   Did duty morning and evening. Churched and christened. Sir B. Graham took up his quarters at Blyth's.

8th.   Called on Mr and Mrs Dawson at Azerley.

9th.   Called on Mrs Morley at Kirklington. Dr Whaley came to Anne. Put on a new pair of knit pantaloons.

11th.   Dined at Mrs Howard's with Mr and Mrs Dawson, the Harrisons, Mrs Lucas, dined Thursday at Mr Morley's.

12th.   Mrs Morley, two Misses and Mr Morley, Mr Harrison, J. Newsam, Mr and Mrs Dawson and Miss Harrison at dinner.

13th.   Did duty in the morning and evening.

14th.   Morley told us he was going to Northallerton Sessions to qualify. The Rainton people promised to mend their part of the Hutton Moor road. Dined at Kirklington with Mr Headlam and Mr J. Newsam.

15th.   Went to Jerveaux through violent rain, got wet thro' and so did Miss S. Williams who was in the gig with me. The rain ceased the moment we got into the house,

16th. and today has been a remarkably fine day which enabled us to see Aysgarth Force in high beauty and to call at Wensley in our way, the Rector and Mrs Maude followed us here to dinner and Mr J. Newsam joined our party yesterday.

17th. Wrote to Mrs Fendall, received a letter from Mr Meade which after detailing the impossibility of visiting us this year ended by saying they were ready and determined to come.

18th. Went to Aysgarth Force, was much pleased with Miss Claridge's friend Miss E. Boodle; called on the Costabadies, found Miss Tyler arrived at Jerveaux during our absence.

19th. Heard Mr Powlett would not go to any place to dine where Mr Claridge was invited because he was a steward, how soon Mr Powlett seems to have forgotten that he is a son of Orde a country attorney,[1] however this might be of some use to Miss C to know when she is great and grand and teach her that in the scale of society and in the opinion of it too she is below the children of those to whose profession the greatest man in the land cannot object merely on the profession's account; I make this remark from the high hand with which she seems to carry herself towards the Costabadies, never having seen breezes of that sort towards my girls. Called on Mrs Hardcastle on our way home and got home between 3 and 4.

20th. Did duty morning and evening.

[1] Mr Powlett (the Hon. Thomas Powlett Orde-Powlett) was a son of Thomas Orde, who had married in 1778 Jean Mary Powlett, illegitimate daughter of the last Duke of Bolton and heiress to Bolton Castle upon his death in 1795. Orde became a Privy Councillor in 1778 and was created Baron Bolton in 1797.

21st.   Received a note from Mr Claridge announcing the death of young Woodpecker yesterday morning. Received three dozen of Lissa wine by the canal and also a letter from Canon Williams giving but a poor account of Benjamin.[1]

22nd.   Thunder and lightening.

23rd.   Thermometer 102 at 9. Bedale Club, Elsley, two Monsons, Morley, Serjeantson, Newsam, Gale, B. N.

24th.   Mr and Mrs Botfield called here.

25th.   Thermometer 109 at 9.25.

27th.   Did duty morning and evening.

28th.   Read Mrs Carter's letters to Mrs Montagu, enough to prove she was a very good woman which every one knew before. The letters have no interest in them, she was decidedly good but her opinions of men and manners want decision and the editor's notes are weak endeavours to bring himself constantly to the reader's notice as Mrs Carter's nephew. He panegyrises my old acquaintance Cooper Willyams who was a very good natured chattering little fellow with some taste for drawing with no learning or strength of head. Received a letter from Mr Thompson with an account of his wife's death but without any expression of regret for her. Read some of Burns's correspondence. Wrote to Sir J. Nicholl and Mrs Wilmot. Received a letter from Capt Symonds giving an account of Mr Keate's having died suddenly as he was dressing to go to dine with Mr Glossop at Wolverton.[2]

29th.   Thermometer 109 at 9 today.

[1] Tenant of Newton's farm at Brecon.
[2] The Rev. William Keate (see p. 3) was Rector of Laverton, Somersetshire, and brother of the Rev. John Keate, D.D., Headmaster of Eton from 1809 to 1834.

30th. Costabadie came to us last night from Ripon where he had been taking his four sons

31st. and stayed till today. I promised to go to Wensley on Thursday. Costabadie told us some curious stories of G. C. and the mode in which Mr Moore, Mrs Carter's father, made his fortune by answering an advertisement when he was a hackney writer in London. He found the person who had advertised for a person to read to him was the first Lord Holland, Charles Fox's father. At his leisure hours he got a few lessons from an acquaintance in French and when he went to give a specimen of his reading Lord H gave him a comedy in which were a few French words which he dashed at with pretty good success at the accent, and Lord H said he thought he would do. Lady H said you can never bear his coarse loud voice, Oh, said his Lordship, I am a little deaf and he is the very thing. He engaged Mr Moore who turned out a useful and an honest man and Lord H pushed him on from employment to employment till he was enabled at his death to leave his daughters £15,000 apiece though he had eleven children. The young men under Anthony's tuition for confirmation answer my questions to them much better than I expected and they appeared to me better qualified than any of the girls except Auton. Dr Whaley called to visit Anne. Read Currey's life of Burns.

August 1st. Received a letter from J. Fendall still at Java giving an account of a severe illness he had, does not leave the island till May last. Read Life of Burns.

2nd. Thermometer at 107. Baptised a child of Smith of Melmerby last night which had its thigh broken in being brought into the world, it did not seem to be in pain or anyways ill. Wrote to J. F.

3rd. Did duty morning and evening, christened a child and churched a woman. Mr Hattersley followed me into my room to tell me that Wells's settlement was not at Melmerby which I thought great impertinence after writing to him to tell him that the Magistrates at York Gate had determined the settlement to be at Melmerby and I told him it was a marked incivility to myself considering the relations in which I stood to Wells and that if he persisted in such conduct, I would turn him off and pay him only the ten pound half yearly for the school.

4th. Heard nothing of Mr Hattersley.

5th. Mr Hattersley sent Wells's boy away with a letter saying that the respectable people of Melmerby say he does not belong to them. Dined at Col Serjeantson's with Mr, Mrs, Mr J. and two Miss Newsams, Mr C. Elsley.

7th. Went to Wensley, saw Mr Maude, etc, and his rectory.

8th. Went in tremendous rain with Mr and Mrs Costabadie to Richmond to the Visitation, dined about forty, heard an admirable charge and a very good sermon from Mr T. Collins, Rector of Bammingham, though there seemed to be some opposition in the tenets of the Bishop and the preacher who seemed to incline a little to Calvinism. Returned to Wensley after having drunk tea with Mr and Mrs Robinson.

9th. Returned home, called at Jerveaux and promised to meet the Bishop of Chester there tomorrow at dinner. Found Mrs Commeline and Henry Fendall at Wath who told me that John and William[1] were on the road and would arrive on Tuesday.

10th. Did duty morning and evening and went to dine at Jerveaux with the Bishop and two Miss Monsons who carried me to Bedale at night and gave me a bed that I might be ready to meet the Bishop

11th. this morning who breakfasted there, confirmed 984 of which 40 were my parishioners, after the Confirmation the Bishop ascended the pulpit and gave the young people a most appropriate and excellent address. This Confirmation was far better conducted with more regular decency and quiet than I ever saw it before, for which Mr Monson deserved very great praise, particularly for having carpeted the Church to take off the noise of the country people's hobnails against the flag stones. I returned after having dined with the Bishop at Mr Monson's and drank tea with him at Mr Morley's, well convinced of his being a very good Bishop both in the Church and out of the Church, a conscientious and a very agreable man. Found John and William arrived.

12th. Went to Jerveaux to meet Mr Byng (commonly called Poodle) who was there with Mr Bidwell. Byng's footman insisted on not going to bed unless he has a room to himself. Found Byng reading at the door at Jerveaux having had enough of moor game shooting between 10 and 2 and his friend was gone to bed.

14th. Got up, went on the moor at ten, got four shots, killed one bird which I lost and returned at 2. Col Wood, M.P. for Breconshire, and his father dined at Jerveaux and a

[1] Fendalls.

very pleasant gentlemanly man I found him. Mr Claridge would not let him go without canvassing me which he did in a way that was very kind and genteel and I accepted a frank from him to Mr Hildyard in which I enclosed £2 to him for Mr Skipwith. Forgot to mention having driven Mrs N to Thorpe on my way to Jerveaux to call on Mr Milbanke and Lady Augusta who had sent us all an invitation to their ball on the 27th. Returned. William and Henry Fendall went next morning to Mr Danby's moor, killed one bird and got home as we were going to dinner.

16th.   Drove and rode to Ripon. Rained all night.

17th.   Did duty morning and evening.

18th.   Drove Mrs Commeline to Hackfall.

19th.   Dined with Mrs C, W. F. and Mary at Mr Morley's who with his sister dined here and danced quadrilles as did Newsam, J. Harrison, T. Harrison and their sister on Monday evening. Mrs Wilmot arrived while we were at Kirklington.

20th.   J. and H. Fendall, Anne and Caroline dined at Kirklington.

22nd.   J. and W. F. set out for York races.

23rd.   Rode with Mrs N and M. N. junior to Theakston.

24th.   Did duty morning and evening. J. F. told me a girl of 12 years of age when brought before the Magistrate Wetherall to give in her complaint of having been ravished declared it was entirely with her own consent and that she had been at her uncle's pleasure ever since she was eight years old. This girl was daughter to Rees Hopkins the Fendalls' overlooker in the Forest.

26th.   Mr Claridge, Henry, Miss, and Miss Boodle at dinner and dancing quadrilles.

27th.   Ball at Thorpe. Everything managed with the greatest propriety and regularity. 160 about the number present. Mr Powlett, Lady Emily Monions, Sir E. Smith, Wyvill, Serjeantson, Carter, Robson, Newsam, Hutton, Dundas, Wentworth families, got home about 7 in the morning.

29th.   Masham Turnpike meeting, Mr Danby, Batley, Strangeways, Harrison of Oldborough, Ibbetson.[1]

30th.   York Gate meeting, Morley, Mr Stanley, Col Serjeantson. The Meades arrived while we were at dinner without having given the previous notice Mrs M's last letter taught us to expect. Read Ricardo. Difficult to comprehend his first propositions but worth the attention required as it is very sensible and clever. Mrs N went to Thorpe to invite the Milbankes. Continued rain the greater part of the week. Began cutting oats and wheat. Complaints about the wheat in many situations being *deaf*. Mrs N and I were obliged to go to Mrs Fall's to sleep so that now our house is full and we have five who sleep out of it.

31st.   Did duty in the morning and evening. Meeting at the Oak Tree. Mr Morley and Mr Stanley there, Col Serjeantson and I did all the business. Morley had asked me to spare Mr Hattersley till the middle of October to him to do the duty at Kirklington which I consented to. Mr Baines the Rector of Tanfield told me he had received a letter from

[1] Julius Caesar Ibbetson, the artist, lived at Masham under the patronage of Mr William Danby of Swinton Park. He died in the following October.

Hattersley which I had desired him not to send about the school at Wath.

September 1st. Went with all the Meades to Studley, met two Scotch gentlemen there who enquired whether there was anything else worth seeing in the neighbourhood, on my mentioning Hackfall and giving him the best description of it that I could said he supposed it must be very like the Highlands of Scotland. There were eight carriages when we came out of the gardens one of which was Mr H. Elsley's, with Mrs Sharp, Mrs Fendall's aunt, for one of the party.

2nd. Mrs N went to Theakston and took a spaniel puppy to Miss Carter.

3rd. Went with all the Meades, a party of 12, to Hackfall. I forgot to mention I sent the carriage horses with Mrs Wilmot yesterday to Ripon who left us to go to Mrs Pares at Ashbourne Green on her return towards Bath. Met Lord Grantley at Hackfall with three ladies, two of whom he recommended to my care to walk about the place while he proceeded with the other to visit Mr Danby. The two ladies were very coy and repulsive, neither Mr Meade nor I could bring them into any conversation during the whole walk which lasted over two hours, nor to take a sandwich with us after the walk was over. The heat this day was very great and we did not get back to dinner till six o'clock. The lady who went to Swinton with Lord G was a Miss Norton, who our companions were we knew not except that they came from Surrey.

4th. Agricultural Committee meeting, fixed the show for 2nd October.

5th. Oat and wheat shearing. Mr and Mrs E. Carter, Charlotte Costabadie and Mr Newsam at dinner and quadrilles.

6th. Settled a dispute between a Stewart and Brathwaite of Tanfield.

7th. Did duty morning and evening.

9th. Buried young Cuthbert Allanson.

10th. Went with Mr Meade to Wensley, called at Jerveaux on our way.

11th. Went to see Mr Maude's collection of minerals, also Mr Billington's the Catholic Priest's at West Witton, Mr Jackson a brandy merchant's at Leyburn.

12th. Left Wensley with Mr Costabadie and Mr Meade for Arkendale, travelled over a moor entirely covered with ling to Reeth, a beautiful little town situate in Swale Dale and surrounded with mountains covered with ling, called on Mr Hall who has a fine collection of the produce of the Yorkshire, Cumberland and Durham mines, did not see Mr H but Mrs H shewed us the collection, met there with a Mr Harland a particularly handsome man who gave us a few specimens of carbonate of barytes with which the Swale Dale and Arkendale mines particularly abound, bought also a few at a shop and a few at the Inn. Proceeded from Reeth to Arkendale with a letter of introduction to a Mr Tilburn who seemed at first not to know what a mineral was tho' he was a principal clerk in the lead work, however he found us a conductor who led us towards the mouth of the level which he said was about a $\frac{1}{2}$ mile from Tilburn's house; when we had passed the smelting and roasting mill which is on a very large scale and belongs to a company of Londoners and walked about a mile

to the place where some very handsome girls were washing
the lead the guide pointed out the mouth of the level about
a mile and ½ further off on a very high point of ground which
as it was near 3 o'clock was too laborious for us to attempt,
we therefore returned to Mr Tilburn who gave us a few very
good specimens and our guide having brought us also a few
and having picked up a few from the miners living in the
village of Arkendale we returned to Wensley tolerably well
loaded and got there at about ½ past 7. The girls and H. Costabadie had ordered dinner before I arrived and had eaten part
of it. Mrs C and Mr Meade did not arrive till we had finished
and Mrs C was very angry at the young ones having gone
to dinner before our return as Mr C dined out that day at
Leyburn Book Club.

13th.   Having had a good deal of fun about dividing the
fossils between Mrs C, Mr M and me we left Wensley and
called at Jerveaux calling at Otterville Woods and passing
over Middleham Moor in our way and get to Wath safe about
½ past 4.

14th.   Did duty morning and evening.

15th.   J., H. and W. Fendall dined with Capt J. Dalton, I
sent him a bean stem with 45 pods on it for a challenge.

16th.   Set out for Brimham Crags with Mrs Meade, her
two daughters, my three girls and the three Fendalls and
though we went all the way through a drizzling fog were
highly pleased with the sight which is certainly unique and
only to be well described by a drawing, the general character
of the rocks may be given by saying that they are in general
detached masses with the upper parts much larger than their

bases, from 15 to 35 ft high and some of them have such a resemblance to works of art that nothing but their stupendous size is sufficient to satisfy the mind that some enormous giants have not been displaying their skill in fantastic masonry with little stones of about 40 tons weight apiece. I describe four. The first has a cylindric hole about nine inches diameter and 30 feet long drilled thro' it so strait that you look through it with the same ease as through a telescope and Herschell would do well to go to Brimham and fit some glasses to it. The second is a ravine in the rock at least 50 yards perpendicular and about ten feet wide into the top of which 20 feet above the ground which surrounds it are pitched two wedge shaped stones of about six feet thick and 12 feet long and which must have fallen into the chasm at the same instant of time, as had either of them dropped in by itself it must have fallen through into the valley fifty yards below had it not been supported by its brother acting as a keystone does to an arch. The third is an immense rocking stone fourteen feet long and ten foot high and ten foot thick, the upper surface of which is flat and the under one rounded so that by the application of a man's shoulder at one end this great weight is easily rocked to and fro. The last I describe is a stone thirty feet high and seventy feet in circumference supported on a stem only seven feet in circumference and exhibits at a distance the appearance of a great tree supported at bottom by a slender stem and cut into nearly about the middle like a wasp. This stone we measured, by getting under the projecting part we were able to measure the stem at the smallest part about two feet from the ground and the other part about six feet from the ground; supposing these circles or circumferences to be as the squares of their diameters they are to each other as 100 to 1. Need I say anything more to enhance the idea of this phenomenon?

17th.   This relation has made Mr Meade all afire to see these rocks and J. Fendall has promised to drive him there.

18th.   Called on Mr Allanson and get from him Mr M's Rout to Chester.

19th.   Brewster Sessions. Mr I'Anson brought St Clair's opinion as to the power of the Magistrates to enforce a woman to filiate who lives in service and has children by her master. The opinion goes no further than to say he would not recommend magistrates to interfere between men and their mistresses as his legal friends tell him it is not the practice. N.B. This opinion was given 1792 and regarded Priestly of Melmerby. The opinion is unlike a lawyer and ruinous to parishes if they cannot on complaint before magistrates get the children of such women filiated.

21st.   Did duty morning and evening.

23rd.   Dined at Mr Howard's, christening and went to the Ripon Ball. Received a haunch of venison from Mr Allanson and a pike from Mr Claridge. Sir B. Graham's keeper came to me to complain of H. Fendall's having been shooting at Norton, I took the opportunity of telling him that I considered Sir B. Graham to have given me the most unlimited leave to shoot on his manors both for myself and my friends. He produced a written order from Sir B cancelling all former leaves, I told him I considered myself as in a different situation from anyone else as I had purchased the leave by letting Sir B have the deputation of Wath when I might have had it myself and I remonstrated on the excessive impropriety of

SIR BELLINGHAM GRAHAM, M.F.H.

his constantly beating my farm the first in his beat and told
him I sent H. Fendall to Norton on purpose and that I would
write to the effect of what I had said to him to Sir Bellingham
as I had mentioned his conduct to Mr Claridge who told me
he considered it was shameful and would see Sir B on the
matter. I wrote to Sir B the same. Mrs Lawrence, Lord
Grantham at the Ball and about 120 more.

24th. Book Club at Bedale. Mr W went with J. Fendall
and Mr Howard to Brimham Crags. Caleb Redshaw told us
the Barons of the Exchequer were thus distinguished, one
gentleman and no lawyer (Richards), one lawyer and no
gentleman (Wood), one neither lawyer nor gentleman
(Garrow). He told us too of a man who got a living by
preaching at Hinchinbrooke before the Duchess of Gordon.
He said the King who made the supper for the marriage had
good right to be angry with those who refused to come as
the piece of ground the man had bought would be there on
the morrow as it could not run away, the other who bought
the yoke of oxen could have proved them as well on any
other day, but the greatest fool of all was he that would not
go because he had married a wife as he had nothing to do but
to have taken his wife with him.

25th. Mr Howard, Mr Gabriel and Miss Compson at dinner.
Finished my large wheat field the glass having fallen most
rapidly.

26th. Wrote to Lord Ailesbury. Sir S. Romilly[1] told Smith
that Judge Nares once in condemning a man said "You will
shortly appear before another, and give me leave to say an
abler judge". Received a letter from J. F. N. giving an account

[1] A prominent barrister and Whig member for Westminster.

of his having been ordained on Sunday last and that Mr
Sandiford was very civil to him and not very puzzling, he
says the Bishop is in good health but his eyes fail him and
that he could not be licensed till he got a house. Received
a letter from J. Commeline q.v. dated 11th.

27th.   To Ripon with J. F., paid Mr Meade and Betty
Goodenough's allowance.

28th.   Did duty morning and evening. Mrs Commeline
unwell, sent for Dr Whaley, worried at being obliged to stay
here to wait for Lord H. Kerr who does not come before the
10th of next month. Mr Meade desired me to purchase
Otterville Woods chimney piece of Dent marble and Sir
C. Pole is to write to me about it. A letter from Mr Claridge
tells me he has sold Brother Peter to Sir B. Graham for £400
down and £100 more if he wins the Produce Stakes at
Catterick. Finished my wheat harvest and oats. A tem-
pestuous wind in the night of the 27th threw down the stacks
and all the sheaves of wheat and barley in the country, many
trees broken and thrown down and the uncut corn greatly
damaged by having the heads or ears snapped off and blown
away.

29th.   Mr Carter sent a cow here to rest on her way to the
show at Ripon.

30th.   Mr Howard and Mr Gabriel called. Received a letter
from J. F. N. from Fulmer with a very false idea of Biddisham
given him by Mr Parfitt. The Meades left us yesterday and
were obliged to send John back from Hutton for a great coat
they left behind by which they lost more than an hour. The
last three days I have been much annoyed by the toothache
which seems tonight to decline.

October 2nd. Agricultural Meeting Dinner, made up my mind to withdraw from the great stupidity that prevailed at the dinner which was a most excellent one and from the praemiums having no effect whatever in inducing others to become new candidates, but every person who got prizes at the first meeting has continued to get them at every succeeding one, witness Booth, Wright, Brown, Robb.

3rd. Partridge shooting, saw only five and got no shots.

4th. Finished carrying all my corn except my beans which I finished cutting this day. Captain Dalton dined here.

5th. Did duty morning and evening.

6th, 7th, 8th. Taking up potatoes.

9th. Richmond Races, saw Sir B. Graham's mare Duchess[1] win the Cup and the Whitelocke colt that was the favourite for the Doncaster St Leger win two sweepstakes beating D.I.O. who with Rasping had no chance. Returned that evening having travelled our horses 46 miles besides riding them five hours on the course.

10th. Brought in part of the beans.

11th. Potatoes. Breakfasted with two Fendalls at Mr Carter's, went hunting with Mr Milbanke's hounds at Theakston where we had very little sport.

12th. Did duty morning with Sacrament and evening.

13th. Gave Mrs Commeline a good lecture for being so dissatisfied after had a letter from Maria yesterday who was the one she seemed inclined to think was ill and it appears to have done her a great deal of good as she seems better in

---

[1] The Duchess had won the St Leger in the previous year.

health and much more quiet in mind. Received a letter from Mr Ramsden about the conviction of Fletcher and the penalty not being to the poor of Rainton. A thorn that A. F. N. got into her foot four years ago at Little Bedwyn after having given her great pain and bled profusely so that Mr Hague suspected it was an aneurism came out of her foot since when the foot has gradually got well. She struck her foot against the stump about a fortnight before and it had pained her ever since. Physicked Lady Sarah. Finished getting in all my potatoes which were the most abundant crop and the finest of their kind I had ever seen.

15th. Invitation from Mr Gilpin to dine at Hollin Hall either on Thursday or Friday to meet Mr Guise. The same irritation seems to prevail in Mrs C on being disappointed from setting out on Monday which Miss Compson refuses to do. I am heartily sorry to see her such a victim to selfish ill humour which is only kept dormant while every possible whim has its full gratification.

16th. Began wheat sowing and got in all my beans which finished my harvest.

17th. Dined at Hollin Hall, met Mr and Mrs Faber, Mr Powell Guise, Mr Bernard Gilpin. On my complaining of the toothache Mr Faber (the writer on Prophecy) said he heard the toothache accounted for in the following manner by a friend of his and he gave the account as if he believed it. He said that certain minute epemerae of the butterfly species flying about are accidentally taken into the mouth and that they then make a nidus in a rotten tooth where they deposit their eggs which in process of time are hatched and produce minute grub which immediately begin feeding on the nerves of the tooth and cause the intolerable pain which is experienced and that the remedy applied by his friend was to procure the seeds of henbane, make them very dry and then set them on fire under a tin funnel, the small end of which is to be directed so that the smoke may issue against the offending tooth which will immediately kill the grubs, and that the friend had ejected several in the saliva after the operation and seen them very distinctly with a lens.

18th. Finished sowing the Clover Lay with the wheat. Received a letter from Sir B. Graham, very different from what I expected.

19th. Did duty morning and evening. Baptised a child and churched a woman. Called to enquire after Mr Pearson of Melmerby who I heard had a paralytic stroke on Friday which seemed to settle in his leg and cause violent pain which still continued. Gave H. Fendall a Variorum Plautus.

20th. Ripon Book Club, Dr Whaley, the Dean, Dr Harrison, Allanson, Williamson, Oxley, B. N. Received the first new half sovereigns at Coates'. Lent T. P.[1] £40, promised to be returned on Saturday.

21st. Mrs Commeline, Lord H. Kerr, and Miss Compson left Wath at 9 and went towards Redmarley. Spoke to Coates about making housekeepers filiate children they have by their masters and he said there could not be a doubt about Justices having the power and indeed being obliged to do it at the request of the overseer of the parish likely to be burthened.

22nd. Bedale Club. Present Dr Scott, a new member, late chaplain to Lord Nelson who died aboard the Victory in his

[1] Thomas Proctor.

arms. He appears a gentlemanly man who has seen much of the world but seems to have an idea he is sent here to inform the natives. Dr Dodsworth, who ate an enormous dinner for an octogenarian, Mr Monson, Mr G. Monson, Mr J. Monson, Mr Scrope, Mr Elsley, Mr Newsam, Mr Robson, Mr Pulleine and B. N.

23rd.   At Boro'bridge fair, bought my wife a habit and myself a pair of smallclothes.

24th.   Turnpike meeting at New Inn, Col and Capt Dalton, Tim and D'Arcy Hutton, Messrs Bell, Clarke, Monson, two Baines, Leafe, Harrison. Elected (Curtis) a new surveyor. Mr Bell offered to meet us with the hounds on Monday at Skipton Bridge.

25th.   Justice meeting, appointment of overseers of the Highways, appointed myself and Mr Whitwell. Dined at the Howards with Mr and Mrs Gilpin, Mr and Mrs Askwith, two Miss Baines, Morley and Mrs Lucas. All Tories but Askwith who descanted largely on the merits of the Morning Chronicle and demerits of the Dean of Ripon. Killed the last of Hunton's Scotch wethers.

26th.   Mr Claridge called on Friday and we had a conversation about Col Dalton's laying an information against Frank Alman, Wells of Bury Hills, and Thompson of Kirklington for shooting on W. Fall's farm who was with them. Sold a tup at Boro'bridge Fair. Did duty morning and evening.

27th.   Hunting with Mr Bell's hounds at Skipton Bridge.

28th.   Ripon Ball, saw Col Dalton and he consented to lay the information against Alman, Thompson of Pickhill and Wells of Leeming Lane before some other Magistrate as

Alman was one of my parishioners and I have since heard that the Colonel has excused them in consequence of their having taken my advice and begged his pardon.

29th.   J. Fendall went to Aldborough and the Howards came here bringing Anne and Caroline who slept there after the ball.

30th.   J. F. did not return from Aldborough.

31st.   Went hunting about 2 o'clock, drew Melmerby and Hutton Moor without finding.

November 1st.   Went hunting to Thorpe, large field and had two good runs without killing, one from Watless Whin to Clifton Castle and then from High Burton to Nosterfield and Well and Near Kirklington. Lady Darlington, Lady Augusta Milbanke, J. Monson, Harrison, Strangeways, Carter, Col Pulleine, Coore, Clough, Worsley, etc.

2nd.   Did duty morning and evening. Mr Hattersley at dinner.

3rd.   Mr Morley and Mr Wigglesworth, a friend of Mr Morley's, at dinner.

4th.   Coursing on my farm with Mr Morley, coursed four hares and killed one. I forget to mention that I killed the first partridge I have killed this year yesterday. Morley afterwards killed a fox at Tanfield. The Howards and Anne returned to Ripon with them.

5th.   We went to Jerveaux and J. F. to Mr Howard's on his way to Cambridge. I went hunting and found a fox at Sleningford which ran to Hollinhead Wood. Henry took my mare back from Masham. The weather so foggy I could scarce find my way thither. Mr Claridge told me that Ralph

Robb, a tenant of Lord Egremont's at Topcliffe, went to Falkirk Fair and bought twelve thousand head of cattle on his own account, this he accomplished by carrying £30,000 in Bank of England bills besides drawing long drafts, etc. This is the same farmer that bred Otterington that won the St Leger.

6th.   Middleham Fair, bought a score of Scots wethers; it is supposed that there were 5000 more cattle on the Moor than last year. The Costabadies dined at Jerveaux.

7th.   Rode with Mr Claridge to Hutton Hang over Kilgram and back over Ulshaw Bridge by Thornton Steward and Danby. Had a woodcock for dinner every day at Jerveaux. Had a conversation with him on Sir B. Graham's letters which I showed him and he agreed entirely with me as to the terms on which the deputation of Wath was given to Sir B, to whom I defer writing till I see Col Serjeantson.

8th.   Returned from Jerveaux after having been grievously shocked by the intelligence in a Gazette extraordinary of the amiable Princess Charlotte having been delivered about nine o'clock on Wednesday night of a stillborn son and having expired in convulsions about ½ past 2 the next morning to the inexpressible grief of the Regent, the Prince Leopold her husband, the Royal Family and the nation at large. Certainly the loss of any other branch of the Royal Family would have cost less regret. Her most amiable and sensible deportment in many trying dilemmas had endeared her far beyond any other member of her family to the British nation and her domestic life was such as no person in her line of life had ever exhibited on the stage of European Royalty. The hopes of her Father, Mother, Husband and all her supposed future subjects received the death blow. The Succession becomes a matter of no interest if not of regret and now stands over to the Dukes of Kent, York, Clarence, Cumberland, Sussex, Cambridge, the Queen of Wurtemberg, the Princesses Elizabeth, Augusta, Sophia, the Duchess and Duke of Gloucester, the Princess Sophia of Gloucester, the Duke of Brunswick, the Princess of Wales, which still leaves the nation without an heir from the issue of the Princess Sophia of Hanover without going to Denmark for the King who is the issue of the younger sister of George the third. On our return from Jerveaux called on Mrs Ibbetson at Masham and looked over her late husband's rough sketches, which are so very slight as to be of little use to any but artists and which I fear will produce very little at Masham where artists are not likely to see them. Ibbetson's last picture (a view of the Market Place at Ambleside) is the only one almost that she has left to dispose of and is a most beautiful cabinet picture. She values it at 60 guineas. She is an interesting woman and capable of great exertion with a high spirit which prevent her accepting the subscription which was set on foot for her. Mr Newsam returned with us from Jerveaux and dined and slept here. Paid my half year's rent at Jerveaux. Bought a score of Scots wethers of which Mr Morley is to have half. Left Mr Claridge very unwell. Lost a Hereford cow this week which died in calving.

9th.   Did duty morning and evening. Finished the Life of Melancthon, a most amiable character. Received a letter from Mrs Hall about Mrs Shurrah's mother praying me not to mind the law but frighten Shurrah. Mr Claridge perfectly recollected my conversation with Lord Ailesbury and him in Grosvenor Square after my return from Wath in July 1814 about game and understood the arrangement to be precisely as I stated it in my last to Sir B. G. Mr C has Sir B. G.'s letter now by him in which he applied for the deputation of Wath. Heard that Elizabeth Meade was siezed with the measles at Chester.

10th.   Hunting with Lord Darlington at Baldersby Cundall. Weaned my filly, sent six sheep bought at Middleham to Mr Morley. Hired Mrs Humphries' brother to come in Will Houseman's place, at £7 if he behaves himself and 6 guineas if he is not obedient.

11th.   Dined at Mr Morley's with Mr, Mrs, and Miss Headlam, Miss Morley and Mr G. Hartley.

12th.   Dined again at Mr Morley's with the Headlams and Capt and Mrs Dalton.

13th.   Dined again at Mr Morley's with the Headlams, Col, Mrs and Miss Dalton and Mr Wright. Attended meeting at Ripon to put off the next ball on account of Princess Charlotte's death. Miss Claridge came to Wath, brought a woodcock and a brace of partridges. Anne received a long letter from J. Commeline, very entertaining, saying his pupil is very inflammatory but like some coal goes out if you don't poke him.

14th.   Write to J. Commeline and to Eliza. Settled my mowing and reaping account with Smith. Finished wheat sowing.

15th.   Anne returned from Ripon. A violent toothache plagued me all day for which I took James's powder at night. Wrote Lord Ailesbury.

16th. Toothache continued but I did duty morning and evening and determined to set out for the dentist at York next morning,

17th. which I did in Miss Claridge's carriage and got to Green Hammerton intending to take post horses and return leaving my own but the people at the Inn would not come near the carriage and at last when I went to them refused the horses and said they had no boy at home. After waiting an hour we proceeded with our own to York and to my great mortification found both the dentist and his partner gone to Hull for a month. As soon as we had ascertained this we met with Mrs Dixon who invited us to dinner and soon after met Mr Dixon, we accepted the invitation and Mrs Dixon carried me to Mr Atkinson's, a surgeon, to have my teeth out, but he was not at home, she then took me to Mr Drake's, another surgeon, who recommended me not to have the teeth out on any account until I could have another put in as it would most materially affect my speech and the two adjoining teeth would close on the space from which the offending tooth had been removed. So we withdrew, sent our horses back to Boro'bridge and ordered post horses to take us up at 6 o'clock at Mr Dixon's where we dined and get home tooth and all by ½ past 11. I was seized with such a paroxysm that I was obliged to quit the dinner table and go to the fire where I found such instant relief that I thought it was quite gone, however I have had a few other paroxysms but they have not lasted long.

19th. Capt Barton called. The Cape wheat has come up and the wheat is now greener than it was on the 1st of May last. Saw Tweedy at York who gallivanted us and lent Mary

Glenarvon. Mr Newsam called meaning to dine when we were at York but Miss Claridge, Anne and Caroline were too squeamish to ask him for which they are three affected ——s.

20th.   Killed a brace of partridges at one shot. The new surgeon, Mr Appleby, called. Dr Whaley dined here yesterday and seemed to believe in the doctrine of animalculae in the teeth. Vaccinated two children from one of Gatenby's. Saw Dr Chester was dead by the Gloucester Journal, the last of all my mother's first cousins except Mrs Symonds who from having been all her life an invalid has survived the other eleven and most of their children, at least many of their children. I conceive Dr Chester must have been more than 80, but I since see in the St James' Chronicle that he was 77.

21st.   Dined at Mr Askwith's with Capt and Mrs Dalton, Mr and Mrs Howard, Major Hall, Miss Harrison, Miss Becket.

22nd.   Went hunting, found a fox at Gatenby, ran him through Newton Cover near to Morton Bridge where he crossed the Bedale brook and the Swale and ran to Sobergate and back again cross the Swale below Gatenby. Lord D then having lost him drew off towards Newton and I left them. I crossed the beck but not the Swale but stayed on the bank with Col Pulleine. Mr Hartley and one other scarlet man who came from Lord D's, Lord D, J. Monson, Strangeways, Dawson, Newsam, Milbanke, Healey, the whippers in and Serjeantson's groom crossed and recrossed the Swale. Called at Morley's. Promised to lend Newsam Lady Sarah to hunt Monday at Kirklington. Received a letter from Eliza which seems to say John is waiting for his horses to get a fine coat before he comes to Wath.

23rd. Did duty morning and evening. Mr Hattersley at dinner. Dr Whaley called.

24th. Went hunting. Mr Newsam at dinner. Very good sport from Kirklington.

25th. Wrote to Mr Blake the temporary curate of Biddisham to desire he would consider himself the curate till Lady Day. Saw Sam Day of Hinton's widow was married to Mr Parker, by the paper it seemed as tho' she was married by her maiden name, the Hon Catherine Lister.

26th. Snow in the night, melted about noon. In the Hull paper the succession to the throne of Britain is detailed. 12 sons and daughters of George 3rd, all above 40 without issue, 2 of his brother the late Duke of Gloucester, 12 of his eldest sister the Duchess of Brunswick, the present Duke of Brunswick aged 13, his brother 12, are the first in succession from whom issue is probable unless some of the Regent's brothers marry. 6 descendants of the late Queen of Denmark the King's sister, then 10 from George 2nd's daughter Anne Princess of Orange, then 20 from George 2nd's second daughter Mary, Landgravine of Hesse, then 20 from the 3rd daughter of George 2nd, Queen of Denmark, then 40 from daughter of George 1st, Queen of Prussia. The papers are all full of a trial by wager of battle,[1] a trial which ought not

---

[1] A certain Abraham Thornton had been tried for rape and murder but gained an unexpected acquittal. The dead girl's next of kin took advantage of an old statute to obtain a writ of appeal, which Thornton answered by demanding a trial by wager of battle. Although no such trial had taken place for years, the Courts decided that it was in order, and as the appellant was unwilling to take up the challenge Thornton was discharged.

to exist in a Christian country and could have had its origin only in times of barbarism and superstition and is a disgrace to the Statutes Books. Mr Whitehall Davies, Allanson, Mr and Mrs Gilpin, Capt Dalton, Mr and Mrs Howard, J. Newsam at dinner. Blackstone says the last trial by battle urged in the Court of Common Pleas at Westminster (though there was afterwards one in the Court of Chancery in 1631 and another in Durham in 1571) was 13th Elizabeth 1571 in Tothill Fields, Westminster, as reported by Sir James Dyer; Sir H. Spelman was present. But that appears to have been a civil question whereas the present is a criminal one, murder, where the next of kin challenges the murderer acquitted by the Coroner. Blackstone calls it a presumptuous appeal to Providence. A woman, a priest, an infant, a man of 60 years of age, lame or blind, may refuse, and Peers and citizens of London. Bk IV, Chap: 27, where see the form of challenge and battle which must be with batons. In Bk IV, Chap: 33 he says the Normans had the honor to establish it here tho' clearly an unchristian as well as a most uncertain method of trial. He mentions among the improvements in jurisprudence the introduction and establishment of the Grand Assize or trial by a special kind of jury in a writ of right at the option of the tenant or defendant instead of the barbarous and Norman trial by battle. Dined at Col Serjeantson's with his brother and two nieces and nephews and J. Newsam. Found the house which had been left in charge of Henry's wife Charlotte entirely abandoned as soon as we had gone to bed, the other servants being gone to the loosing of Beckwith's apprentice and Charlotte having put old Betty Case to bed with her two children in my garret.

27th.   Finished ploughing the stubble next Jacky Cook's. Humphries the butcher's wife's brother came to live as plowboy.

28th.   Went hunting to Hollinhead and Sutton and Studley where Lord Darlington lost the fox by his obstinacy, and I returned home, breakfasted at Capt Dalton's, the most beautiful day that could be conceived. Received letters from India with J. F.'s will made and executed at Java, he sailed from thence on 29th June and he expected Mr Fombelle's place, gives a very indifferent account of his wife's health and not a good one of his own. Received also the catalogue of Java minerals which he was good enough to procure through the Chief English Physician of the Island and are now on board either the Claudine or the Margaret. He says he has received the most gratifying approbation of his conduct from the Government at Calcutta. Mr Howard went home.

29th.   Meeting at Oak Tree. Col Serjeantson, Mr Morley there. Dined at Mr Allanson's with Mr, Mrs and Miss Howard, Capt Dalton, Mr Morley, Mr Whitehall Davies who tho' a very pleasant agreable man takes the head of the table wherever he goes. He told an anecdote of poor Mr Tennant, of his early taste for chymical enquiry when a child collecting the moon beams in a large concave mirror to see if there were any sensible heat and buttering the mirror to see if it would melt it. He accounted for that oddness which was about him from his never having perfectly recovered a shock his nerves received when his mother who was riding out with him dropped down dead from off her horse. Tennant had lived a great deal in Mr D's house. Heard from

Eliza that she and her husband set out for Mr Cotton's at Thormby-cum-Northam and were to spend Saturday and Sunday there and would be at Wath Wednesday 2nd or Thursday 3rd.

30th.   Did duty morning and evening. Called at Camp Hill on Major Serjeantson.

December 1st.   Dined at Mr Carter's with Mr and Mrs Hunton and J. Newsam.

2nd.   Went with Mary and Caroline to call at Jerveaux. Found Mr Claridge very much recovered but exceedingly reduced in flesh, he rode out for a short time, shewed me two colts he had bought for Lord Ailesbury's carriage, both very fine but one is the finest horse in size, shape and colour for a coach horse I ever saw.   Returned to dinner, had a long discussion about Charlotte Barnett from which I am more than ever convinced that the moment any servant becomes such a favourite with Master or Mistress that the one cannot find fault without offending or shocking the feelings of the other, that is the moment when that servant should be discharged.   For to mark the progress of this discussion whether I am right or wrong in the view I take of Charlotte's behaviour, when the dog barked my wife rang the bell and no one answered and I immediately said Charlotte had left the house and gone to the junketting, she flatly contradicted me, rang again, and at last got up not from any fear that the house was left open to robbers but for the purpose of confuting my uncharitable charge upon her favorite.   She is not afraid of robbers nor ever was.   After she had searched the house and could only find C was gone out and the old woman was abed with her children and she returned to bed, she could not close her eyes even after all the servants were returned, but because I expressed my displeasure at the conduct of the favourite. And tho' till the moment she had detected her she considered the breach of confidence reposed in her so heinous that she could not be guilty of it, as soon as she was convinced she had gone to the dance instead of entering at all into my feelings on the subject she set herself to find out excuses and palliations and to make me think as well of her as before, tho' if I had told Henry that I had given all the rest of the servants leave to go out and desired him to stay and take charge of the house and he had undertaken it as she did and left it as she did he should never have entered it again. Yet am I told because I say I can't think as well of her as before that I am very uncharitable and all the girls with more zeal than either wisdom or duty are drawn in to support this system of favouritism of their mother, who would have done precisely the same let the crime be what it might short of cutting my throat but if it had been breaking open my bureau and stealing my money or my watch my wife's conduct would have been precisely the same. I very much question whether I myself should have been more angry. So much for favourite servants, the best fuel in the world to light a fire of family discord.

3rd. Letters from Lord A and Canon Williams. At 4 o'clock arrived Mr and Mrs John Newton and Master Newton with their maid Betsy, five hours before we expected them. Eliza looks thin but better than I expected and eats pretty well, John looks well but thinner, his boy looks remarkably well and in two or three years from his make and shape may get employ in the training stables at Middleham, does not seem to have forgotten anything he saw three years ago tho' he is not six till February.

5th. Col and Major Serjeantson and Lieut and two sisters at dinner.

6th. Dined at Mr Morley's with his mother, two sisters, Mr and Miss Stanley, Capt Comby, a Navy officer. Miss Stanley rather pretty, the captain very silent. Hunting with Lord Darlington who would not hunt either of two foxes he found because his Lady was not arrived tho' there was a field of upwards of 60 amongst whom were Mr Graham, Mr Chaloner, the Lord Mayor of York, Mr Witham, Mr Vigors Harvey, etc.

7th. Did duty morning and evening. Christened a child. Vaccinated three or four on Saturday.

8th. Snow which melted by noon but seemed to be the beginning of a frost as thermometer fell to freezing point at night.

9th. Dined at Mr Morley's with Mr Caleb Redshaw and Newsam. Frost.

10th. To Ripon with J. F. N. Decided frost.

11th. Thermometer 23 at sunrise. The Morleys at dinner and Mr Newsam. Received a note from Mr Howard saying he could not dine here today, and enclosing one from Miss Allanson to Mrs Howard saying that Mrs Brand's feelings would not permit her to dine in company with any part of the family from Wath tho' she negociated the sale of all her furniture with me in July 1814 so that J. F. N. and I who were to have dined at Mr Howard's tomorrow were forbidden approaching the widow's presence and had to dine at home.

12th. Thermometer 22 at 9 this morning. Received a letter from Mrs Fendall saying the insurance on her life was not paid. Wrote to Joshua and Sir J. Jelf to pay it.

13th. Wrote to Canon Williams to take £55 per share for my Brecon Canal shares.

14th. Having a bad cold J. F. N. did the duty for me morning and evening. Mr Hattersley at dinner. Sir C. Flower who was Lord Mayor of London before Alderman Wood has been lately abroad and visited many of the English amongst whom was Mr Dundas, the grandson and heir to the title of Lord Dundas, who brought home Sir C. Flower's card which was in the following style

Sir Chas Flower
le feu Lord Mayor de Londres

not knowing that *le feu* means deceased.

15th. Hard rain almost all day.

16th. Ditto. Tithe day, a good receipt, only Alman and Mason of those whose payments amount to a pound being in arrears. Heard from the farmers that the Hatters in the neighbourhood of Atherstone annoy Sir B. Graham by never suffering the foxes to break cover.

17th. J. F. N. went hunting to Masham Bridge. Total receipt at Dalton's £640. Bedale Club, Messrs Monson, Scrope, Serjeantson, Pattison, Robson, Elsley, Major Elsley, Glaister, B. N. in the Chair. Discussions on Saving Bank which came to nothing. Lord D had a good run till dark, lost his fox at Studley that he found at Askwith's.

18th. Went with Col Serjeantson to turn a road for Mr Carter from Theakston to Gatenby, called on E. Carter and

J. Newsam. Joshua at my request paid £153. 5. 0. to the
Equitable Assurance office for J. Fendall's policy on the life
of Mrs W. F., sent the receipt to her. Sent 45 bushels of barley
to Ripon to be malted. One of my sows pigged on the 5th
and the other on the 13th of this month. Received a letter
from Mrs Wilmot. An advertisement in the Gloucester
Journal for a County Meeting, the requisition signed only by
Whigs. A letter from Smith refusing to let the stock be
changed and one from Joshua saying it would be a good
thing.

19th.   Dined at Mr Oxley's with Mr, Mrs and G. Allanson,
Capt Horn, Mrs Lucas, Miss Hodges and Anderson, young
Elliot Fenton, Mrs N, Mary and J. F. N. Talked about Savings
Banks, found Mr Collins of Knaresborough was Treasurer
gratis to the Ripon and that the necessary expence of establishing a bank would not exceed £10 beyond the clerk's
salary and the room. One circumstance is to be observed
that though the Bank of England pays £4. 11. 3 per cent and
the Savings Bank pays only £4. 0. 0., yet as the latter pays
interest monthly on all deposits there will not be a clear
advantage of 11/3 per cent to the Savings Bank.

20th.   Went to Oldboro' to meet the hounds, tried Hezlet,
Tanfield, Kirklington, Pickhill and had a blank day. Only two
red coats who with Clerk, Newsam, J. F. N., G. Serjeantson
and Major Hall constituted the whole field.

21st.   Did duty in the morning and J. F. N. in the evening.
Dr Whaley came to Eliza to direct her diet. Heard that Mr
Lumisdon had given a Bengal Cadetship to Henry Fendall[1]

---

[1] Son of John Fendall of Java and Bengal.

and that he is much pleased. Flattered J. F. N.'s mode of reading which is as near as may be after my own manner. Heard that my Java fossils are gone in the ship to Antwerp.

22nd. Coursing. Dined with J. F. N., Mary and Caroline at Mr E. Carter's with Mr and Mrs Tim Hutton, Mr and Mrs Cooper Preston, Capt Taylor and Miss Costabadie.

23rd. Ripon Ball. With Mary and Anne N and Mary Costabadie. The papers full of the trial and acquittal of Hone[1] who defended himself very ingeniously on his being indicted *ex officio* by the Attorney General for a libel on the Book of Common Prayer. The libel was declared to be a parody on several parts of the Liturgy and Litany which were a lampoon on the Regent and his Ministers. There is no doubt that it was an infamous publication as many assert approaching to blasphemy and possibly Hone might have been punished either for the lampoon or the blasphemy, but Hone defended himself by an argument which was incontrovertible that the making a parody on anything was not proof that the person making the parody intended disrespect to the original passages which he parodied and he quoted parodies of the Scriptures by bishops and divines and various productions sacred and profane which had been parodied by others without any possible disrespect intended and I remember that I once parodied Gray's Bard without intending the least disrespect to that fine ode. The occasion was the Lamentation of a coxcomical fellow who on being ordained

---

[1] Hone had enraged the Government by publishing a series of satirical pamphlets. He was prosecuted on three charges of blasphemy but was acquitted on all of them, despite Lord Ellenborough's biassed summing-up. Great interest was aroused by the trial, public opinion enthusiastically supporting Hone's cause of the freedom of the press.

lamented the loss of his queue which all men except the clergy wore in my younger days and it began thus

> Ruin seize thee, ruthless Jack,
> Confusion on thy scissors wait,
> Turn thy murderous forceps back
> And spare the only honors of my pate.

Now no one can doubt that the disrespect shewn was to the clergyman's pate and not to Gray's ode. Hone was tried by Judge Abbot on one indictment and acquitted, next day by Lord Ellenborough on another indictment whose charge to the jury reminded one of the days of Judge Jeffreys as he told the jury it was an infamous and blasphemous libel whereas it has been laid down by law ever since Fox's Bill to explain the law of libel that the point the jury are to try is whether the matter in the indictment be libel or not.

24th.   A haunch of venison from Lord A. Sent a hare, turkey, pig, and two ducks by coach to Joshua. M. Costabadie returned to Mr E. Carter's.

25th.   Christmas Day. Did duty and administered the Sacrament in the morning. J. F. N. did the evening duty. Read an account of Hone being acquitted on a third indictment.

27th.   Dined at Mr Allanson's. The party Mr and Mrs Walker, Mr Charnock, Miss and Miss A. Allanson, Capt Horn, B. N., A. F. N., C. E. N. The most remarkable occurrence was Walker's eating, 1st a plate of haddock, 2nd a plate of fillet of veal and being twice helped to tongue, 3rd three slices of a saddle of mutton, 4th a large wing of a large duck, 5th two plates of roasting pig, 6th half the tail of a large lobster, 7th cheese and then dessert. N.B. He had no wager on his eating. Saw an attack on the Bishop of Chester's sermon on the death of the Princess Charlotte in which he has the expression of praying for the Souls of the Dead as far as may be allowed. This was one of the great points urged by the Reformers, particularly by Luther and Melancthon against the Papists, and it is wonderful that he should have laid himself open to such a charge which is urged with great force and would have been urged with greater force had he not let out that he was sore on the subject of the Bible Society tho' he signs himself a Member of the Society for promoting Christian Knowledge.

28th. Did duty in the morning, J. F. N. in the evening. Received a printed prospectus by the post of an intended life of Robert D. Waddilove, Dean of Ripon, meant as a lampoon on the Dean.

29th. Shooting with J. F. N. Shot nothing.

30th. Dined at Mrs Lucas' with Mr and Mrs Howard, Mr and Mrs Oxley, Mr and Mrs Askwith, J. Harrison, Major Hall. Heard of the death of Mr Sidgwick of Brafferton.

31st. Mr and Mrs G. Allanson, Mr and Mrs E. Carter, Miss M. Costabadie, Mr and Mrs Howard, Mr Hunton at dinner to eat Lord A's haunch of venison and so finished the year 1817. God grant we may all spend the next year better than the last and make us unfeignedly grateful for all his mercies.

1818

January 1st.   Set out with J. F. N., M. N. junior and A. F. N. to Jerveaux where we met Mr Ivison and Mr Hawkes and spent the evening till 2 in the morning.

2nd.   This day very cold. Mr, Miss C. and Hy Costabadie and Mr Cockcroft dined at Jerveaux and brought my Wensleydale stockings which I paid for.

3rd.   Returned in very bad weather from Jerveaux.

4th.   J. F. N. preached a very good sermon on the New Year at Wath. I distributed the Sacrament money to the poor at Wath together with £30 of Dr Samwaies' Charity amounting to near 15/- to each of the poor families of Norton, Middleton, Melmerby and Wath.

5th.   Went to see the school floor which has been new flagged and I fear a considerable expense will be incurred in repairing the seats and desks which are much decayed.

6th.   The Bellerby tenant brought his half year's rent excepting five pounds which he promised to pay Mr Costabadie at Leyburn within these six weeks. Dined all seven of us at Mr Howard's where we met the Allansons. J. F. N. and his wife slept there. Paid Horne for silk stockings and blankets and Henry and Heslop for wine.

7th.   Dined at Mr Allanson's with the Howards.

9th. The Howards, Mr Newsam and Miss Claridge at dinner and dancing quadrilles.

10th. Miss Claridge went home. Hunting with Mr Bell's hounds and had capital sport. Mr Newsam's mare nearly knocked his eye out by throwing up her head. Paid Thompson of Pickhill his bill. Mrs J. F. N. and C. E. N. both frightened in riding my grey poney there.

11th. Mr Newsam still at Wath on account of his eye. I did duty in the morning and J. F. N. in the evening.

12th. Went on Justice business to Col Serjeantson's, convicted George Fletcher in £5 penalty for snigling.[1]

13th. J. F. N. went to Brafferton to meet York Fox Hounds. Mr Newsam left Wath with his eye much recovered. Carpenters making binns in granary, Anthony improving the beast sheds. Met Col Serjeantson on improving the road from Wath towards Kirklington yesterday. Paid Davey, shoemaker's bill.

14th. Dined at Camp Hill with Mrs Lawrence, Mr and Mrs Allanson, Mrs N, J. F. N., A. F. N.

15th. Rode to Ripon with Caroline. Sent 20 Bushel of wheat to market, could not sell. Paid Wath blacksmith's bill.

16th. Hunting with Mr Bell. Mr J. Newsam at dinner. Little sport, very tired.

17th. Finished Ten Virgins. Paid Askwith's bill for post horses.

18th. J. F. N. did morning duty, I did evening. Very cold wet unpleasant weather all the week. Received an invitation to dine at Mr Hunton's on Friday next.

---

[1] Catching eels with baited hooks.

19th. Ripon Book Club, present the Dean, Allanson, Dixon, Howard, Walker, Bury, Charnock, Oxley, Williamson, Whaley, B. N. Bought Peat Manure, West's Life, City of the Plague, Nicholl's Anecdotes.

20th. Miss Claridge came to Wath and we all went to the Ripon Ball i.e. Miss C, J. F. N. and his wife, Mother and I, and M. N., A. F. N., C. E. N., only fifty people.

21st. Bedale Club. Called on Col Serjeantson who told me that Col Dalton was much annoyed at being charged £3. 13. 0. for conveying Fletcher, convicted of killing a hare, to Northallerton, charging 15/- per diem for a cart for four days. We proceeded to Bedale where there were assembled Mr Monson and son, Mr Elsley and son, Col Serjeantson, Mr E. Wyvill, Mr Clarke, Mr Robson, Mr Jas Robson, Mr Carter and son, Mr Newsam, Mr Scrope, Dr Dodsworth, Mr Pattison, Mr Tim Hutton, Mr Fielding, B. N., to consult on the best method of establishing a Savings Bank at Bedale which I shall always take the credit of having originally projected the first of anyone. We subscribed £50, of which I put my name down for £3 and we advanced so far that I trust our books will be open by the first week in March. Rode Tuesday to Grange with Mrs N.

22nd. Rode with Eliza to Camp Hill. J. F. N. went to Kilgram Bridge to meet the Duke of Leeds' hounds and returned having had very little sport. Yesterday was little Jack's birthday, six years old. J. Humphries brought me back a Bank of England note received of T. P. and also a light guinea received of Mr Henry the wine merchant. Convicted Rainforth of Rainton of killing a hare this morning on his own confession. I expect he caused the information to be laid to avoid being exchequered by Mr Ramsden.

23rd.　Dined at Mr Hunton's with two Messrs Richardson, Major Elsley, Messrs Newsam, Glaister, Pattison, Carter and J. F. N.

24th.　After reading Junius identified with a Living Character I am pretty well satisfied that Sir P. Francis was the man. Went hunting today with Mr Bell's hounds, saw Mr Barstow who returned with his bride on Wednesday. Dr Whaley called. The ox that was hurt having been obliged to kill turned out much better than I could expect. Took my Heligoland beans into a barn.

25th.　Mr Claridge at dinner.

26th.　Mrs N at Mr Barstow's (wedding visit).

30th.　The Howards at dinner. Hunting with the Boro'-bridge hounds.

31st.　Meeting at the Oak Tree.

February 1st.　J. F. N. did duty in the morning. Mr Claridge came and took away his daughter.

2nd.　Mr Morley called. Mayor's feast at Ripon. Dined there. My health drunk with three times three (*inter mingendum*) by the Mayor (Terry). Invited to dine tomorrow with Mr Fk Robinson who came down on being appointed Treasurer to the Navy in the room of Mr G. Rose for the Borough of Ripon, I was introduced to him by the Dean and declined the honor of dining with him.

4th.　Went to Jerveaux and

5th.　to Middleham and the school at E. Witton of which

I prophecy the fall unless supported entirely at Lord A's and Mr Claridge's expense.

7th.   Returned from Jerveaux by Sleningford to Ripon and brought home M. N. junior from Mr Howard's, called at Langdale to correct the press for the rules of the Bedale Savings Bank. Found a letter from G. Serjeantson to say he would buy the mare Lady Sarah for £65, also from Mrs Wilmot with an account of the settlement of Mr Farquharson's property now settled by Mr Smith and which induces me to write to Mr Thompson to put in a claim for Mrs Fendall's[1] share to Mr Smith to give it to the Farquharsons in such a way as not to preclude Mrs Fendall having a share.

9th.   Letter from W. Fendall giving an account of the surgeon of his regiment being sent for and sending word by the gentleman's servant who came for him in these terms, "Go tell your master I'll be with him before you return". On my telling my grandson that the reason the hearse did not return to the house of the deceased as well as the mourning coach was that it had only brought the dead body to the church and there was no further use for it, "What", said he, "did it not bring the legs and all?" Buried Mrs Walker of Melmerby. Rode with Mrs N, J. F. N. and Eliza to Carthorpe. Mr Hattersley at dinner yesterday.

10th.   Received £10 from Mrs Fendall in part of payment for piano forte.

11th.   Capt Dalton and Mr Newsam at dinner. Dined yesterday with Col and G. Serjeantson, E. Carter, T. Hutton, Major Elsley and J. F. N. at Mr Newsam's.

[1] Mrs John Fendall was a Miss Farquharson.

12th.   Rode with J. F. N. to Northallerton.

13th.   Sold Lady Sarah to G. Serjeantson for £65. 4. 0. into my pocket and all expenses, grooms, etc, paid. Best Hereford cow miscarried, the proper time not being till the 20th of March, however the calf seems inclined to live. Sent Wells to Northallerton Fair. Paid Hester her wages. Winnowed fifty-three bushels of wheat, took in a bean stack, paid J. Humphries £10 on account. Received a letter from Mr Thompson enclosing the one he had written to Capt Farquharson on the subject of his mother's property. Sold Capt Dalton 4 qrs and Mr Newsam 1 qr of oats. Visited Mr I'Anson who had his brother with him to make his will, tried to persuade him to receive the Sacraments. N.B. I was called upon Thursday night about one to administer the Sacrament to T. Clarkson's wife which having done I recommended them to send for Dr Whaley which they seemed disinclined to do as they said she had made up her mind and was very resigned, however they afterwards consented and she is now in a fair way to recovery. After having read the accounts of the trial of the Glasgow rioters as managed by the Lord Advocate and as it appears by the debates in the House of Commons on Lord A. Hamilton's motion I think a more disgraceful stain was never affixed to the character of any lawyer and the four worthies of the day ought to descend united in infamy to posterity. Oliver, Castles, M'Conochy and Sidmouth.

15th.   Did duty in the morning, J. F. N. in the evening.

17th.   Ripon Ball, no one went from Wath but myself.

18th.   Bedale Club, 16 dined. Col Pulleine, Dr Dodsworth, E. Wyvill went before dinner. Ordered M'Cleod's Journal of the Alceste. Dispute at Club as to the spelling of expence. No one but Mr Monson and I supported the above mode but both Universities print it so in last Bibles.

19th. Hunting at Myton with York Fox Hounds, no sport, eight hours on horseback.

20th. Dined at Mr Allanson's.

21st. M. N. junior received a letter from J. C. junior saying his pupil had determined to stay in Florence until May and then return to England. *Quel bête*. Mr Fenton, Mr Howard's clerk, walking in the town of Ripon with Mrs Howard met a gentleman whom he knew to be no favourite with the lady, in fact he had heard her say that the gentleman they saw was her abhorrence, Fenton mistaking this word said, Here comes your abortion.

22nd. J. F. N. did duty in the morning and I in the evening. Sat up last night till 2 waiting on Dr Whaley who had come to see young Clarkson who was in great agony. The Doctor found his disorder to be an inflammation of the peritonaeum, took 50 ounces of blood from him, blistered, glistered, purged him, gave salines, etc, and he was almost immediately relieved. The Dr thought he would not have lived 24 hours if he had not been sent for last night. Began to make a sermon on "It is not lawful to take the children's meat to cast it unto dogs". Perceived Charlotte[1] to be getting very big again. Went coursing with J. F. N., his wife and A. F. N., coursed four or five and killed one.

23rd. Went hunting with Mr Milbanke's hounds to Thornbrough with J. F. N., Miss Claridge and Eliza, met Capt

---

[1] Charlotte Barnett, the Newton's maidservant.

J. Dalton, Major Elsley, Mr R. Pierse, Mr E. Carter, Mr G. Clarke, Mr Milbanke.

24th. The Howards at dinner. Rode with Eliza to Ripon. Paid Langdale.

25th. Called at Mr I'Anson's, found him worse. Dr W seems to have but little hope.

26th. A bad night from soreness and oppression on my chest. Wrote to Mrs Commeline about a school for Chs Commeline. Having read Hutton's life of himself which afforded me much amusement I mean to get a book and attempt something of the kind though aware I have not his memory, industry or energy, it may gratify those we love, or rather those who love me, to peruse it, as it shall be true if it be nothing else. Wrote to Joshua and desired him to lay out £11 for me in John Waters' name which makes together with the £5 I laid out before his year's wages due November last.

27th. Col and Mrs Serjeantson, Mr and Mrs Barstow, Miss Jones and Mr Morley at dinner. Very unwell with sore chest, drank no wine.

28th. Meeting at York Gate.

March 1st. Too hoarse to do duty. J. F. N. did it morning and evening. Mr Hattersley laid up with cold, little Jack very poorly with cold which seems now to have gone through the house and I think inflammatory colds have the appearance of being epidemic. Read Paley's Evidences.

2nd. Oxleys, Humphries, Mr Askwith and Morley at dinner. Heard Harrison's sister and mother of Melmerby had murdered a bastard child of the former at Ripon, buried it a mile

off near Ripon, heard they were suspected, went to the
sexton to request he would bury it in the Minster Yard, took
it up from where it had been buried at Hawick in the bank
of a hedge, called in Yorkshire a cam, and opened the coffin
to shew it was not murdered when Grimstone the surgeon in
taking it out of the coffin discovered it had been struck with
a knife or some such instrument in the back so as to cause its
death. Report says the mother did it unknown to the
daughter and that the girl will so plead. It is not her first child
and she studiously concealed the birth and both mother and
daughter denied the pregnancy when the parish officers urged
her to filiate. Much better today.

3rd.   Went hunting to Skipton Bridge, sent home by the
wet.

4th.   Rode with J. F. N. and Eliza to Ripon.

5th.   Dined with Morley. Coursed two hares and killed
them both. Mr I'Anson very unwell, no alteration for the
better. Read Walpole's Turkey and M'Cleod's Voyage of
the Alceste to China. Letters from India announcing the
arrival of the Fendalls at Calcutta and his being invested
with an appointment of £7000 per annum which had been
kept open for him for some months. Wrote an account of it
to Lord Ailesbury. Met Mr Bourne, a most silent man, at
Morley's with Col Serjeantson and Barstow. Morley talked
about coal like a fool. Grey filly got strangles, the extreme
wet weather seems to have made this disorder also epidemic
at present. Went with Morley on Monday to Sinderby to
examine a pauper and make an order for his removal and
suspend it.

6th. Went hunting with Boro'bridge hounds and had great sport. Mr Claridge called yesterday and took away his daughter who had been flirting for three weeks with J. F. N. in such a way as to make Mrs J. F. N. dislike her exceedingly and my wife vows she will never ask her to stay here again when J. F. N. is in the house. She assumed the character of Lady Grave-airs for a time but though she said she thought a quiet manner the most interesting, hoyden came uppermost at least ten times a day. The sooner she is married to prevent her laying in the hedge the better. Eliza's manner was quite perfect to her. I think her more agreable every day. She has the most and the best sort of what the French call *naïveté* I ever saw. Her wit is so playful that it cuts blocks like a razor tho' the blocks are insensible of the gashes tho' they are very deep. Dr Whaley has called more than once and I find his sitting breeches stick closer to the chairs than ever. Wrote to J. Fendall about sale of stock which my trustees have delayed selling till the funds are fallen 5 or 6 per cent and the dividend is just ready to be received.

7th. Wrote to India the account of Jas Farquharson's letter and his mode of proceding on his father and mother's will. Sent Thompson a copy of Col Smith's letter. Heard from Little Bit[1] that G. Thompson, though in debt, was to be married directly to Harriet. Get on but slowly with Bede and here I have to record the loss of an old and faithful friend in my little dog Pam who was unfortunately killed by my son's horse laying upon him in the stable where he was sent to dry himself after having been washed and was forgotten to be taken into the house again at night. He was 12 years old,

[1] Mary, daughter of William Fendall.

very sagacious and affectionate, particularly handsome and never had any descendants at all equal to him in beauty. For many years he slept in our room. He was of a very amiable disposition and had as far as I am able to judge no evil propensity. He was grave but could be gay. Interpreter not only of looks and actions but often as I thought of words also. He remembered his friends at any distance of time and expressed himself with pleasure at seeing them after a long or short absence.

8th.   Did duty in the morning and J. F. N. in the evening. Sent back the gown ordered at Cambridge.

10th.   Attended Groves' sale.

11th.   Read M'Cleod's Voyage of the Alceste, his account of the island of Lewchew is an account of the most amiable pagans I ever read of. N.B. Little or nothing is said of the females. A letter from Mr Bell to desire me to vote for an old servant of his as surveyor of the Masham and Thirsk roads.

12th.   Administered the Sacraments to Mr I'Anson, found him much altered.

13th.   Administered the Sacraments to Betty Case and Mr Squire.

14th.   Dined at Mr Howard's, convicted a man of Dishforth in setting snares and catching a hare in £5 penalty. Coursed for the last time this year, killed a hare.

15th.   Did duty in the morning and J. F. N. in the evening.

16th.   Heard this morning Mr I'Anson of Melmerby was dead. Applications from Britain of Howgrave and Ward of Middleton for the place of High Constable lately held by

I'Anson. Mr Hattersley at dinner yesterday. Transcribed and altered a sermon of my grandfather's on the text "And if I be lifted up will draw all men to me", bought a new pair of gaiters.

17th. Went to Bedale to the Savings Bank in which £730 had been paid on Tuesday and today. The attendance was respectable, Messrs Monson senior and junior, M. Wyvill, Newsam, Clarke, Tim Hutton, Pulleine, Serjeantson, B. N., talked over the appointment of a new Chief Constable with the Colonel. Called on Newsam.

18th. The first spring day. Began drilling beans. Having lately read Chalmers' sermons on Astronomy in which he has expressed the highest admiration and respect for I. Newton's modest and firm faith in Christianity I am inclined to put down his opinion on infidelity as given by Dr Hartley, a physician at Bury who was contemporary with Sir I. N. and very probably acquainted with him. Sir Isaac used to say infidelity would probably prevail till it had quite banished superstition but would then be swallowed up in the great light and evidence of true religion. Dr H goes on to say, he seems to have conjectured well upon this no less than on other matters. I think so too, we have seen in our days in France the Roman religion first become indifferent to the mass of the people and then proceed to open infidelity and the natural progress is this, the ordinances which superstition has grafted on true religion must necessarily fall and it is perfectly natural to be the case that it should carry with it a part of its support that many articles of our belief should be brought into doubt together with those that are evidently trivial or false. I conceive Christianity to be progressive.

I may be recording an opinion that possibly is not orthodox but I think that when once infidelity has banished superstition the religion of Jesus Christ may proceed to be more and more spiritualised in the actions and faith of its professers as to be able to subsist without the aid of any human institutions. The prevalence of faith and practice shall ultimately be so universal that before the second coming of our Lord even the Priesthood or more properly the Christian Ministry (except for the administration of the Sacraments which our Saviour at their first institution commanded to be continued till his coming again) may be unnecessary and it may not be required that the preacher should say to his congregation "Know the Lord", for the knowledge of the Lord shall be as universally diffused in the hearts of all men as the waters are over the sea. After those days, saith the Lord, I will put my law in their inward parts and write it in their hearts and will be their God and they shall be my people. And they shall teach no more every man his neighbour and every man his brother saying, Know the Lord, for they shall all know me from the lowest unto the greatest of them, for I will forgive their iniquity and I will remember their sins no more.

19th. Rode to Pickhill with Anne and Mrs Newton, and the former this morning (20th) complained of a violent shivering before we went to Church and which made her sisters prevail upon her not to go, on coming from Church (where J. F. N. read prayers and I preached and administered the Sacraments) we found her alarmingly ill and immediately sent for Dr Whaley who gave her a dose of calomel with salts and senna which however seemed to yield no relief to her head which continued most excruciating and she was scarcely anything relieved this morning (21st) when three leeches applied to her temples seemed to give a slight relief. Dr Whaley came at one and applied eight more which seem to take off the pain from her head but as a large blister was applied to the nape of her neck which reached down between her shoulders she is left this morning (22nd) much exhausted from want of sleep and much evacuation. J. F. N. went hunting yesterday on Mrs Fall and I to Wright's sale where I bought two ewes for £11 and a calf for £3. 13. 6.

22nd. Easter Sunday. J. F. N. read prayers and I preached and administered the Sacraments. Mr and Mrs Barstow and Miss Jones came to Wath to receive the S.S. in order that he may qualify at the next Quarter Sessions as a Justice for the North Riding. I had the happiness of hearing on my return from Church that my dear Anne was more improved than Dr Whaley could have expected. Buried Mr I'Anson on Thursday last, the funeral was attended by a mourning coach and two chaises.

24th. Ripon Ball with J. F. N., Eliza, M. N. junior. Sold two cows at Bedale Fair for £30. 9. 0.

25th. To Bedale with J. F. N., Eliza, M. N. junior and from thence to Richmond,

26th. thence to Catterick Races, having been charged and paid two pounds sterling by Mrs Yarker at the Inn at Richmond for our beds which the Inn being as she pretended full she procured for us at a taylor's about three doors off. I have been considerably quizzed and laughed at as a fool for submitting to this charge and very poor comfort from Col Serjeantson who upon my telling him of the charge for the beds declared that at the same inn they charged him six and thirty shillings for a bushel of oats at a time when the market price was only twenty four shillings the quarter. Had good sport at the Races and were highly gratified at seeing Mr Claridge's horse win the Produce Stakes. This horse was sold by Mr C to Sir B. Graham for £400 on condition of receiving another 100 if he won these stakes. Mr Jacques of Easby had three colts which ran and all won. They as well as Claridge's were well rode by Billy Pierse. The first day the course was so covered with snow that they were obliged to drive a flock of sheep round to tread it down before the horses ran, and the riders were covered with mud, every vestige of turf was destroyed as much as in a fallow. Returned to Wath about nine, there we found Mary Fendall and Sam Commeline had arrived about one o'clock in the day.

27th. Sale of Sir B. Graham's stock, 15 head fetched £430. Mr Morley and Capt Dalton at dinner. Went in the morning to the New Inn to attend a turnpike meeting to elect a clerk or surveyor and on finding there were sufficient to elect without us Capt Dalton came away to Sir B. G.'s sale where Mr Askwith told me that he had taken the Hall at Norton Conyers and 95 acres of land for five years.

28th. A Justice Meeting at York Gate to appoint overseers of the poor where I met Col Serjeantson and Mr Morley who agreed to recommend Mr Walker of Melmerby to the Court of Quarter Sessions to succeed the late Mr I'Anson as one of the High Constables for Hallikeld. Received the Venerable Bede and some other old writers on English history from Mr Howard who procured them from the library at Ripley for me.

29th. Did duty in the morning and J. F. N. in the evening and signed Mr Barstow's certificate of having received the S.S. at Wath Church last Sunday. Mrs N took Sarah Anne[1] to Mr Askwith's yesterday and I lent her brother a poney to carry him to Ripon on his way back to Worcester where he is obliged to attend the Assizes on Wednesday next. Smith invites me to partake of his continental tour against which I have at least 24 reasons, the first of which is my unwillingness to put myself under any man's control for six weeks, especially as Miss Bayley gave him a terrible character for fidgetting on a journey. I am however greatly obliged to him and Mrs Smith for the kind offer but I shall enjoy very little in absence from my family, to every branch of which I feel so attached that nothing would make up for a total separation from them for half the time my projected tour would take up. My dear Anne left her room for the first time today. I bless God for her recovery.

30th. Went to Jerveaux and Middleham Races with J. F. N., Eliza, Mary Fendall and M. N. junior, little sport but we had woodcocks for dinner.

31st. Middleham races, no sport. Morley left Jerveaux for the Sessions. Whistling plovers for dinner. Dined at a $\frac{1}{4}$ past 7 and at 8 yesterday. Paid my rent.

April 1st. Returned from Jerveaux, called at Mrs Hardcastle's, paid her for Mrs Ibbetson's sketches, took Eliza to shew her Hackfall and called at Mrs Askwith's on Sarah Anne Commeline, found Mrs A had been brought to bed of

---

[1] Sarah Anne Commeline was a niece of the Rev. James Commeline and sister to the Thomas Commeline who later married Anne Frances Newton. She was engaged as governess to the Askwiths' children.

a daughter last night. Found one of my ewes dead. Received of J. Williams Benjamin's rent up to Michaelmas 1816 and a promise to send the last year's rent by his son to J. F. N. Paid Dalton the glazier.

3rd. Dined at Mr Barstow's with Mr Bell, Col Maddison and Mr Morley.

4th. Rode to Ripon. Morley said Hunton had requested Serjeantson to propose him to the Bench and that Serjeantson did not do it.

5th. Did duty in the morning and J. F. N. in the evening. Lost a sheep which takes Wells' time up to hunt for. The weather appears quite changed, being very warm and dry. Called on Mason of Withernwick who appeared to be in a very bad way, I much fear in a consumption. Received a chest of tea from Joshua. Read Golownin's Captivity in Japan, well told but he was a silly man, suspicious yet not cautious. Read Rob Roy.

6th. Went to Thirsk, had the grey mare covered by Grey Orville.

7th. Received a letter from Mr Guise to say they would be here on Monday next.

8th. Miss Claridge called.

9th. Snow.

10th. Went in gig to Ripon. Administered the Sacrament to Mrs Raper.

11th. Snow and rain all day. Read Pegge on the English Language, Sir J. Sinclair's Code of Agriculture, proceeded with notes on Bede. Mr Cline in his paper on breeding is

quite decided that animals take more after a dam than a sire.
I conceive that it depends much on the species of animal. It
may be true of horses, pigs or sheep, but Mr Colling the
great breeder of short horns is not of that opinion as far as
it regards neat cattle and my experience proves that the calves
follow the bull. I have tried and seen tried a Hereford bull
with all sorts of cows, Gloucestershire, Scot, Suffolks, Yorkshire and Durham short horns and I never saw a calf that
did not take the exact colour of the Hereford bull, white face,
rose on the shoulder, small mark near the eye, but I conceive
there is something particularly permanent in the breed of
Hereford cattle for even the cattle that have been got by a
Hereford bull produce calves more like themselves and the
grandsire than the sire.

12th. Did duty in the morning and J. F. N. in the evening.
Disgruntled at his not doing it at my request in the morning.
Mr Hattersley at dinner. Dr Whaley's horse which he lent
me taken ill of the strangles. No pigeons yet fit to take. Snow
has thrice covered the ground during the last week. Peaches
and apricots in blossom. Great floods in the Eure from the
melting of the snow. Mr Morley sent an invitation to me to
dine at Kirklington to meet Lord Tyrconnel, etc, I conceive
he might mean to ask more of us especially John Newton but
all the party said it was the rudest thing they had ever known
and he meant no such thing but merely to have me and no
one else.

13th. Mr and Mrs Guise came to dinner.

14th. The Howards came to dinner.

15th. The Allansons came to dinner. Mrs A seemed dis-
composed at my taking Mrs Guise out of the room before

her but as Baronets' sons have a degree in the scale of precedence there can be no doubt but that Mrs G ought to precede unless she chose to wave it.

16th.   The Guises left us. J. F. N. and I went to Peacock's sale at Carthorpe and hearing no more of Mr Morley I called at Kirklington on my return to say that I could not dine there tomorrow.   Col Serjeantson called to say he was going to London tomorrow and mentioned Hunton's having applied to him to propose him as a Magistrate at Quarter Sessions but that somehow or other he did not do it.   Morley told me he heard the Rector of Bedale meant to oppose his being made if he was proposed, I suspect the truth of this knowing that Hunton and Morley hate each other. Visited Mason and Mrs Raper on the 17th and swore in W. Britain Bailiff Constable to execute the commitment and convey a man from Howe for bastardy to Northallerton.

18th.   The man came to request me to take his own bond which as the Magistrates at the Petty Sessions refused to do I could not.   Consented to keep J. F. N.'s chestnut mare till Christmas.

19th.   J. F. N. did duty in the morning, I administered the Sacrament to T. Mason and did duty in the evening.

20th.   Rode with Mrs N to Ripon Book Club.

21st.   Application for a warrant for Mr Ramsden for assaulting collector and refusing to pay his assessed taxes. N.B. Which is the Comissioners of Taxes' business. J. F. N. went to Nottingley and had his mare covered by Caliban. The father of the man sent to Northallerton offered to become his bail. Letters from Chesshyre, Costabadie about the wine and Guise about the barouche.

22nd. Dined at Capt Dalton's with Mr, Mrs, and two Miss Allansons, Col and Mrs Dalton, Mr Askwith, Mrs N, J. F. N. and Eliza and M. Fendall. Application made to me for a warrant for Mr Ramsden for not paying his assessed taxes. Sent a letter to the keeper of the House of Correction to let out W. Downes sent there for not going security in a matter of bastardy.

23rd. Received a stock receipt from Joshua from which it appears he sold the Settlement Stock at £60 and put it into the 5 per cents, £6183. 4. 6. Visited Mason of Withernwick and Mrs Raper, both of whom I fear are past recovery. Rode to Pickhill with Eliza and Anne, fetched Mary Fendall from the Grange on the 24th and on the 25th I spent all the morning at the Oak Tree justice meeting where I was met by Major Elsley, the principal business was a complaint from almost all the paupers of Leeming against the overseer and an information against one Jordan of Brafferton by the exciseman which went off for the present, the exciseman being the informer and could not be sworn as a witness.

26th. Did duty morning and evening and prayed with Mason and Mrs Raper, published J. F. Newton's *Siquis* having heard from Parfitt that the Bishop of Bath and Wells was too unwell to ordain on Trinity Sunday but would give letters dimissory. Received a box of fossils from Torquay from Mr Meade which would have been more acceptable had they consisted of uranite and tourmaline only as the nailheaded crystals and sulphates of barytes are much finer in Arkendale than in the South. I received also a parcel for Mrs Costabadie. I wrote to Costabadie to desire him to sign J. F. N.'s testimonial and offer him part of the pipe of wine. Received a letter from Joshua enclosing an affidavit for me to make respecting H. Barnett's stock.

27th. Drove Mary Fendall to Aldborough through a continued rain, sold a heifer and calf there for £10.

28th. Last night was a most tremendous storm of thunder and lightening which however did not remove all the snow from the Hamilton Hills. Rode to Bedale to the Savings Bank, made the affidavit for Henry's money and was agreably surprised by Mr Monson's very kindly offering to sign J. F. N.'s testimonial which Mr Glaister signed also, sent the fossils from Bedale to Wensley and left my gig to be new rung, felled and painted.

29th. Went with Eliza and J. F. N. and the three girls to Studley. Newsam dined here. Received a letter from Florence from J. Commeline, also one from Mr Barstow covering his draft for £60 for the wine of which I received a letter to apprize me and to say the price was £105, casing, etc, £1. 6. 6. and that it was sent by water to the care of Mrs Hogg. Wrote to the Bishop of Chester and enclosed J. F. N.'s testimonial to him and also to Joshua desiring him to purchase £16. 5. 6. 5 per cents to make the stock lately purchased even £6200 and pay the rest of the proceeds of Henry Barnett's sale into Esdaile's, apprizing me of the amount. Read Vth and VIth Vol. of Clarke, admired his account of Pyramids, Catacombs and hatching of chickens but think he lies when he says that after providing the oven and the fuel to heat them and persons to attend the process and providing the eggs of which half perish in the hatching they are still of so little value when hatched that they will not be at the trouble of counting them but heap them up in measures of about a gallon which they sell for a para or little more than an English farthing. His supposition and argument that the Soros in the chamber of the Great Pyramid might have contained the body of Joseph delighted me much by its ingenuity. That the Israelites were employed during the latter part of their sojourning in building the Pyramids is probable for on what else could 600,000 men be employed in brickmaking for? Granted a warrant to a man at Thornbrough for his nephew who lives at Yafforth who robbed him in November of lard, saddle, etc. Newsam paid me for the oats and dined here.

30th. Went to Ripon, saw Mr Collins and Mr Rowcliffe paid me for beans. Mr Newsam dined here.

May 1st. Went with John and Eliza to Newby, found the gallery painting and the statues all in confusion.

2nd. Mrs Raper of Melmerby died, visited poor Mason and Mr Blyth, the former past hope of recovery, the latter much better.

3rd. Found the black mare had foaled a remarkably fine horse foal which was found dead, supposed to be smothered in the cawl. Did duty in the morning and J. F. N. in the evening. Yesterday E. Carter sent to pay me for the beans. Wrote to Parfitt on John's ordination, enclosed a Title and *Siquis*, having previously sent his testimonial to the Bishop of Chester requesting him to forward it when countersigned to the Bishop of Bath and Wells. Mary Fendall returned yesterday from Aldborough.

4th. Today being Northallerton Show J. F. N. and I rode there and found neither buyers nor sellers.

5th.   Dined at Mrs Harrison's, present Dr and J. and M. Harrison, Mr and Mrs Oxley, and Mr and Mrs Allanson, J. F. N., Eliza and Mrs N, and I lost my money.

6th.   Miss Claridge and Mr Ramsden called.

7th.   Left home with J. F. N. and rode all the way to Stokesley in the rain, having heard that Mr Prince of Melmerby was dead having had a paralytic seizure in the night before and Mrs Raper was buried. We dined and slept and breakfasted at Stokesley and went through a thick mist to Skelton Castle to Mr Wharton's sale intending to buy the carriage which was advertised but found it was not to be sold. The fog prevented our seeing the sea from the castle which commands a view of it in fine weather, it is a magnificent looking house but the hall does not look as if it belonged to a castle, being floored with deal and neither large or grand. The situation is very fine, the ground romantic and well wooded with a muddy piece of water close up to the castle windows, the extent of which is but awkwardly attempted to be enlarged by shewing it goes to the bridge but at the same time by shewing it does not go beyond the bridge. The exciseman refused permits which did not prevent the wine being sold at very high prices, £5. 4. o. the Port, £4 the Sherry, there were 470 dozens of different sorts. The wax candles sold at 4/6 and 4/9 per lb, the wine glasses at 14/6 the dozen and other things in proportion. No refreshments was to be got and we paid a shilling apiece for our horses to the coachman for putting our horses and feeding them in the magnificent stables. We passed close to Roseberry Topping on the very point of which we were told there is a spring of water which is a curious geological fact considering the very pointed shape of the hill and the circumstance of its being basaltic, as I suppose, as the neighbourhood is chiefly of that description and the road by it for some miles is made of it. No sensible difference appeared between the forwardness of the spring at Skelton, Stokesley, or Guisboro' and Wath. I admired the stone posts tho' I was a long while before I could meet with anyone to ask for what purpose they were intended, which is that they who bring materials for the roads may know how and where to place them without laying them by the roadside where the road is narrow. These stone posts are always placed at some waste part where there is room to lay the stones till they are broken. Tho' this was the country for Cleveland Bays we saw but few horses of that colour. The country was deluged with wet tho' the agriculture was respectable, we past my patron's estate of Swainby and saw his old baronial castle of Whorlton. Were it not for the shambles in the middle of one of the squares, for there are three at Stokesley opening one into the other, it would be a very pleasant and good looking town. The wall of Guisboro' Abbey containing the East Window is a handsome bit of Gothic ruin. We returned through a continued rain and found the water so out on the road that J. F. N. who rode his wife's poney was obliged to dismount oftener than once in order to have his poney led through the streams while he went over the footbridges by the roadside. We got home to Wath without being wet through and went two chaises full to dine with the Howards.

10th. Whitsunday, went to Church, did the whole duty, Sacrament, etc, Mr Hattersley being gone to Kirklington to do duty for Mr Morley and J. F. N. not being in Priest's orders. Received a letter to say the Bishop of B and W would give

J. F. N. letters dimissory and inclosing 4 half £20 Langport
and Wells Bank bills. J. F. N. did duty in the evening.
I visited Thomas Mason at Withernwick and found him very
ill. Prince of Melmerby died this week and was buried at
Topcliffe. He was well on Saturday and found speechless in
his bed on Monday morning.

11th.   The Howards dined here and John Harrison called in
the morning. With the Howards came Mr R. Howard and his
daughter and J. Howard's daughter and a Mr Chandler, a
clergyman and Magistrate of the West Riding, a sensible man
and not disagreable though I could discover that he is of a
very irritable disposition.

12th.   Went to see poor Mason at Withernwick, when near
his house was met by his brother who told me he was dead
having expired about two in the morning. Thus have three
of the principal farmers of the parish died in about a month,
I'Anson, Prince and Mason.

13th.   Ripon Fair, saw Mrs Prince of Melmerby the widow
very gay at Fair today, bound old Ripley the Miller of
Tanfield in a recognizance yesterday to appear at Sessions for
assaulting Emanuel Inchboard and paid him a bill which I
had paid before. Finished Curwen's letters, I have recorded
my opinion of the style, the commonplace of abuse of tithes
pervades the work tho' he fails more than most of the ad-
vocates for their abolition. He proves indeed that in many
cases the tithes are high, but he proves universally that the
rent is higher than the tithe and unless he can prove that the
tenth in the hands of the clergy costs the landholder more
than the other nine tenths in the hands of the landlord he
proves nothing to his point. I have also read Gisborne's

Natural Theology. The design and matter of the work are excellent but it is exceedingly deficient in that plainness and perspicuity in which an argument of so very popular a description should be pressed on the attention of common readers. In the beginning of the book and in some other places there is an imitation of Paley's manner of putting an argument but the manner is very inferior and fails of that striking effect which is so peculiarly a fort of Paley.

14th. Rode with John and Eliza to Pickhill and wrote to Lord A.

15th. To Ripon, paid Stephenson £71. 17. 0. and visited Mrs Orde at Norton, found her in a deep decline and rode with J. F. N. to Boro'bridge. Eliza and my wife went with me to Ripon and called on the Allansons. Wrote to G. Moultrie to buy Smith's Bede. Had the red cow bought of Mrs Fall to Ward's bull and the black cart mare to Ledstone, had the sheep washed.

16th. Wrote part of a sermon from Gisborne's Natural Theology.

17th. Did duty in the morning and J. F. N. in the evening.

18th. Administered the Sacrament to Mrs Orde and in attempting to do it to T. Lancaster found him unable to receive it. Mr Newsam dined here. Sent my mare called Mrs Fall to Ardrossan but she refused him. Lancaster died about two o'clock.

20th. Bedale club. Sat next to Dr Scott who told wonderful stories of the effect which Bell's Mode of Education had caused at the Charterhouse. Rode yesterday to Ripon and

get my banking book from Coates's. Some of Watson's life
which I brought from Bedale and notwithstanding the abuse
bestowed on this Bishop by the last Quarterly I think posterity
will pay as much attention to what he says of any of his
contemporaries as to any of his brethren on the Bench. His
integrity and his veracity stand high. His doubt about the
ordinary gifts of the Spirit seems to me the most heterodox
of his religious opinions and seems quite in opposition to
"I will be with you always to the end of the World". From
what I saw of Dr Scott I think him more calculated to amuse
than to instruct, a good-natured man whose assertions may
excuse a sceptical man for wishing some other confirmation
of what he says, especially with regard to the Charterhouse
boys at their examination rather challenging and daring
Messrs Mant and D'Oyley, the Archbishop of Canterbury's
chaplains, than being at all timid or hesitating what to reply,
and more particularly the story of all the boys examined being
able to dispense with having any books before them when
examined in Horace and that they could all not only repeat
the whole of the Odes and give them in elegant language
but that where one left off any other boy could take it up at
the place and proceed repeating and construing.

21st.   Rode with J. F. N. to Ripon. Mr Costabadie with the
three girls with Hugh came here Tuesday, took M. N. junior
to Ripon, brought her back and dined here Wednesday after
consulting Dr Whaley about the eldest who is I understand
in an alarming state. Saw my gig at Bedale which is to be fit
for travelling Saturday and took the carriage lamps to have
them put on. Get my books back that Langdale was to bind
for me.

22nd. Finished planting potatoes. This week has been remarkably fine, dry and hot. Began reading a Tour in Denmark by Von Buch translated by Black with geological and mineralogical notes by Professor Jamieson. He gives a curious account of the immense quantity of deals brought to Christiana which are piled up by the peasants as they bring them so as to form long streets and when they are delivered the proper officer marks the quantity and the amount on the peasant's back with a piece of chalk who goes immediately from the quay to the counting house where he is immediately paid the amount, the clerk then brushes the chalk marks out of the man's coat and this is his acquittance. M. N. junior and Mary Fendall walked over to dine and sleep at Ripon. I went to pray with Mrs Orde at the Hall and found Sir B. Graham was in his cellar there. I did not disturb him but left a message to say I should be glad to see him at dinner at 5 o'clock but he was going to Lord Grantham's. Newsam dined here after having been fishing all day with J. F. N.

23rd. M. N. junior and M. Fendall returned from Howard's.

24th. J. F. N. did duty in the morning. Finished my sermon from Gisborne. Smith shewed my epigram on the Prince of Hess[1] to John Hobhouse and J. Hobhouse to the Duke of Sussex. Smith says he is more like a beast from Exeter Change than a human being. Poor dear Anne is again an invalid with a very bad cold.

25th. Costabadie and his three eldest girls and son came to dine and went to Ripon in the evening, leaving his eldest daughter and Charlotte here.

[1] Prince Frederick of Hesse-Homburg married in this year Elizabeth, daughter of George III.

26th.   Mrs N went to Ripon. Mr Claridge and Miss at dinner. Two or three children are now ill at Wath and their disorder is pronounced to be water in the head.

27th.   Sheep shearing.

28th.   To Ripon. Bought breakfast china and ten dozen of Cape Madeira from Henry.

29th.   Militia meeting at the Oak Tree where there was also one of the Commissioners of Taxes. Present Mr Carter, Mr E. Carter, Major Elsley, Rowcliffe, Hunton and Newsam.

30th.   Meeting at York Gate, Mr Morley, not much business.

31st.   Did duty in the morning and J. F. N. in the evening.

June 1st.   Inspected Topcliffe Bridge. Mr Askwith at dinner. Anne seems recovering.

3rd.   J. F. N. went fishing to Hackfall with Mr Newsam. Dr and Mrs Whaley called.

4th.   Another of Von Buch's miraculous tales. On the coast of Norway are many rocks on which the seafowl deposit their eggs. When the owners come in quest of the eggs the bird knows them and remains quiet for he knows by experience the superfluous eggs only are taken and one always left. The bird flies to a short distance, looks quietly on the spoliator and then returns to the nest. But if a stranger robs the nest of the whole of the eggs many thousands rise at once and fill the air with frightful cries and if the robbery is repeated they leave the place and lay there no more. Rode to Ripon with Mrs N in the morning, paid for wine and clover, called on Mrs Whaley, Howards and Mrs Lucas. Ripon Ball. Mrs J. N., M. N. junior, J. F. N. and

C. Costabadie went from Wath. This is the nineteenth hot day without any rain. *Voilà* Mr Buch once more. At Skey eagles are much dreaded, not content with lambs and smaller animals they even attack oxen and often master them. The eagle plunges in the waves, then rolls itself in sand, then hovers over the unfortunate victim, throws sand and stones into the ox's eyes and beats him with its wings. The oxen run racing till they dash themselves to death from some cliff. The eagle then mangles him undisturbed. Von Buch praises Professor Schytte.

5th. Mr Costabadie, Mary and Miss Milnes and Henry at dinner and Mr Newsam, Mary Fendall and Anne returned from Masham, Caroline fetched them in the gig. The thermometer at 7 in the evening was 80 in the shade on the east side of the house. Received a canvassing letter from Mrs Cowper and one from John Williams saying he had sold the Canal shares and was reconciled to his cousin at Penpont and Davies was got well and gone to St David's.

6th. Von Buch says that it is only lately that the Holy Sacrament has been better understood by the Laplanders than that they took a cloth always into Church with them into which they spit out the Sacramental Bread which they then wrapped carefully up and divided at home into numerous small crumbs. Every beast of their herd received as long as any remained one of these crumbs and the Laplanders were convinced that by this means the flock would be secured from all injury. Lent J. F. N. £10.

7th. Did duty in the morning and J. F. N. in the evening.

8th. Letter from Mr Claridge saying he had hinted to Lord A that a Residentiaryship at York would be a good

appendage to living of Wath. Unluckily Lord A has no
influence with the Archbishop. Finished two sermons, one
from Gisborne's Theology, the other on the Syrophoenician
woman.

9th. Wrote to Mr Claridge. The Howards, Mrs Lucas,
Morley, Newsam at dinner. Mr Claridge mentions Mr Skey
having gone mad and being sent to a place of confinement at
Salisbury, he mentions too that Lord Lascelles declines
standing for the County of York. Canon Williams in a letter
received says he has sold my Canal shares to Maybery for
£60 a share.

10th. I begin this book[1] on the 24th day of such weather
as I never remember for twenty years past there having
been scarce a cloud to be seen for far the greater part of
the time either by night or day and it having not rained
since the 16th of May. The thermometer has been very
generally above 60 by night and 70 by day. Sent to Boro'-
bridge for bottles. The thermometer at 4 p.m. was 75 in the
shade, 108 in the sun.

11th. Went with J. F. N. and his wife to Wensley in great
heat.

12th. Went to Aysgarth Force, never felt it hotter. Mr and
Mrs Vincent dined at Wensley.

13th. Returned to Wath, had thunder and lightening both
yesterday and today. On our return J. F. N. found a note from
the secretary to the Archbishop of York saying he received
no letter dimissory from the Province of Canterbury and
ordains no one who has letters dimissory unless he has been

---

[1] The diary was written in a series of note-books.

examined by his Diocesan Chaplain. On which I wrote to
Mr Wrangham saying I knew the Archbishop had ordained
Mr Caldwell both Deacon and Priest within a few months
who belonged to the Province of Canterbury and who had
not been examined by his Diocesan Chaplain, which produced a letter from Mr W full of hard words and convinced
me that he is what I heard of him before, that he was a man
who talked a great deal and said but little, and that he said a
great deal and meant nothing, so my son has to seek Priest's
orders elsewhere. When it is considered that the trouble (if
one can use that expression for performing that which is a
duty) of every curate who baptizes a child is about ten or
twenty times as much as ordaining one additional candidate
at a public Ordination and that the refusal to ordain is
attended with at least forty times as much expence as the
refusal to baptize, one would hardly think it possible for any
man of common civility, at least for any gentleman, to refuse
on so slight an inconvenience to himself, and yet we are told
that the Archbishop of York is a man of amiable and gentlemanly conduct and manners, what a pity then that making
an Archbishop should unmake a gentleman. It is like the
Popes styling themselves *Servi Servorum Dei* at the moment
they were exercising Imperial power in all the Kingdoms of
the Earth. Had my son been a man of spirit he would have
gone to York and said, My Lord Archbishop, I am confident
I am qualified for the office of a Priest according to the laws
of this land and the usual acquirements and am ready to be
examined and your chaplain Mr W has declared that he is
willing to give his part of the trouble. Your Grace's trouble
then is merely to lay your hands on seven heads instead of
six and by so doing you will save me forty guineas. Now

I am confident if you were not an Archbishop or any Bishop but only a gentleman and I was introduced to you as a respectable young man who could get forty guineas if you would be pleased to put your hand on me you would not refuse. If then the imposition of your hands not only gave this candidate such a sum at so slight an expence of trouble, can the refusal be justified on the plea that you would have conferred an infinitely greater favour on the candidate by conferring on him those spiritual gifts which Episcopal Ordination is supposed to confer and enabling him to be of greater and more important advantage to the flock over which he is appointed to preside? My idea is that a resolution not to ordain a candidate properly qualified and properly recommended is neither civil, gentlemanly, Christian or Episcopal.

14th.   Did duty in the morning and J. F. N. in the evening. I forgot to mention that Charlotte Costabadie went to Wensley with us and returned to Wath to her sister.

15th.   This was a melancholy week as my dear children and grandson were to leave us at the end. I hope yet to have them established at no great distance of time in the neighbourhood before I am quite got down the hill and unable to enjoy their society. I trust my behaviour to them during their visit will prevent their ever again mistaking my motives of action towards them. I gave J. F. N. a discharge of all monies due to me previous to the 1st January last, to my belief about £400, and I lent him £85 for which he gave his note of hand to his three sisters and a promise to pay it as soon as he could and at all events on the marriage of either. I also promised to give up all the profits of Biddisham and to try and get it resigned to him, only that I am not to pay curate since Christmas last or stand to repairs, but I give up all arrears after paying curate up to Christmas last and the business of the Priory is for ever set at rest between us. This day we went to Carthorpe to drink tea with Mr J. Newsam where we met Mr E. Carter and Mr Morley. Six went in the carriage and three in the gig.

16th.   Dined with my wife and J. F. N. and Eliza at Morley's who gave us a most splendid dinner and won our money afterwards.

17th.   The Bedale Club. Mr Monson not there but two Elsleys, Newsam, Morley, Carter, on my return bought a mare at Burniston on the recommendation of Mr E. Carter who came down from Theakston with us as I had driven C. Costabadie there and left her while I went to the Bedale Club.

18th.   Sent for the mare, visited Mrs Orde who is in the last stage.

19th.   Went with J. F. N. and E. Carter and Newsam to Boro'bridge Show. The two latter dined at Wath.

20th.   Lawson elected member for Boro'bridge, the Parliament having been dissolved on the 10th ult. Canvassed by Webb at Gloucester but received a letter from Mrs Commeline saying they had paired me off against my old friend Dr John Roberts. Canvassed also for the Brecon County election but by which party I cannot tell as there was no signature to the letter nor anything by which to judge who it came from.

21st.   Did duty in the morning and J. F. N. in the evening.

22nd. Went to Boro'bridge Fair with Mr Morley and H. Costabadie and saw Polito's wild beasts, two lions, a boa strictor, a tyger, a Nilgau, zebra, two hyaenas, kangaroo, jackalls, pelican, cassiowary, etc. This day J. F. N., Eliza and dear Jack, M. N. junior and Mary Fendall left Wath for Redmarley.

23rd. Went to Ripon, Mr Morley, Newsam and H. Costabadie went also and dined here.

25th. Went to York County Election with Mr Morley and returned to dinner. Lord Milton and Mr Stuart Wortley returned without opposition. Bethell and Wortley spoke well. Bottled a pipe of Port this week, half for Mr Barstow and a $\frac{1}{4}$ for Howard.

26th. Dined at Mr Howard's with Capt and Mrs Gabriel, Mrs Lucas and Miss Hodges and Mr Gilpin. Received very bad accounts of Bullo Pill. Answered W. Fendall's letter about his father's affairs.

27th. Meeting at Oak Tree, very little to do. Col Serjeantson who returned from London on Wednesday and Mr Morley there. N.B. Saw Mr Claridge at York and consented to give £140 for the barouche if it could be got down free of expence.

28th. Did duty morning and evening. Churched, catechized and christened. Mrs Orde died yesterday.

29th. Mr Askwith, Mr Morley, and Mr Allanson called. Settled with Mr Askwith that he should have the deputations of Norton and Melmerby and I would try to get those of Wath and Middleton and Mr Allanson who had met Mr Askwith on the road very kindly said that he would give me the deputation of Middleton.

30th. Drove Anne to Ripon, left her at Mr Howard's, took up Mrs Howard and went on to Ripley Castle to call on Capt Garnet and carry back the Venerable Bede and the other books he had lent me, found the library not very large but very well stocked with ancient British history, Camden, Dugdale, Hoveden, Shype, Malmesbury, etc. Walked over the farm. Saw the chamber in which the King slept guarded by a Miss Ingleby, who walked about all night with a brace of pistols in the antechamber while the castle was besieged by Cromwell. This is the only part that is ancient, the modern part of the house being built on to it and the way to it is through a blind door out of the modern drawing room. The only thing of high value is Venus of Canova, admirable. She is in the act of catching up the drapery to hide herself on the supposition of being accidentally seen naked. The drapery is drawn up nearly to her mouth, hides part of the body from the neck to the feet, while it leaves enough exposed to show the beauty of the form. The stooping attitude is just sufficient to show that the Venus de Medici had been studied by the artist without its being a copy and indeed hardly an imitation. The back of the figure is entirely naked from head to foot. There are two German game pieces with dogs very well painted. The portraits are all daubs, not excepting the late Lady Ingleby by Sir Joshua, as only the black and white remains. The place is capable of more improvement than it is likely to receive under the present master of the works whose education was being Mr Penn's gardener at Stoke. They talk of expending 7 or 8000 pounds on a range of hothouses and greenhouses when 2000 spent on a conservatory to adjoin the west end of the drawing room would make the place ten times more complete than all the money to be spent at such a distance from the house that the ladies may not be able to visit the greenhouse above once a month in the winter season. Returned with Mrs Howard to Ripon, set her down and brought Anne home to dinner after having heard some very strong insinuations against one of the Ripon Banks. Paid the girls up all that was due up to midsummer.

July 1st. Mr Morley called on Justice business, afterwards drove Mrs N to call on Mrs E. Carter, Mrs Serjeantson and Mrs Morley, found them all at home. Began mowing Monday last and the fine weather continuing promises a very short hay harvest. Wrote to Lord Ailesbury and Mr Claridge to request the deputation of Wath and heard from Mary Newton. Received a letter from Ivison requesting me not to go to Brecon to vote against Col Wood. Tonight the thermometer was below 50 for the first time since the 16th May.

2nd. Mr and Mrs Gilpin called. Finished mowing White Field and Red Field. Heard that Harriet Fendall was married to G. Thompson[1] on the 4th January, that Capt Berkeley had lost his election for Gloucester and that Cooper and Webb were returned. Also that Scudamore had lost at Hereford and Cocks and Col Symonds returned.

3rd. Heard from Mr Claridge that he had bought Lord Ashton's barouche for me for £140 including a new boot and painting the crest.

4th. Sent Mr Claridge the money for the barouche by order from Mr Coates and get in 2/3 of my hay into pike. Rode to Ripon, saw Capt Gabriel. Wrote to J. F. N. Got in the

---

[1] Their son, Sir Rivers Thompson, became Governor of Bengal.

greatest part of my hay which began to be mown only on Monday last.

5th.   Mr and Mrs Howard came to Church in the morning and spent the rest of the day here. Wrote to M. N. junior.

6th.   Mrs and Mr Morley, Col Serjeantson called. Finished hay making. A long letter from J. Commeline from Naples and in it he says he hopes to be at home by Christmas.

7th.   Attended as visitor at Bedale Savings Bank, Mr Monson and Col Serjeantson there, received £87. 12. 6. The whole deposits amount to more than £4200. Called on Mr E. Carter and Mr Morley. In the evening a thunderstorm and violent rain from the South. Heard Brougham had lost his election for Westmoreland.

8th.   A violent shower began about 8 and lasted till near 10 which made the Stell overflow till 8 o'clock in the evening. None of the rain reached Ripon as we learnt by our postboy and immediately after the shower the barometer began to rise, the wind went to N.W. and we have a prospect of dry weather still continuing. Planted the mangel worzel. The girls went to Ripon and we planted out our first crop of brocoli and some Savoys.

9th.   Dined yesterday and today *tête à tête* with my wife for the first time since we have been at Wath. The girls came from Ripon. Heard from Lord A who will give me the deputation of Wath and I received that of Middleton from Mr Allanson. Paid for covering the two mares by Ledstone.

10th.   Dined at Kirklington with my wife, A. F. N. and C. F. N., Mr and two Miss Morleys, Capt Comby, R.N., and Mr Ridsdale who lives near Nidd. Was called at 12 to pray with old Mr Squire who had a seizure about 7 or 8.

11th. Found Mr Squire not much worse than usual. Put on a new black silk waistcoat yesterday. Dined at Camp Hill with Mr, Mrs and two Miss Morleys and Mr Newsam.

12th. Did duty morning and evening. Administered the Sacrament to Mr Squire, churched Charlotte Barnett.

13th. Rode to view a road with Col Serjeantson and Mr Morley at Kirklington. The Bellerby tenant brought half a year's rent, all but £6. I told him that as his father had got into gaol the trustees would expect him to bring a security for the rent or that he otherwise would have notice at Michaelmas to quit at Lady Day and he promised to bring the £6 and the security the end of August or the beginning of September. Gathered French beans which were much too old. Began clover stack. The thermometer in the shade at the north side of the house 75 the greatest part of the day, did not go out except into the village till 8 in the evening.

15th. Bedale Club, present Dr Scott, Col Serjeantson, Mr Monson, Mr Newsam, Mr Elsley, Mr Morley and B. N. in the chair. Paid for the flags for the school £8. 15. 0. Heard from Mr Claridge that he would bring down the barouche.

16th. Ripon Market, the thermometer in the sun at 9 a.m. 118. Heard that the heat this day in the sun at Ripon Market was so great that three butchers broiled their steaks for dinner on their cleavers in the sun without fire.

17th. Mr Newsam at dinner and heard from J. F. N. that he had been ordained Priest last Sunday at Wells by the Bishop of Gloucester.

18th. To Topcliffe Fair. Mr Newsam and Capt Gabriel at dinner. Heard from M. N. junior that Mr Watson was Lord Somers' agent and a very gentlemanly man, a great friend of Capt Gabriel's. Heard Lord A was coming into Yorkshire 27 strong in 3 carriages and with 9 horses. Received a printed letter from the Bishop of Chester requesting me to preach a sermon for the repairs of Chester Cathedral. Thunder in the afternoon but no rain. Thermometer 75 in the shade all day, at night 63. Saw Mr Livesay at Topcliffe and he gave a good account of Sir B. Graham's health. Saw L. Booth and Hutton of Sobergate. Dent the Justice wanted to buy my mare but would not give £25 for her, bid £22. 2. o.

20th. Set out for a tour without having determined which way to travel any further than Wensley where we had promised to dine in our way either to Hawes or Askrigg this evening as the Costabadies were so full with all their young folks at home that it was not in their power to give us any beds. The first blunder we made of which I shall give account in order to make the history of our tour a history of blunders, which will be easily done, was setting out without either of those friends which had occupied the attention of at least two of the party for some days, not to say weeks before, and being obliged after travelling the first three miles to send John back for the road book, and telling him we would wait his arrival at Masham where we found Mrs Hardcastle at ¼ past 10 not risen, however by the time I had fed the horses at the Inn the elderly lady made her appearance and after we had experienced the wonderful capacity for news which is the exclusive property of antiquated vestals and found that their powers of devouring and digesting news are inex-

haustible in as much as she had three continual streams
poured into her by my wife and two daughters for the space
of an hour and a half and yet seemed none the fuller, John
arrived with the road book and a letter from Mr Claridge to
say Col Wood had got his election by a majority of 28, and
having brought the horses after feeding his own, we started
for Wensley and reached Middleham without any further
accident and as Mr Costabadie's man had driven us through
the ford the last time we came from Wensley were proceeding that way, when exactly at the turn of the street that
leads down to it we met Mr Brease who told us it was very
unsafe, we therefore continued up the town and over the
moor thro' excessive heat and labour for the horses and a
very considerable quantity of rain upon the new bonnets
which were projected on a certainty of fine weather and when
we arrived at the top of the moor and were to descend the
steep lane down to Wensley the ladies had to descend from
the carriage and found their shoes could not be used for
walking, the carriage was unpacked and reckoning our
blunder about the ford as the second, the improper state of
the bonnets and shoes may well pass for the third, without
adding to which we arrive at Wensley where we found all
the family well, about $\frac{1}{2}$ past 2 and sat down at four to an
excellent dinner and to an excellent story of my old friend
about an acquaintance and I believe relative of his, the rector
of Finchampstead in Essex, a man of fortune, who kept his
coach and four and made his two sons postillion calling one
son of a whore, whom he had by his wife who was his
housekeeper before marriage, and the other son of a bitch
whom he had by her afterwards. The weather threatening we
were pressed to sleep at Wensley and found the capacity of

our friend's house exactly like Mrs Hardcastle's curiosity, capable of being stretched to any extent and that to overfill it or make it seem fuller was impossible.

21st. Breakfasted at Wensley and set out a little before 9 for Askrigg, a very good road with little hill, had thence 5½ m to Hardrow where we got some oats for the horses, and my wife got some water to drink with her bread and cheese, the water was brought in a white basin, they had an egg each and the charge was 5/- for their eating, so much for laking. The drag chain broke both the first and second time having been mended after the first. From Hardrow we set out after admiring the Scar and the beck that comes down close to the alehouse, for Sedbergh, 15 miles, very much uphill for about five miles till we got above the source of the Eure and on turning over the point of the hill came to the rise of another rivulet which runs into the Western Ocean. The point in the road from which the rainwater runs into the Eure and so to the German Ocean, and also down the Garsdale Valley into the Western Ocean I take to be about 9½ miles from Sedbergh. This Garsdale is for 5 or 6 miles a beautiful Dale, the road for the most part running close to the river walled up from 6 to 20 feet above it without any fence between the road and the river. The singularity of the Dale is that after having gradually widened from a mere ravine to a valley half a mile wide it is suddenly shut up into a ravine again and the road carried up the hill a considerable way and then descends gradually as the Vale opens out again over a handsome new bridge to Sedbergh, which is the narrowest town I ever saw, the street in no place exceeding

8 to 10 feet except for about 20 yards opposite the shambles which stand directly above the church and churchyard. In this place all the boys and girls and women are knitters employed in knitting not stockings but blue woollen caps of yarn which makes all the children look as if they came out of a dyeing factory. A circumstance obtains in many of the small towns in Yorkshire, Middleham, Askrigg, Sedbergh, etc, which I have not seen remarked, which is that of making the groundfloor of the houses merely lumber rooms, stables, cowhouses, etc, and throwing a flight of steps up out of the street to the floor above which is the part inhabited by the family. Almost all the children of Sedbergh wear wooden shoes and make a great clatter in the street. The church seems calculated to hold not only all the people but all the houses. No Cambridge man ought to leave Sedbergh without seeing the house and taking off his hat to the memory of the late Mr Dawson, an apothecary of this place who for more than half a century sent a continual supply of young men excellently grounded in the mathematics to that University. I find on enquiring the old gentleman is still living in this place with his daughter but that he neither instructs the ignorant or heals the diseased any longer, many who were my seniors in the University had been his pupils. Dinner at ½ past 6 at Sedbergh. Trout, loin of lamb, cold beef, tarts and rum pudding, good Port wine etc. A good knitter knits 12 caps *per diem* which on examining must be worn by convicts and prisoners, they are knit very loose on wooden pins. I omitted to say that the ale which was brought us at Hardrow was brought in an old silver tankard very much battered and mended at the edges with tin and had engraved upon it "Masham Plate. 1725".

22nd. Left Sedbergh very early this morning to breakfast at Kendal which we did not reach owing to a fifth blunder at taking the road to Kirkby Lonsdale instead of Kendal, till half past ten, being full three hours in travelling the eleven miles, the road lying all the way over mountains and some of the highest in Westmorland, with scarce a symptom of cultivation or habitation for more than six miles out of the eleven. We got an excellent breakfast at Kendal, walked a great deal about the town and among other places to the Church where there happened to be assembled a numerous body of the clergy and a sermon was preaching for the benefit of poor clergymen and the widows and orphans of the clergy by a gentleman who had one of the most powerful voices I ever heard and a very good delivery, making some allowance for a North Country dialect. His sermon must have been a very long one as it lasted I should suppose at least 25 minutes after we got into the Church and I should think was half over. He embraced a great number of topics, and among others lamented the acquittal of Hone in three several trials and said if the laws in being were insufficient to punish a parody-maker new ones should be enacted. On going to a druggist for an ounce of tincture of rhubarb, the druggist asked me if I had a phial to carry it in, and on my answering in the negative he took up one which ran out and on putting it aside was unable to find another and obliged to go out to buy one. The road from Sedbergh was so hilly and had nothing but ling to be seen on it, so I made a sort of vow never to tour it again that way. A little before 2 we left Kendal and travelled for the first three miles up and along a most glorious terrace I ever yet travelled, we at length got up on the moor, the ups and downs of which were very steep and

we had well nigh lost our way by the Jesuitical language of a
finger post which instead of saying "To Bowness" says "to
Ambleside by Bowness 8 miles" and on another finger "To
the Ferry" which as it is Bowness ferry perplexes a stranger
which road he is to take to the Inn. We were much favoured
by the weather, which though it threatened rain the greater
part of the day, just as we were in the most interesting part of
the road broke up and showed the landscape and the distant
hills with the finest broad lights and shades that can be
imagined. As it was only nine miles, after ascending and
keeping on the mountain for seven miles I grew very im-
patient for a sight of Windermere and at every step the horses
made I stretched my neck in vain to see it and owing to its
breadth being narrowed by Mr Curwen's island, did not get
a view of it till we were quite descended into the Vale, which
however highly gratified us, when we did see it. And I
cannot conceive how it is possible that anyone's expectations
can be disappointed, except by their expecting that to be
sublime which is only beautiful in the extreme, smiling, not
frowning, not terrific but enchanting. We arrived about 4 at
Bowness, a beautiful little village, too much cannot be said
of its beauty or its littleness, the excellence of the White
Lion as an Inn, the prospect from the windows and the odd
but natural situation of the house and garden. As soon as
we had dined we ordered a boat and got into it with two
lads in order to be rowed to what is emphatically called the
station but they landed us on Mr Curwen's Island not far
from his house and said nothing. Here our blundering again
became conspicuous. We walked round the island and returned to the place in which we had been landed and found
no boat, we waited half an hour, the evening drew on and the

wind began to whistle and to threaten rain. Some poor men
who had had their boat unmoored and taken away were in
the same predicament with ourselves, they immediately went
to Mrs Curwen to borrow a boat that was very neat and kept
in a boathouse which she lent them and coming down to the
landing place advised us to avail ourselves of the opportunity,
but we had sent our man in search of our own boat, and the
men who had potatoes and many other things to freight their
boat with were not going to Bowness. We thanked Mrs
Curwen and presently after had the satisfaction of seeing our
man coming with the two lads in our boat. While we were
waiting we had an opportunity of observing some of the
productions of the island, oaks that would not have disgraced
the Serpentine Walk in Savernake Forest, eating chestnuts
nearly as large, one growing at the landing place, close to
the water's edge, nay almost in the lake, was at least seven
yards in circumference six feet from the ground, Portugal
laurel of great size and vigour, larches and ripe cherries on
standard trees in abundance. I hope Mr C will excuse my
having plucked some few, to have an opportunity of marking
and recording the climate and the season by the circumstance
of having picked and eaten them on the spot. One thing only
surprised me as contrary to my expectation, and that was
that this luxuriant isle in the hands of the first agriculturist
in the kingdom with an abundance of grass sufficient to
fatten 20 or 30 shorthorned cattle should be stocked with
only about half that number of Scotch or Moorside sheep.
I had an opportunity of enquiring of Mrs C when the show
at Workington would be which she obligingly told me would
not be till 19, 20, 21 August and not being quite sure applied
to Mr H. Curwen who much to my disappointment con-

firmed it, as it will be too late for me to attend it. I was much
gratified by perceiving the facility with which the poor
fishermen obtained the boat from the Laird and Lady of the
Isle. At Dinner—trout, perch, jack, beef steaks and tarts.
Good Port.

23rd.   I forgot to mention that the church at Kendal is very
handsome and the lightest within that I ever saw. Walked
down by the North end of the church and was particularly
struck with the view of the lake from a timber yard about
200 yards above the place where you take boat. My wife got
up without a hint from me before 7 o'clock. This is the first
time since we were married which makes me remark an
occurrence that happens but once in 30 years. Potatoes are
selling from a cart at tenpence a stone. Rowed to the
Station, the wind was rough enough to put me somewhat in
fear, however we were most highly gratified particularly with
the view up the Lake, we met with an *extempore* poet who
wrote verses on the Lieutenant who was lost last year by
the upsetting of a sailing boat on the Lake, and also some
verses on the death of a young clergyman who was killed by
the overturning of a coach, with which we were more than
satisfied, though it was but a moderate shillingsworth. On
a gentleman giving some commendation, he seemed as well
satisfied with himself as Walter Scott or any other gentleman
poet; as he said "Yes, he was very well for what he was, no
grammarian". We met at the Station with a clergyman and
his friend and with Mr Henry Curwen and a friend of his and
with these four I ventured into conversation but with two
very gay dandy officers of the Sixth of Dragoons whom we
had seen yesterday I did not venture; the length of their

spurs quite daunted me. On returning I had the boat anchored close to another boat in which two gentlemen were fishing which gave me an opportunity of entering into conversation with them, also our blunder about the boat last night was a very happy one as the evening was so hazy and foggy that we should have had a very inadequate view of the Lake from the Station had we not seen it lighted up as it was today by the glorious light of a glowing day. When we came back to Bowness, which we did when I had gratified myself by catching two brace of fish in the mere, we encountered a funeral consisting of a hearse and seven or eight carriages following; it turned out to be that of Mr Allan, the father of the gentleman who married Kitty Smith of Coniston who died last year. He had come on a visit to a friend in the neighbourhood, was suddenly taken ill and buried at Bowness. The *extempore* poet would have given us the history of all the people in the neighbourhood had we had time and inclination to have listened to him. He abused a rich neighbouring Colonel, said he was an odious character. I found the poet was a Brougham and the Colonel a Lonsdale man, enough to excuse his opinions if we would not judge of him by harder rules than we judge his superiors. When we came to pay our bill they had charged us only for breakfast omitting both dinner and tea, and being ordered to mend the bill again omitted the tea. All things however being righted, we set out for Lowood Inn by the Bishop of Llandaff's and making only one blunder in the road arrived through excessive heat at ½ past 2 and meeting with two other gentlemen I beguiled the time with conversation with them till the pike was ready. One of them who was an old tourist knowing the lakes told me there was one view from Dunmaile Raise which could only be seen in perfection by bending down and looking backwards at it through your legs. On my remarking that was rather awkward for ladies, he said that was not the case, for that soon after he was married he was travelling there with a large party of ladies and that they all looked at the prospect in that way except one old maid and that she always continued an old maid. On consulting the landlord of the Inn how to make an evening tour he recommended Lough-rigg Tarn and Elter Water, which we set out to see, leaving Ambleside on our right we coasted the head of Windermere and were highly gratified with the mountain scenery which was really and truly sublime, especially from Elter Water. We then turned down to Skelwith Bridge and Skelwith Force, which Force was a very small Force indeed, but being one of Mr Green's views which we had got at Kendal Anne seemed desirous of visiting it, and we got back to Lowood at 8 o'clock to tea, where I found the landlord Mr Ladyman had been a servant of the old Bishop Barrington, knew Rendcomb, Craike, Sir William and Powell Guise, Mr Webb etc, and has kept this Inn about six years. Saw the proprietor of Rydale, Sir Daniel Fleming, in a hack chaise going to Grasmere and the landlord said he was awkwardly situated with his wife who was gone to France which prevented him living at Rydale. Mr Ladyman told me the waterfall at Rydale exactly represented a woman standing on her head. I hope I may be excused not filling my paper with epithets respecting prospects from the works of Sir John Carr, Gilpin, Walter Scott etc, as I shall have blunders enough without naming God's creatures as some of them have done and drowned their half ideas in seas of words which some people think very fine and some very foolish. Our tour this evening

might be about 11 miles, our port was very good, our dinner,
pike, eels, Scotch collops and gooseberry pye. The drive this
evening was on the whole the most level this side of Askrigg.

24th.   Rose before 7 and set out to breakfast at Grasmere,
passed through Ambleside by Rydal and Rydal water, soon
came in sight of Grasmere and turned out of the road to
Grasmere Inn, a little retired house behind the church kept
by a little farmer and his wife who were civility personified,
but here a sad disappointment occurred to the pleasure I had
promised myself in enjoying this place with my dear Anne
who was so ill as to be obliged to go to bed and lie there till
3 o'clock. In attempting to sit up was again obliged to go
to bed till near six. As soon as breakfast was over I walked
out to find my way down if I could to the lake in which
I succeeded and passing by the Church I peeped in at a
window of the chancel and to my great surprise saw the
Communion table, the rail at the altar, the seats, the windows,
every part of the Church crammed with all sorts of tawdry
and ridiculous things, stuck upon sticks, hoops, crosses and
made to stand upright. These sticks etc were some papered,
some covered with coloured paper, red green and yellow,
flowers of all sorts, roses, sweet williams, straw etc.   On
going down to the water I saw a gentleman's servant fishing
in a boat moored about 200 yards off in the lake who very
civilly pulled up his anchor and asked me if I wished for the
boat which I declined and went back for my wife and
Caroline who walked down with me to the boat and as soon
as we got there we were joined by the servant's master, a Mr
Burley from Lancaster, who hailed his man and we all embarked, he and his man rowing us round the island to our

great delight, for a more lovely scene in the same distance it is impossible to behold. Mr Burley and his man fished some time without success and I then went back to the Inn and finding it very unlikely that Anne would be able to move till the evening desired my wife to order dinner, tried in vain to catch a trout in the river with a fly and meeting with the rector of Grasmere begged him to explain the reason of his church being so fantastically ornamented, which he did by telling me that the seats in the church had no flooring but the bare earth, that there were very few appropriated seats and that there was an ancient custom of strewing the seats with rushes which was annually done the day after he had gathered his tithe wool. The old rushes were taken away and all the boys and girls in the parish brought a bundle of fresh rushes to strew the seats with and each carried a garland made after their own fancies which they deposited in the church fixing them up as and where they pleased; after which they were regaled at the expense of the parish with cakes and ale and gingerbread and had a dance in the evening in the barn belonging to the Inn, which led me to look into the said barn and I was surprised to see it floored with a good oak floor from one end to the other, the said barn being over a good six stall stable and a large cowhouse. Mr Burley's carriage had been turned out of the barn for the fete and it required five stout men to wheel it up the inclined plane that led to the door of this exalted barn. Mr Burley told me he had been $3\frac{1}{4}$ hours in ascending Helvellyn from the Inn at the foot and that last week it had large quantities of snow on it. After some fine pike, beef steaks, peas, Westmoreland ham and apple pye we left Grasmere, Anne being much recovered and never in my life did my eyes take in such a draught of

pleasure from viewing scene of nature as in my ride to
Keswick where we arrived at 9, the road barring the hilliness
the best that can be travelled; it would have been unpardon-
able to have hurried over it. The forms of the mountains are
the most grotesque and at time the most sublime that can be
imagined. We had no sooner lost sight of the lovely Grasmere
than Leathes water stretched itself before us and passing
nearly three miles down to it and two miles along it its loss
was fully compensated by the mountain scenery that surrounded us, till we got sight of Keswick, Derwent and
Bassenthwaite Waters and walking down the steep descent
to the turnpike arrived at nightfall at the Royal Oak at
Keswick, where not being able to obtain a sitting room in
the house we proceeded to the Queen's Head where we had
been recommended by the landlord at Lowood; a boy knowing us for lakers put handbills in our hands to tell us of all
the wonders to be seen at Keswick and its neighbourhood.
I was happy to see my dear Anne somewhat revived and
having treated her and her sister with six doses of calomel
and my wife with a bottle of essence of anchovies from a
facetious druggist who did not know the difference between
a barometer and a thermometer though he told me he was a
Scotchman I drank some tea and so lay up for tonight, the
thermometer at 11 at night being 68.

25th.   The thermometer fell in the night to 62 and I have
not much to record today except my joy and gratitude for
the recovery of my dear Nanny. The principal business of
this morning was inspecting museums of which I saw three,
my daughters and my wife one. They are certainly well for
the distance from London, and the few opportunities which

one would think would offer in these remote parts to a collector. The first had but an indifferent collection of the minerals of the country; I bought a few small specimens of lead as they say the mine is exhausted or lost as it does not like other metals lie in veins but in detached pieces larger or smaller as it may happen, from a few grains to many pounds. The only specimen I had any liking for was a green fluor but on hearing the price I liked half a guinea better. I saw a fine live eagle five years old taken at the Isle of Mull, his keeper was afraid to approach him without a stick though he has had him so long and as his wings are not cut it seemed to require some strength to hold him by the chain that was round one of his legs when he attempted to fly. We dined early intending to drive as far as Bowder Stone, Anne and the horses not wishing for much, but it threatened rain and I rode on horseback just as far as Mr Pocklington's when the rain increasing and threatening much in Borrowdale I turned about and came home to tea, after taking a beautiful station in a field between the road and the lake about $\frac{1}{2}$ a mile on the Keswick side of Mr Pocklington's. After tea Mrs N, Caroline and I walked in the rain as far as Crosthwaite Church and I wrote to Mr Commeline. Pike, leg of mutton, currant pyes, jellies, peas and sherry. Made no acquaintance today, found that my greatcoat was left at Lowood and congratulated myself that it was an old one. The houses slated and whitewashed very neat, the people civil, the museum keepers Jews, the streets clean, Keswick market very full, have seen no waggon since we left Wath, very bad mowing, scythes six feet long, a small cart load of coal costs from 6 to 12 shillings, the people as thick as in a Welsh market. No church in the town, the museum being the tower.

The museum keeper told us the bell on which the town clock struck was cast in 1001. He had a good Oliver Crown struck before the mishap to the dye and a Queen Anne's farthing, a Henry 3rd and 4th. The earliest British coin was one of King John's. Had an arrival of ladies this evening and saw the names of three old acquaintances written with a diamond on the window in our sitting room, viz: Mrs Rewe, Mrs Price, Miss S. Hatton, Sep 1793. The glass though frail has long survived the two and for all I know Miss H also.

26th. Got up at 8, it rained hard. We each took an umbrella and went to Crosthwaite Church, heard a most excellent reader and preacher deliver an excellent sermon in a most excellent style from the verses "Father, let this hour pass from me", "Father, glorify thy name", in the 12th St John. I could only learn that he was Rector of Coldback without learning his name, but if it were tolerable weather and I was at Kendal again I would ride to Coldback though it is 12 miles to hear him. The singing was very well conducted. The clerk went out of his place after the second lesson to sing the *Jubilate*, as it was so very wet I suspect the whole choir were not at church. The music with the exception of one flute was wholly vocal and they had one woman. They sang the *Jubilate* and six verses of the 95th and six of the 34th Psalms, both new version, to tunes quite different to any I had heard. The vicar of Crosthwaite's name I understand is Denton, rather an elderly man. They have only one sermon on Sundays, but he expounds after prayer in the afternoon, passages of the New Testament. The church besides the singularity of being a mile from the town and having no village or hamlet near it has one or other things belonging

to it that I do not recollect seeing before. The seats are all
floored with stone and the aisles with boards. There is a
regular ascent from the great door on the south side up to
the altar and also up to the west end of the church but the
ascent to the altar is by a gradual rise of about an inch in a
foot whereas the rise from the door to the west end is nearly
a foot in a yard and the singers standing up in front are all
seen one above the other sloping from the bottom to a height
of ten feet from the floor. The great window over the altar
is not near in the center. On one side room is left only for
one tablet, on which is painted the Belief, on the other side
are two tablets on which are the ten Commandments, this
makes too the south aisle much wider than the north. The
churchyard is large and the people do not seem to have the
same prejudice against burying on the north side of the
church as they have in the South, there being nearly an equal
number of tombstones on all sides of the church which is
very large and light and owing I suppose to the wetness of
the day would have held more than twenty times as many as
were there. I should think the proportion of men to women
was nearly twenty to one. The clouds above and below the
hills were a contrast to the almost unclouded sunshine we
have hitherto enjoyed. In the next room are the most unceasing talkers that can be imagined, they seem to be counterpart party to ourselves, father mother and two daughters.
Heard from Mr Claridge that Lord A had postponed his
journey into Yorkshire, I think he might as well have said
abandoned it. Dinner today, Little Jack to put me in mind
of my grandson, ham, two chickens, loin of mutton, jellys,
cabbage, lettuce, cucumber, potatoes, gooseberry pye, excellent cheese and Portwine. The rain continues to prevent

any laking today. The Miss Greens who shewed their father's museum were very nice well-behaved good-looking young women, the youngest quite handsome. In Crosthwaite museum was a remarkably fine-toned gong. My wife's devotion obliged her to change her shift being thoroughly wet through in coming from church. I have not yet remarked that alteration of countenance that some people pretend to observe in travelling north long before they reach these latitudes, especially in the cheekbone being much higher and resembling the Scotch countenance. As I lately read a touring man who remarked it I have been particularly attentive to it especially in the females and if I may venture any remark it is that the female figure is in general remarkably good, the countenance not handsome but pleasing, not strongly expressive or hardly marked, not ruddy like a young Welsh girl, nor weather-beaten like a middle-aged wife of a farmer in Brecon or Monmouthshire, in short a quite different face from what I had set down in my own mind (whether rightly or wrongly I pretend not to say) as peculiar to the mountainous parts of the South of the Island. Indeed I think that a Herefordshire woman differs in appearance as much or more from a Hertfordshire, Kentish or Essex woman than a Cumberlander or Westmorelander. The weather clearing about five o'clock we sallied out down to the lake about 6 and the evening was so clear that every part of the landscape was equally distinct. The furthest and highest points of Skiddaw were as plain to the eye as the dripping tree whose overhanging leaves wetted you as you past. Having walked along the gravel walk which the Governors of Greenwich Hospital have very kindly allowed to be made for the accommodation of travellers and the people of the town we saw Lodore Fall

very well across the lake and heard it roar tho' more than
two miles distant as if it was within a quarter of a mile. At
the end of the walk we met our landlord who here became
our guide and would have pointed out all the beauties of the
spot which no human being with his senses about him can
miss, we rather availed ourselves therefore of his offer to
conduct us up Castle Crag which he very civilly did and we
were if possible more highly delighted at reaching the summit
than we had been at the end of the gravel walk. We not only
commanded the whole of the lake and all the islands (among
which the first place is held by the one formerly called
Pocklington's Isle on which Col Peachy has a house) the
Lodore waterfall, Mr Pocklington's house, the mouth of
Borrowdale, Castle Rigg and on the opposite Latrigg and
Lord William Gordon's, but turning to the north west we
saw the whole of Bassenthwaite and the glorious Skiddaw
with Crosthwaite church and the town of Keswick at our
feet. The ravines and points of the mountains of Skiddaw
were sprinkled over with light coloured bits of clouds that
hung on their dark sides as thin as the gossamer and changed
their shapes at every instant and we spent two hours in as
high a state of gratification as to do away all repining at our
having waited all day for the rain to have cleared the atmo-
sphere so effectually as to varnish the whole picture and
bring out the most brilliant and transparent colours. The
landlord told me he rented a farm of Greenwich Hospital
and that he paid near £4 per acre for the land. His hay a
very poor crop and his wheat a very good one so good that
it was the first I had seen lodged by the rain. He said the
late valuers among whom our friend[1] took the lead were

[1] Mr Claridge. See p. 81.

pretty merciful and the advance had not been very considerable the land having been high rented before. He
shewed us the residence of the poet Southey who has changed
his residence and his politics *outrement* from the Tagus to the
Greta, from Jacobinism to Sidmouthism, Castlereaghism
and Regentism. He shewed us also Sir George Beaumont's
cottage which was the late Mr Bunbury's and which Sir
George not occupying last year he lent to the Wetheralls,
and the Merewethers while they were enjoying an expedition
to one of the romantic views of the neighbourhood had all
their schemes of pleasure blasted by finding on their return
that one of Mr Wetherall's children had been smothered in
their absence by falling into the privy, this child was about
four years old. Such events may well chastise our enjoy-
ments even of the purest kind, one of which I hope and trust
the pleasure we all receive from the contemplation of these
wonderful and beautiful works of the Creator may well be
reckoned, especially to those who gratefully look up thro'
Nature's works to Nature's God. My landlord told me Mr
Curwen would have joined Lord Morpeth to stand for
Cumberland against the Lowthers, who seem more disliked
here than in Westmoreland but that Lord Morpeth would
not join Mr Curwen; the expense of turning out the Lowthers
would have been at least £50,000 if it had succeeded at last.
I think nothing we have yet seen has exceeded the Vale of
St John, till my senses fail I think they will retain the impression received in travelling down the eight miles of the
road from Grasmere to Keswick.

27th.   Rose at ½ past 6, rained a little, thermometer 58,
wind N.W. Cleared up at 9 and we set out for the Lodore

fall and the Bowder Stone. The peculiar brilliant clearness
with which objects are seen amid this mountain scenery can
hardly be conceived by those who have not experienced it,
and the quantity of rain was sufficient to make the Lodore
fall the most picturesque possible, that is it had as much
water in it as it can have without falling in one sheet, as
Green's large view represents it, we saw in going from the
bottom in the far side the bridge from Keswick and on our
return we got the key at the public house and went up the
side next Keswick which seems to be the side and the way
laid out for visitors to visit it and I should apprehend that
there is no waterfall in England that can in any degree rival
it, when seen after rain as we saw it. How fortunate must we
think ourselves for, as an Irishman would say, had we seen
it only three days ago before the rain there would not have
been anything to see. Instead of seeing a river as large as
the Eure at Wensley tumble over rocks only not perpendicular, from the height of Cheddar Cliffs, with a deafening
yet most agreeable sound. We proceeded to the Bowder
Stone which none of our party ascended by the rustic ladder
placed against it of forty steps but Anne. This rock is placed
in the jaws of Borrowdale, which some one describes as the
receptacle for all the refuse of creation after the world was
made; but the valley opens about a quarter of a mile above
the stone, before it shuts up again into an apparently
impassable ravine. We returned by the way we came to view
a second time the sublime Lodore and then walked again
down to the lake. After dinner we left Keswick for Cockermouth, passing along the east side of Bassenthwaite over
Ouse or Ews bridge to Cockermouth. The lower end of the
lake from which you see the whole length and down into

the very mouth of Borrowdale as far as the Bowder Stone
with Skiddaw on your left and a mountain on the right that
shoves its base quite into the lake is uncommonly fine. The
head rises perpendicularly exactly as if artificial and the road
to Ews bridge passes over it and the issue of the Derwent
out of the lake has an artificial appearance also, as there is
no gradual contraction of the lake but the river issues at
once through a narrow channel of uniform breadth at once
out of the lake and the bridge is fifty yards from where it
issues. The road to Cockermouth is over a green mountain
with the Derwent at no great distance all the way to Cockermouth, and after the scenes we had left had no interest till
Cockermouth Castle and the bridge just as we descended
with the setting sun into the town. Dinner, trout and leg
of mutton, tarts, jellies, cucumbers and sherry. The last hour
was so cold that it made me wish for my greatcoat though
the sun shone brilliantly upon us. The Globe at Cockermouth
was so full that there was a demur when we arrived at the
door whether they could take us in and give us beds or not
but the demur was got over and we find ourselves well
accommodated. I have adopted the plan of zigzagging, that
is, when there are two opposite inns at a place I enquire at
the inn I leave which is the inn at the next town they drive
to and then I drive to the other; this in travelling through a
country for the first time gives you an idea of both sides
and their prices. I perceive sixpence a bottle difference in
the Port wine, sixpence in the charge for breakfast and sixpence in the charge for beds between the Bowness and the
Low Park sides. The Bowness is the cheapest and best.
Anne continues to improve and complains of nothing but
hunger.

28th. Rose soon after seven and walked up to the Castle but could not find any way into the interior but on enquiry was told if I rang the bell they would admit me. Returned to breakfast and had some of the best cakes ("*pains*" we should call them) I ever ate. I had just seen enough of the Castle from the top to make me see more, as I got a view of a fall of the Derwent which literally washes the foot of it for on attempting to pass between the Castle wall and the river I found I could not and was obliged to return. From 5 o'clock there seemed as much noise in the streets as if I had slept in the Strand. All the carts in this neighbourhood are under the guidance of females, excepting the lime carts, and most of the children of Cockermouth were without shoes or stockings. I observed too that the cows were driven about the town by women at Keswick, a girl rode a poney between two barrels of about a foot in diameter and two feet long to serve the town of Keswick with milk. After breakfast I took my wife and two girls up to the Castle and rang the bell boldly when the gate was opened by a female who let us in, said nothing, and departed, after we had wandered within the walls for some time without being able to get a good look out from it, a gentleman came to us and shewed us up to the top by a circular staircase in very good preservation and beautifully finished at the top. From the roof we had an exceedingly fine view and the gentleman, who was Lord Egremont's agent, entertained us with an account of his Lordship's vast possessions in these parts, extending over Skiddaw, Grasmere, Cockermouth, Buttermere, Egremont, told us great part of the land was very highly rented, as high as five and six pounds per acre and had been let during the high times as high as £7. He told us that Mr Wood at the

Globe was a great renter under Lord E and that the 28 large oat stacks which we noticed standing in a row by the road side as we came to Cockermouth last night all belonged to him and that till very lately there were many more which darkened the road for a length of way. He then shewed us the rooms which Lord E had fitted up for himself in the Castle and very spacious they were, said his Lordship had written to say he was coming down to shoot moor game, that he had never seen this fine property till after he was fifty; took us through a window to walk outside the Castle wall and shewed us a table of curious construction which his Lordship has attached to all his sophas. We parted and went down to the inn and sate out for Scale Hill where we saw what the gentleman told us, the great spirit with which agriculture is carried on in the neighbourhood of Cocker-mouth, where the potato oat was accidentally discovered. We saw land just enclosed breast plough and burnt limed with several waggons load per acre and literally cut to pieces with drains that were not more than three or four yards asunder for fifty acres together on the moor within two miles of Cockermouth on the Buttermere road and a fine white thorn hedge planted all along the road side. No attempt has been made to reclaim the hills in South Wales at as low an elevation above the sea and in a latitude three degrees to the south. Q. Why not? As ten quarters of oats of a finer quality than were ever seen in the South of England are the produce of an acre under Cumberland management. We proceeded along a hard but roughish road to the very neat and comfortable little inn at Grasmere where after having ordered our dinner of a nice looking woman somewhat in the stile of a dairy maid but well looking and well behaved

we desired to have a boat and walked down with the boat
man near a mile to the Crummock Water, who immediately
stripped to his blue check shirt, very much the Cumberland
costume, and rowed up the lake, which is near four miles to
Buttermere. Crummock is for beauty the third or fourth and
for size the third. Borrowdale mountains are here again
visible and preserve the selfsame character of rugged sub-
limity which we saw at the Bowder Stone at the other end
of the Dale. Buttermere is quite a peaceful little village and
the lake after Crummock appeared of less consequence than
I had expected, not being more than one third the size, and
presenting little which we had not seen from Crummock.
The walk from where we landed and back to regain our boat
was full two miles, we saw the inn where the famed Mary[1]
belonged and saw a successor washing potatoes for whom
I think no man would feign himself a gentleman. There were
two parties at the inn whom we followed on our return to
Scale Force, rowing for about a mile and a half along the
west side of the lake and then walking up a steep hill for
upwards of a mile we climbed into a ravine overgrown with
oaks to see the famed cascade and well rewarded we were
with the sight of the waterfall fifty-six yards in one un-
interrupted sheet. The sheet indeed was a North Country
sheet like the one breadth of calico which was literally all
that was allowed at one of the inns of our tour for my wife
and myself. It was however a most beautiful and surprizing
scene, a fine counterpart to the fall at Lodore which was
wider and more broken, with a much greater quantity of

---

[1] Mary Robinson, the 'Beauty of Buttermere', an innkeeper's
daughter and subject of a well-known ballad. A rogue, parading as a
gentleman, deceived her into marriage.

water, yet this was I think more unique of its kind. That was
the first and grandest of its class. This the only one of its
kind. Having descended to the boat we again embarked and
with the wind in our favour and an excellent boatman we
reached the point we left in the morning in half an hour and
arrived soon after five to dinner after a most delightful expedition that took four and a half hours to perform. We
dined on roast chickens and some capital chops from a leg
of mutton and gooseberry pye, excellent porter and cheese,
set out again in the carriage to see Lowes Water about $1\frac{1}{2}$
miles from the house which was not uninteresting but would
have been more so had it been seen before the others, and
coming back to the inn finished our day with a good deal
of fatigue but which we thought we were most amply repaid
for, and the evening having served all our purposes to the
utmost of our wishes set in for rain almost as soon as we had
left the carriage. The thermometer this morning was about 54.
On seeing a man mowing and thinking he did it very awkwardly we went to him and I requested he would let my man
shew him how they mowed in other countries in order to
examine his meve and tackle, when I found that the blade of
his scythe was full six feet long which he wetted as in Brecon
with a square piece of wood with grease and sand upon it
instead of a stone rubber and the mode of mowing was as
follows. He raised himself as erect as he could and at the
same time throwing his scythe as far as he could with both
his arms to the right and then with all his might towards the
left he stooped his body quite low as the scythe passed from
right to left and drew up his body again at the same moment
as the scythe quitted the swathe. My man who mows as they
do in the South without ever quitting the stooping attitude

could not make near such good work but had to mend it
every time as the strait scythe left a piece of grass standing
almost every stroke he took. The grass was a poor crop of
moist wiry meadow ground. The landlord and the mower
both assured us that there were men who could mow two
acres *per diem* in that way but that was not the universal mode
of the country as many made use of the paddling mode. The
price was about three and sixpence per acre. In mowing in
the paddling method the man turns first to the right and
makes four steps during the interval of every swathe.

29th.   Rose at 7, the weather rainy a little and threatening
more. Thermometer 60, wind nearly south. Soon paid our
bill and get to Cockermouth where I could hear no intelligence of my greatcoat, as soon as we had breakfasted we
sate out for Allonby, found the road very intricate and very
bad, however we arrived at the Ship Inn about 2, having
been two hours and a half going the ten miles and on asking
if they could take us in and being answered in the affirmative
we dismounted but soon found they would not lodge us but
we might live there and we asked the expense and my wife
was so much surprised when they told her 4/- per day that
she would not believe the landlady. However we soon found
that we were to breakfast when we pleased, to dine at three,
to drink tea at six, and sup at nine for our 4/- per head. We
therefore hastened to dress and at 3 I as the last comer sate
at the bottom of a long table at which with my wife and
daughters we made 17 women and 5 men and the dinner was
nearly as under; a dish of trout at top, a fine piece of salmon
and a pair of soles next me at bottom, a fillet of veal, a ham,
a couple of boiled fowls, a round of beef, a loin of mutton,

with plenty of pyes and puddings, a dessert followed of gooseberries, currants, cherries; and shrimps, roast rabbits, roast apples, cold ham pyes, cold round of beef, potatoes, etc, for supper. I got acquainted with a Mr Merest, a friend of Mr Hills of Snailwell, knows Dan Gwilt, Mrs Dalton of Bury, Mr Whaley near Axbridge married his sister. De Visme junior was curate of Topham, acquainted with Mr and Mrs Isherwood, he has a very elegant wife. There was a Mr Graham and his son and two daughters, Mr Preston, Miss Clerk and these are all the names I have as yet picked up. When we went up into the drawing room before supper we found a party at whist and another at backgammon. My wife and Anne eat ravenously. The beach is beautiful, quite as good as Weymouth. We were sent to a nice cottage for two beds and the woman of the house seemed so dejected at having her two remaining bedrooms let without the sitting room that we agreed to give her half a guinea for the week for it. The bed rooms are small, we are to pay 1/6 per night for them and the drawing room looks upon the sea which now roars and has been roaring ever since we came here very violently.

30th.   Rose at 7. Thermometer 60. Rained a little but soon cleared and gave a fine view of the Scotch coast for many miles towards Port Patrick and I saw Nelson's pillar near Dumfries very distinctly. I walked for an hour before breakfast and then went to the inn where we were as plentifully served with meat, eggs, etc, for breakfast as we had been yesterday at dinner and supper. Walked again on the sand with Mr Merest, found our party consisted of Mr Preston, his wife, sisters and daughter, Mr Graham, his son and two daughters (the father has a living in Rutlandshire, the son is at St John's College, Cambridge and takes pupils), a Miss Robinson. Mr Graham senior told us he came in a vessel to Maryport from Liverpool and was but indifferently accommodated tho' only 20 hours in their passage. The girls have found one of the ladies to be a governess to a pretty looking girl of about 13. I find Mr Merest is not a clergyman as I at first thought, he told me he thought Mr Preston had been an agent of the Lowthers during the late elections, which I find was the case. I walked a considerable time on the beach admiring the beauty of the Scotch hills and saw Nelson's pillar very distinctly on a hill near Dumfries. I afterwards rode along the sands as far as Bedfoot near five miles and found it very delightful either for walking, riding or driving, and I was considerably surprised at seeing a field of barley completely ripe close to the village of Bedfoot. This being the first time I had ever seen barley ripe in July, I thought it more extraordinary that it should be in Cumberland and within ten miles of Scotland across the Firth of Solway. We had again an excellent dinner, trout top and bottom equalled only by Lord Ailesbury's Grafton trout before the cutting of the Kennet and Avon canal, boiled leg of mutton, quarter of lamb, ducks, apple pyes, puddings for dessert as yesterday. For supper as yesterday nearly, with raspberry cream, minced veal, apple pye, etc. Anne bathed in the tepid bath above 80. Walked after dinner and again after tea. Some of the party to whom I mentioned the ripe barley said they had seen barley already cut. The whole of this day was extremely delicious, the wind at south dying away at night into a perfect calm. We understand that nothing is paid for beds by those who sleep in the house.

31st. Rose at half past 7. Thermometer 60, hard rain. It appears that the liberties in eating and drinking my wife had taken did pretty well as long as she was moving but the salmon, gooseberry, currant and apple pyes now she is stationary seem to tell. I gathered a few specimens of granite but the shore is very unproductive of pebbles or shells and has nothing of boldness about it. My wife was not able to dine at the ordinary and continued ill all day and all night and I was affected much in the same way and cannot account for it except by eating trout which gave me a violent lax which I have experienced from eating salmon. I ate indeed a good many shrimps but they are considered as wholesome and my wife ate none. We had for dinner trout, roast beef, ducks, rabbits, veal puddings and pyes, and a ball at the Ship in the evening to which were invited the party from the other inn amounting to three gentlemen and a lady. We supped at eleven and got home before twelve. I find Mrs Merest was a Cumberland heiress and he a Cumberland man but I have not made out what took them to Soham where they live. I was rather surprised at the selection of words used by one of our ladies, as they were very appropriate and her language above the common run.

August 1st. Mr Preston is a plain likeness of Dr Blackman, rather like in voice and manner than in person, but as I said before a plain likeness. Miss Blamire may be called a little ugly Mrs Hillter, being half the size and not a quarter as handsome. Rode today with Mr Merest to Maryport, a very neat little town on a hill sloping down to the port and pier. We were lucky in arriving a little after high water. Saw one ship enter and one run aground but happily got off again

just at the harbour mouth, about 170 tons burden. Mr and
Miss Gawthorpe arrived today from Kendal and Mr Ferguson
from Carlisle, the latter I hear is a little mad. Mr G gave
Lord Lonsdale for a toast which was very readily drunk. On
Mr Merest giving Mr Brougham he immediately put his
stopper in the bottle and walked away. Just heard that Mr
Blamire was arrived. N.B. I mounted Mr Merest in his ride
to Maryport on Mrs Fall. I forgot to say that I danced two
dances with Miss Blamire and two with Miss Parkinson.
Songs after supper by Mr Ferguson, Mr Graham junior and
Miss Robinson.

2nd.   Went to church, heard a very good sermon from
Mr J. Graham who if he corrected one or two peculiarities or
rather provincialities would read and preach exceedingly well,
but he never pronounces the letter i in the words necessity,
adversity and says ud for ed at the end of participles, viz:
endud for ended, adversutty for adversity. He reads in a tone
gruffer than his natural voice, quite in a falsetto base. This
is a most delightful day, the Isle of Man visible. The thermometer below 56 in the night. The singing very good at
church, a large choir of female voices some of which were
very sweet, they sang the 100th, part of the 118th and part
of the 4th, new version. About 200 persons who filled the
church completely and the heat was very great so as nearly
to make the ladies faint. Mr Studholm and Mr Dobinson
arrived. I read prayers in the evening. A mischievous tame
jackdaw stole my thermometer which lay in the window of
the bedroom and threw it down and broke it. A scheme was
projected tonight of going to Dumfries at ½ past 8 tomorrow.
Mr and Miss Gawthorpe, a pair of twins aged 56, appeared.

He is said to be a lover of Miss Clerk and to have offered to have kept her a carriage and a pair of greys, was refused last year and then again this and so they say does Mr Dobinson try the eldest Miss Robinson. Saw the finest bed of mignonet in Mr Cowan's garden, the clergyman of Allonby, that I ever saw. Mr C said it had been sewn ten years ago and had ever since been selfsewn.

3rd. A large party intended availing themselves of Mr Ferguson's offer to take them to Dumfries in the vessel which he had hired and was to sail about ½ past eight this morning. Another vessel sailed for Scotland about that time with about twenty young men and girls, servants and suchlike, who went over to the Scottish coast in an hour and a half and returned in two hours after having been two hours in Scotland and drank so much whiskey that when they came back they could not tell the place where they had landed. In about twenty minutes after this party had sailed Mr Ferguson went aboard his vessel and Mr Graham senior and his daughter and three Miss Robinsons. As soon as they were aboard Ferguson said they were in too deep water to take in any more and pushed off without Mr Preston or young Graham and a lady or two more who were to have been of the party. Spent the morning principally on the beach with the telescope in my hand and saw more than a dozen vessels pass, had it not been rather hazy could have seen more as it was the highest tide at one o'clock. Both girls bathed and were highly delighted. Rode along the beach about one o'clock for two or three miles and drove Mr Merest and Mrs N and the girls in the carriage in the evening. Mr and Mrs Merest leave this place tomorrow for Workington and the whole of the present party quit Allonby this week with the exception of Mr and Miss Gawthorpe, most probably never to meet in this world again. The evening was remarkably close and the horses were more heated and as much distressed as they have been at any time since they left Wath though they had not been out more than an hour and a half and walked a good part.

4th.   Rose before 8 with a very threatening appearance of rain. I find the gentleman whom I heard preaching at Kendal about Hone's trial was a Mr Walker, vicar of Ingleton, and that the very excellent preacher we heard at Crosthwaite was Mr Lynn who married one of the Bishop of Carlisle's (Goodenough) daughters. Mr Brisket of Grange, brother-in-law of Major Brooke of Littlethorpe arrived, a sensible well informed man, vicar of Grange. Rode with Caroline and Mr Graham to the Treestone quarry as it is called in the Wigton road. Dined a fine salmon, veal, lamb, ducks, peas, ham, pyes, puddings. Took leave of the Merests who went to Mr Curwen and promised to get me a sight of the Schoose farm, ordered the bill which was moderate and cheap enough and I was well satisfied with the place and the people I met; should much more readily repeat my visit there if I or any of my family should want sea bathing than go to Coatham, Redcar or the east coast. When I left the inn there were no tidings of the party who went to Dumfries but a sailor said he saw the vessel go about midday into Caith on the Scots coast but Mrs Ferguson arrived to look after her husband about 11 at night and people seemed distressed for her as he had escaped from her to Annan races, it was not more than a month since he had been confined closely. How the three girls, the Robinsons and old Graham and his daughter could trust themselves to his management seems very strange.

5th. As I had intended to rise early and breakfast at Workington in order to see the Schoose farm and being rather restless I got out of bed at $\frac{1}{2}$ past 3 to look at the weather and saw the ship that carried the party to Dumfries just returned and the party in the act of walking up the beach from the vessel. I got up at 6 and about $\frac{1}{2}$ past I left Allonby on the mare leaving John to drive the ladies and arrived at Workington $\frac{1}{4}$ before 9 where I saw Mr Merest ready to conduct me to the Schoose; as Mr Curwen was obliged to be from home he desired him to attend me and we rode up immediately to the farm where I was most highly gratified by the sight of a greater number of fine shorthorned cattle than any other person in the kingdom can produce amounting to 118, none of which had ever cropped a blade of grass as it grew or left the post to which they were tied since they were put there and some had stood there fifteen years without quitting their post except for the bull. Thirty or more cows stood in a row in sheds open behind them and a place for the food with which they were soiled which happened in one shed to be vetches and in another sourish grass mown from under the plantations and on this plan they are kept as long as grass, clover, tares, or green food can be mown for them, they then have turnips and straw but never oilcake, hay or corn of any description. The bull was a six years old bull and hired, Mr Curwen had no other bull except three calves, the eldest about five months and the youngest about two months old. His crop of reared calves this year was 28. I saw two working bullocks and the men said they had just taken two more two-year-olds to work. I took a cursory view of the farm. They were making cock's foot grass into hay, a bad crop much stained by the weather and I understood the bailiff to have nothing to say in its favor if the crop and the weather had been good except that sheep would eat it. The land appeared a poor sand almost universally through the farm. There was a fair crop of clover, a good crop of wheat, some good turnips, a piece that had failed, 16 acres of good swedes and 58 of potatoes. The tares they were cutting was a good crop but not extraordinary. Clover was sown in the wheat, the wheat which was all red lamas was drilled and had been hoed at which time, April, the clover was sown. The clover promised to be a good plant. Mr Merest returned to the Hall and I to the inn to our respective breakfasts. I was shewn into a room with two travellers, one of whom was a very decent civil man and the other an intolerable coxcomb. I walked down to the quay and into the market, it being market day, and found the bushel in Cumberland which is in universal use to contain three Winchesters[1] I then proceeded along the docks to Wallace's yard where there were two or three vessels building but all of whom I enquired assured me the coal trade and the building trade and the general trade declined and laid the blame upon Lord Lonsdale insisting so high a price for his coals, which seemed an absurd reason while so large a coal proprietor as Mr Curwen was close at hand to undersell him. They told me here that coals were not put on board under 18 shillings per ton but this must have been a mistake as the Lonsdale men at White-haven assured me that they were put on board at 16 shillings

[1] The old 'Winchester' measure was abolished by Act of Parliament in 1835.

the waggon and that a waggon held more than two tons.
Mr Curwen's steam engine is one of the Bolton's 160 horse
power, has three boilers, draws 700 gallons a minute, draws
all the water with ease in ten minutes, there is only one pit
which is 135 fathom deep and is 16 ft over, allowing for the
bucket pumps as well as the coal from three different gangs
of colliers to be drawn through it. When I returned I found
Mrs N and the girls arrived and having baited our horses we
sate out for Whitehaven and we were all extremely pleased
with the approach to the place which is a moderate descent
down a narrow valley with the bay gradually opening all the
way down till the port, the town and the meadows sloping
quite to the water's edge lay directly under our feet. We
went to the Black Lion and the girls who had never seen a
port before were greatly pleased with walking all round the
quay to the pier head. Here were many vessels sailed out
just as we got to the town and one after our arrival. We now
ascended one of the steepest flights of steps that can well be
imagined and in some places the road overhung the sea with
only about a yard unprotected to pass; this appeared to be
nothing to those constantly in the habit of passing and re-
passing but it made our heads dizzy and my wife who I
thought would not attempt to scale the top sate down and
called a woman to help her. At last we got to the top of the
inclined plane and went into the enclosed place in which the
waggons pass and repass up and down it. The plane lies at
an angle of about 40 degrees and it was astonishing as well
as gratifying to see with what facility the waggons containing
upwards of six ton of coal were let down by a single man
who regulated their rapidity and with equal facility brought
up three empty waggons to be filled and returned down the

railway again. At the bottom of the inclined plane the waggons travel along a covered way under the floor of which is an immense coal yard and at different parts of this covered way are shoots which shoot the coal out into the vessels laying forty feet or more below them. These shoots are at an angle of about 70 degrees and that they may not overshoot the coal by the velocity acquired in descending so far so nearly perpendicular a man has a mode of stopping the coal about midway in the shoot and as soon as he stopped it let it go again immediately and the shoot drops the coal into the hold of the vessel moored against the quay side, which without this contrivance would shoot the coal over the vessel into the sea. We found a better way out at the bottom of the plane and got a most excellent dinner of soles and oyster sauce, loin of mutton, lamb fry, chicken pye, peas, potatoes, gooseberry pye and bread puddings, and so having ended our repast we sate out for Calder Bridge when having driven in a narrow street rather beyond the turn I ought to have taken the ostler laid rather roughly hold of Mrs Fall who plunged and reared till she threw herself down under the pole and in doing so tore off one of her hind shoes. A blacksmith lived near and we stopped to have the shoe replaced and the number of children, men and women who collected to see the shoe put on was quite surprising. We proceeded under Miss Caroline's conduct very happily to Calder Bridge and were all most exceedingly tired with the heat and exercise of the day and after our tea were very glad to get into the most comfortable beds we have had since we left Wath. We were agreably disappointed in this day's road, it being for the most part very good indeed, excepting the stoniness of the last part from Egremont very good. The castle of Egremont is a very picturesque ruin and the village is a large paved one, the Church I did not see, it was dusk when we passed it.

6th. Rose soon after 7 and wrote a note to Mr Stanley to say that we would call on him as soon as we had breakfasted and received for answer that they should be glad to see us as soon as we could come as he was going out as soon as he had breakfasted and we saw the posthorses from Cockermouth going towards his house as soon as the message arrived, we therefore set out at once and were ushered into a room into which Mr S came immediately and shewed us into the drawing room saying he would not take us into the breakfast room as there was a party there who were all strangers to us. He then shewed us his house, garden and grounds, the first is very large and handsome, the second had more fruit in it than I ever saw in any garden and the nectarines and grapes in the hothouses were indescribably fine and abundant. The grounds through which the Calder winds a rapid course in a very deep and rugged channel were highly picturesque and romantic, his wheat and clover very good and his swedes which were transplanted better than Curwen's, and his meadows and pastures very rich. We now returned to the house and were introduced to the breakfast party which consisted of Mr and Mrs Brydges, two Mr Lutwyches, Miss Stanley and the second Miss Senhouse of Calder Abbey. The gentlemen departed for Carlisle and Miss Senhouse invited us to go to the ruins of Calder Abbey which stand close to a handsome new built house and have a fine Saxon arch and an oven large enough to bake thirty bushels being 16 feet across. The Abbey was a cell to Furness, founded 1145, and the sleeping cells of the monks, two of

which remain, seem to have been on the ground floor.
I thought the ladies who owned and shewed it were the
prime of all I had seen since I had come in the North and on
our proposing to go to Wass Water and the elder proposing
to ride with us I determined to put John to drive and escort
the lady and to return to Calder Bridge. So we sate out
taking Mrs Brydges with us to Wass Water and were extremely delighted, though we did not get back till half past
six overtaking two lakers from Keswick on the pyebald well-
known nags and Mr Hutton the guide, botanist and minera-
logist for their conductor. These two men wrote their names
at Calder Abbey as the Rev Mr Lowndes, Magd. College,
Oxon, and the other as Mr Howard of London. The former
is a friend of Mr Tho Collins and is going after conducting
his friend back per Keswick to spend some time at Knares-
boro' and Harrowgate. He told us Mr Collins had written
to him to say he was very shortly to be married, he strongly
recommended the Sun at Ulverston and told us there was not
the least cause for apprehension in crossing the Lancaster
sands with the coach. On our return we found our landlady
had got ready a couple of boiled fowls, a ham, a leg of
mutton with apple dumplings and rolled puddings of prunes.
We dined and went to Mr Stanley's to drink tea with Miss
Stanley and Mrs Brydges and the Miss Senhouses were of the
party. Soon after 10 they moved and their servant not being
arrived I had to attend them to the Abbey and return in
the dark. The principal conversation at Ponsenby Hall was
abuse of our unpopular friend at K,[1] in which the Cumberland ladies are as unanimous as both sexes in Yorkshire. They
told us Miss Morley would be Mrs Comby before we arrived

[1] Mr Morley of Kirklington.

at Wath. We then went to the inn sufficiently tired and very soon went to bed determined if a fine day to start for Ulverston betimes on the

7th, so at 8 o'clock we left Calder Bridge for Ravenglass where we arrive at ½ past nine and I went to the shore which abounded with muscles and every stone was covered with balani. I put up a specimen and also two or three hard pebbles, perhaps jade, I found on the shore. I heard Mrs Grice (Miss Lutwyche, Mrs Carter's sister) lived at Ravenglass but we were puzzled about the road and the tide and I had not a minute to spare, so we at last started for Brampton and in order to see Muncaster Castle we took the road over Black Combe, a mountain, a steep nearly three miles long entirely over moor game shooting, but we were most amply repaid by the view of Muncaster Castle and the view from it. The situation far exceeds anything I ever yet saw of any house in the kingdom. We left the carriage and walked to the front of the house. And had we not seen Muncaster Castle we should have been sufficiently gratified with the descent from the mountain and the view of the Duddon valley. Nothing can exceed the richness of the view from the bridge just before we enter the village or town of Broughton, as I knew not which to call it. We had a little flying shower just as we came down the hill but have been singularly fortunate in our weather hitherto. The crops of apples on every tree whether close to the sea and exposed to the north or not are truly astonishing. At Ravenglass, which is on a ridge running into the sea, the apple trees were loaded. We dined at Broughton roast lamb, veal cutlets and apple pye, and set out for Ulverston at 5, arrived at ½ past 7 at the

inn when the house was so full that my wife would not have
the beds that were left on account of their straw mattresses,
to say truth however comfortable they may be in great houses
when they have a good woollen mattress and a good feather
bed upon them they are in general in inferior inns only an
excuse for no feather beds or next to none. By inferior inns
I mean the best inns in places of little thoroughfare. The road
was extremely hilly but I think we have had few finer rides
than this evening through High Furness down to Ulverston
to the Braddyl Arms, as we refused to go to the Sun, though
it appeared to be the superior inn, on account of the beds, as
we saw at the inn door three or four livery servants. The most
provoking thing is that we are obliged to leave this place
without seeing Whitrigg iron works or Furness Abbey which
was the principal reason of our coming here, to have the
disagreable alternative of passing the sands or going 25 miles
about to get to Lancaster, and besides the day after tomorrow
being Sunday no coach goes on that day or Monday and as
we conceive that to be the best guide we must not lose the
opportunity, and in addition to this unless we move home-
wards we shall not have enough money to carry us home as
it runs very scarce.

8th.   Rose at 6, a fine morning. Breakfasted at 7, sate out
at 8 behind the coach to cross the sands. The water nearest
Ulverston was up to the top of the fore wheels of the coach
and over mine but the boxes on the platform of our carriage
were not wetted, excepting half a mile the sands were very
hard and allowed trotting. The harvest was everywhere
commenced. The first sands were I should think barely four
miles over and the last barely nine, we were little over four

hours in travelling the 21 miles, waiting for the coach passengers to get up and down and the coachman made three stoppings. The first part of the coast is very grand and picturesque seen from the Cartmel sands, the coast seen from the Lancaster sands is far tamer. The road excepting the sand admirable. I consider the whole to be easily accomplished in three hours in a gig. Excepting the waters there seems little need of a guide; over the Lancaster sands I rather guided the coach than the coach me as I was generally before it. The approach to Lancaster is very fine and the bridge one of the most magnificent in the kingdom. But the commanding situation of the castle as a fortress is better calculated to shew the shape and strength of our forefathers' fortresses than almost any I have seen. There was not much water in the Lune but Cockermouth Castle and the Derwent seemed Lancaster in miniature. We arrived at the King's Arms, the most magnificent inn in appearance of any we have entered since we left home. I see a Mr Waithman's name opposite the inn. I felt an unpleasant apprehension at passing the sands but at this time of year I conceive that with a guide or following the coach as we did, which is still better, there is no sort of danger. I fancied the tide was coming in when we mounted Hest Bank, but for the last two miles had we been overtaken by it we could easily have driven to the shore so as to avoid all danger, though possibly we might have incurred great inconvenience in being driven off the sands where there was no road. I forget whether I noted an Irish Lord Tara, one of the largest men I ever saw, with two yellow and white spaniels, less than Sprite but longer legged, living at the inn at Cockermouth. We walked out after dinner to the quay which seems to have seen its best days. Only three vessels were in the harbour, most of the warehouses were unoccupied and the grass grew all along the quay walls. We saw one large vessel building the opposite side the river. One fine arch of an old bridge which led directly to the quay remains standing in the middle of the river, the two which attached it to the land on each side having been carried away and not a vestige remaining. We then visited the courts which are very magnificent and well contrived. Over the Judge's seat in the Crown Court is a picture of George the Third on horseback and in the civil court are full lengths of the present members for the County. We then visited Mr Gillow's celebrated cabinet warehouse in which I was much disappointed as there are fifty warehouses in Moorfields which have a greater quantity and greater variety. There was one very magnificent set of very wide tables which would probably hold thirty persons or perhaps forty. I wonder Lord Derby should not have employed his neighbour but when I was in town I saw a large quantity of furniture which they told me at Morgan and Saunders' in Catherine Street was for Knowsley. I found the Miss Senhouses were Whiggishly inclined though they complained the Edinburgh Review had fallen off and many of their neighbours had exchanged it for the Quarterly. They told me the Cumberland Stanleys were all Tories and seemed to insinuate that the Rev E. Stanley was a deserter. They rejoiced as men of all parties seemed to do at the dismissal of Mr Satterthwaite from the chair at the quarter sessions. The blocks of stone that were lying at the Castle to build a new tower were some of the finest I ever saw and Lancaster is greatly indebted for its appearance to the stone with which it is built. The Church and the Castle are all of the same. Apples are everywhere presenting themselves in abundance. For dinner we had some most excellent crimped salmon, beef steaks, broiled fowl and mushrooms, apple pudding and jellies. Had a little rain the greater part of the afternoon. It cleared in the evening. When we were at Wass Water we examined the view with Green's book in our hands and nothing could be more correct. On the east side the lake scarce a symptom of vegetation is to be seen from the mountain's top to the water's edge. Ulverston is a place of more importance than I imagined, as on further enquiry it supports a coach to and from Lancaster every day and as it appeared to us supports it well, as there were not fewer than a score in, on and about the coach which left Ulverston this morning. As the coach meets no other at Ulverston and goes no farther it is a strong proof of the consequence of the place or at least of the population of the neighbourhood. We saw many persons passing the sands with their shoes and stockings in their hands and indeed they are useless appendages to the feet and legs, for the sands are covered all the way with a glazing of water which would wet the feet if there were no river intersecting the sands to pass, one of the principal of which is that which issues from Windermere under Newby bridge. I have seen two chimney pieces of the Dent marble like that which was so much admired by Mr Meade at Mr Wood's in Wensleydale, one at the inn at Lancaster and the other at the inn at Workington where the rider told me Mr C had 12 natural children by one woman he was well acquainted with and that once on an insurrection by the colliers and his haranguing them and desiring them to return to their work he gave as a reason that he had been quite a father to them, an old woman who was by bawled out to him that what he

said was very true of half of them but not of the other half.
This not only shut his mouth but drove him off.

9th.　Slept remarkably well $9\frac{1}{2}$ hours and rose at $\frac{1}{2}$ past 8
and went to Church where the vicar of Lancaster preached
a sermon for the repairs of the Cathedral at Chester according
to the Bishop's direction. He made but a poor hand of it and
I am very willing to believe no one could make more of it;
he avoided very wisely the topic of the Chapter not keeping
the fabric in repair themselves but kept close to Solomon and
the propriety of all possible honour being paid to the Deity
and said that earthly Princes have palaces in order that their
subjects may respect them without ever touching on Carlton
House and the propriety of the Regent's contributing to the
Cathedral a small part of his expences at Carlton house and
the Pavilion. The preacher's voice was so like Captain
Gabriel's that I could hardly believe it was any other than
himself. We were shewn into the Duke of Hamilton's seat
by the desire of the landlord of the inn. The prayers were
read very well by another gentleman, five banns were published, there is a very good organ with a most delightful
flute stop, two voluntaries were played and the psalms sung.
The Mayor's Mace was hung at his seat door the opposite
side the aisle to which we sat and it was a very superb and
handsome one, two smaller ones were carried in front of him,
then two serjeants, then the Great Mace, then the Mayor and
one other Alderman without gowns, which surprised me.
The Church is a very fine light Gothic building and all the
pews were occupied promiscuously and the poorer sort
seemed to have the seats nearer the reading desk and pulpit,
the genteel people were mostly in the galleries and excepting

the Duke of Hamilton's where we sat I saw no people of condition near the pulpit. The Vicar was a Lancashire man, said shud for should. The chimney piece I mentioned as being Dent marble I found was Kendal marble and cost £2. 10. 0. when put up. Mrs Pritt the landlady a very civil nice woman and the inn very comfortable but the charge for beds and breakfast higher than anywhere since we have been out. We left Lancaster at 1 and drove through a beautiful country along the bank of the Lune on an excellent road to Hornby where we heard the bells ringing for church and ordering a mutton chop to be got ready against our return went to church where there were only prayers and no sermon. Service was commenced by the clerk and two other men singing the 100th Psalm, new version, to the old tune and ended with the same persons singing the Evening Hymn with whom the school girls joined. The clergyman's name is Proctor and he did the service well. He sent the clerk to ask us whether we would like to sit in the gallery with Mr Marsden, the proprietor of Hornby Castle, but we refused being already seated near the pulpit. The church is new except the tower which is a most elegant Gothic octagon building and disgraced by not having two or three of its pinnacles repaired, as the Church is by the patchwork of the old pews being cut and spliced in the Church and by two very awkward old miserable looking pews in the Chancel. One may imagine that the Church as well as the Castle is under Mr Marsden's regimen as the gates up to the Castle and one or two houses within the gates are actually tumbling down, unroofed and quite an eyesore to every person going towards his house. We continued our ride after dining on veal cutlets and mutton chops along the Lune and passing

over a bridge of a river called the Greta soon found ourselves
in Yorkshire, the road still continuing very good and much
more level than I had expected. When we were at Allonby
young Graham enquired with some earnestness of Mr Preston
and me if there were any shoemaker there and on our
answering in the affirmative he desired to know if he were
a good shoemaker, and on our saying we believed so, he said
he wanted only a strap sewn on his gaiter. The collection at
Lancaster was made for Chester Cathedral by the Church
wardens from pew to pew after the sermon and before the
Blessing. They seemed to have collected a large quantity of
halfpence. The sermon ended with the Collect on Charity,
the very bond of peace and of all virtues, etc. He stiled the
Bishop of Chester the Honorable and Right Reverend. The
finest shop I saw in Lancaster was Seward's, the lamp shop.
The inn at Hornby is the dirtiest and worst I have found
since I left home. This also belongs to Mr Marsden and is in
a dilapidated state though the tenant is but just come into it.
We saw several very neat houses, not large, between Hornby
and Ingleton and the churches between the latter place and
Lancaster were very numerous. Ingleborough with his cap
was gilded by the setting sun for the last three miles, and
all before us seems uncultivated moor and mountain, though
the situation of Ingleton is very picturesque on a stream
issuing from the mountain and just at its foot. We heard the
cryer this morning about the town of Lancaster crying
salmon to be sold in the New Inn yard and also a mare which
had been pounded. The public house at Hornby was full of
fellows drinking almost close to the church door and on
opening one of the bedroom doors to see what sort of bedrooms they were I discovered a fellow lying on one of the

beds on his face drunk, from these two circumstances the police of either the town or county seems but laxly administrated and very many shops in Lancaster were open. The only garden where I have not seen the trees loaded with apples was the garden at the King's Arms, Lancaster. Corn was ripe to within about two miles of Ingleton. The Green Devils have haunted me all the way and all the while I have been out. If any one wishes to know what sort of things they are, I can only say they are not quite so bad as Blue Devils, being no other than green peas a month too old to be eaten by me who am very fond of them when young. I have heard Mr Wharton, the member for Beverley, says all women ought to be hung out of the way at forty; peas are like them and should never be brought to anything but pigs after the pods are full. The aqueduct which carries the canal across the Lune about a mile from Lancaster has five very magnificent arches much more lofty than those of Lancaster bridge and as wide in their span. We arrived at Ingleton at 8 and after some good tea in a clean room we are now ready to take our rest.

10th.   Rose at 7 and as soon as we had breakfasted sate out for Hawes, having purchased from a man who pretends to be the guide in these parts some of the slate with the cubic pyrites in it. This guide told us there was a very curious cave about four miles from Ingleton near the road, so when we had travelled about four miles I got out of the carriage and went down on the left to a little village called Chapel-le-Dale where I saw some women of whom I enquired for the cave and was shewn one that was kept locked up about 16 feet over and 20 deep in which the water trickled down the rocks

which were overgrown with wood and romantic and picturesque enough. They informed us the name of this cave
was Hurley Pot but that we must pay sixpence apiece and
that there was another cave about 100 yards off, the admission
to which was a shilling a head; we therefore desired to see
this cave which is called Weathercoat Cave and very highly
gratified we were at seeing it, as it was forty feet deep below
the entrance and a torrent rushed in 40 feet above the entrance which fell to the bottom in one unbroken cascade and
filling the whole with the spray which as the sun shone
displayed the prismatic colours in a most beautiful manner,
being backed by dark rocks and overhanging trees. In this
cave the spectator sees only the fall as the stream issues from
a hole in the rock and falling into another hole disappears
and does not come to light again for $\frac{3}{4}$ of a mile. The whole
of the road from hence to within a mile or two of Hawes is
through nothing but heath over a very fine road, excepting
that it is hilly and uphill till we began to descend towards
Hawes along the Eure. At Hawes we got our dinner and
finding a party of boys going through Wensley to Plews'
school at Ripon I sent a note to the Costabadies to say we
would drink tea with them and if they had no room would
go to Leyburn to sleep. We had a very pleasant drive through
Aysgarth and Bainbridge and Swinethwaite to Wensley
where we found my old friend as hospitable as I could wish,
though from having met Mr Morley and Captain Comby
who had dined there and did not mention that we were
expected I feared my note had not arrived.

11th. We had ordered the carriage to the door after breakfast which was much better than usual and as they pressed

us to stay and I thought I might have a better chance of seeing Mr Claridge in the evening I acquiesced and dined there on salmon and boiled beef and sate out soon after five for Jerveaux where we found no one at home, but having viewed and fitted ourselves into the carriage and all of us having expressed how well pleased and satisfied we were with it we mounted the old rumble tumble for the last time and arrived soon after nine at Wath where we found all well, for which and for all accidents and chances which might have befallen us as well as for all other mercies God make me truly thankful.

12th. Returned last night and found letters from George Wheeler announcing the death of his poor mother after two days illness. She was a very excellent woman and a very highly valued friend of my wife's. A letter from Miss Allanson about a monument to be erected to her two sisters and which they had erected in my absence. I survey my farm on which scarce a blade of grass is to be seen, heard the particulars of poor young Palmer breaking his neck on the hill above Mr Blyth's by falling from the black pony I once saw fall with Mr Blyth in the Tanfield road, so uncertain, were I inclined to moralise, should I say is life. This young man who rode many years a hunting was said to be frequently in liquor, lost his life in riding along a grass field when quite sober from a horse that I had seen fall with his uncle who was more than double his weight and three times his age without receiving any material injury from the fall. I found my oats cut and my wheat cutting in three different fields, my beans vanished through the drought, my turnips very backward from the same cause, my horses all with coughs, my neat cattle and sheep as well as want of pasture will admit.

13th.　Began cutting the poor beans.

14th.　Mrs N went to Ripon. Carried my oats. Mr E. Carter sent us a leash of grouse. Found our apricots rotten ripe. Called yesterday at Mr Askwith's whom we heard had taken up their abode at Norton Conyers since Monday last, saw Mrs A. and S. A. Commeline. Received a deputation of the Manor of Wath from Lord A to Henry Barnett.

15th.　Wrote to G. Wheeler. Mr and Mrs Askwith called. Sent the gig for the two Miss Howards who came to Wath in the evening. The cats ran away with two of the three grouse Mr Carter sent yesterday. Mr Claridge and his son Henry came to dinner and told us of Miss Tyler having gone with Lord Essex to Paris to take care of a natural daughter of his about 13 whom he calls Miss Latouche and that Young the actor was of the party. The ladies are to be settled at Versailles. Received two brace of grouse from Mr Merest.

16th.　Henry Howard and S. A. Commeline at dinner. Wrote to Lord A. Wilfrid's day. Did duty morning and evening. Administered S.S. to Old Squire, and J. Waters' father and mother.

17th.　Carried wheat. Sent Mr Askwith two grouse. Gathered jargonelles. Heard of the Cooper's house at Topcliffe being broken open and silk shawls, stockings and handkerchiefs stolen from shop kept by his wife to the amount of £100. The same time two horses were stolen from another man and nine fat sheep from a third, all during last night. Received a piece of salmon from Mr Claridge by

Thomas, carrier. An account in St James' Chronicle of the assizes at Gloucester being deferred by the Judge (Abbot) not being in time to open the Commission. Ricardo the Sheriff objected to proceeding with the Assizes but Abbot persisted. When the other Judge Holroyd and Dauncey Jervis and the other Counsel were of Ricardo's opinion and sent express to the Chancellor to know what was to be done.

18th. Dr Whaley called. Heard from Mr Merest that he and his wife would dine here Thursday. Sent for the barouche to Jerveaux. A very slight mizzling rain the great part of the morning. John brought the carriage and a note from Mr Claridge saying Lord Egremont and his two sons were just arrived.

19th. Bedale Club. Called on Newsam and Mr E. Carter who told me he and Newsam quarrelled going home from Wath about J. F. N.'s ordination, Carter finding fault with the Archbishop which offended the little divine and he declared he would ride no further than Kirklington Bridge with him. At the Club no one but Mr Monson, Dr Dodsworth, Mr Carter, Mr Elsley and B. N. Drank tea at Mr Carter's. Home about 11.

20th. Mr and Mrs Merest with a man, maid, and little girl, daughter of Mrs M's nurse, arrived. He told me he killed 20 brace the first, 20 the second and 9 the third day of grousing. Cut the first melon which was very good.

21st. The Merests left us about 10. Mrs N went to Sleningford. It was mentioned by Mr Monson at the Bedale Club that the company at Redcar having no place of Church of England worship nearer than the Parish Church at Upleatham which is more than three miles from it get the neighbouring

clergymen to officiate on Sundays in the schoolroom, who
finding themselves largely and respectably attended applied
to the Archbishop of York to consecrate the room who
declined consecrating it but applauded the practice and recommended a continuance of it. Now one question arises
whether clergymen doing Church of England duty in unlicensed houses are not liable to £20 penalty for doing duty
(preaching) in unlicensed houses, and another question is
whether the Court of Quarter Sessions is empowered to
license persons to do duty according to the rite of the Church
of England.

22nd.   Mrs Rob Allanson came to look at the monument
she lately erected to her two sisters in Wath Church and took
away the two Miss Howards with her.

23rd.   Did duty morning and evening and christened a boy.
(Wath Feast.) Expected Mr Assey all day. Received a brace
of grouse from Mr Askwith. Cut another melon. The hot
weather seems gradually declining with the waning year
without wind, thunder or rain as yet. Thermometer generally
under 60. Carried the beans yesterday, easily put four acres
on two carts, began cutting the barley and turned the ewes
from the front of the house. Read Armata, said to be Lord
Erskine's,[1] very unworthy of his name tho' his politics are
displayed which are pretty nearly my opinions and I should
therefore be more inclined to judge favourably. The allegory
(if it may be so called) is not well kept up, but degenerates
into matter of fact and he often slips as when he calls the
representatives of Armata the *Commons* he forgets that term

---

[1] Erskine's authorship of this political romance was afterwards
acknowledged.

applies only to the representatives of the people of England. He talks of an island sitting on a promontory and yet for all that I doubt whether it is his work or not.

24th. Mr Assey did not arrive yesterday, went in the morning to Ripon to elect Managers for the Ripon Assemblies, elected Charnock, Hodson and Morton and put off the first ball till October. Mr and Mrs Askwith, Dr and Mrs Harrison dined here. Mr Assey did not make his appearance today. Mrs A told my wife that Sarah Anne was extremely deficient in common politeness insomuch that she never offered her the least assistance in any sort of work she might be about, never offers to ring the bell, open the door, takes precedence of almost everyone that comes to the house, even of Mrs A's mother Mrs Harrison. Bought a backgammon board and men. Carried the last of my oats and all the wheat that was cut. Saw by the papers that the stables of the inn at Lancaster were burnt down at the Assize and that seven horses belonging to the lawyers had been burnt and two more very much injured on Tuesday night last.

25th. Mr Assey arrived about 12 noon via Leeds from Carlisle. N.B. He is not an Irishman but came from Bowness on Windermere via Kendal and Leeds for the sake of the coaches and at ½ past 7 Mr John Graham arrived by the mail from Carlisle and was set down at York Gate. Mr Assey a very good-humoured agreeable gentlemanly man and quite handsome enough for Little Bit. Graham told us that we were regarded at Allonby after we left it as the proudest of all mortals and that tho' we had associated with him at Allonby and told him we should be glad to see him at Wath, that if he tried us we should not speak to him. That these two girls were good-natured enough girls but that the other who was somewhat older was quite brilliant. Got up early this morning to make the Chester Cathedral sermon and found it but stupid work. Heard of a famous dandy at Harrowgate of the name of Stewart, a relative of Lord Castlereagh, who being asked by the Master of Ceremonies to dance enquired of him if the lady he meant to introduce him to was handsome, and being told she was he enquired if she was rich, and being told she had a good fortune asked if she danced well and being answered in the affirmative said, "Trot her out". When he came to her he took out his quizzing glass and having eyed the lady some time through it says to the M.C. "Trot her back again".

26th. Drove Mr Assey, Mrs N, and the girls to Studley. Mr A went on the box and was somewhat annoyed that Graham did not return on it with me who kept his seat in the barouche with the ladies. At Studley we saw fifteen carriages besides our own of which Sir D. Baird's and his ladies' was one. This was the first time of using the barouche which met with the approbation of us all. Sold eight sheep to J. Humphries for £21 to be killed off by the end of next month.

27th. Rained a good deal of small rain without its wetting much. Hauled two loads of barley. Got up to the sermon without much progress. Played chess with Mr Assey who beat me very much, I attribute it to playing with the red men instead of the white to which I am most accustomed. This evening Mr Graham went in the gig to York Gate to take the mail, he seems a very well disposed agreeable young man who talks rather more than I think is quite pleasant.

28th. Played at chess again with Mr Assey and beat him pretty easily with the white men. G. Serjeantson, Mr and Mrs E. Carter and J. Newsam called. I carried Assey to Ripon in the gig and brought back the two Miss Howards. Assey told me that in consequence of J. Fendall when Governor of Java not admitting of some allowances which were charged in the accounts of a Colonel Yule, the Colonel followed J. F. to Calcutta and calling one morning upon him, told him that he was going to lay his case before the Governor General unless he chose to alter his determination. J. F. told him he had considered the matter well before he had decided and saw no reason to alter his decision. Upon which the Colonel immediately pushed his papers in J. F.'s face, brushed them across it and told him to take it as a personal insult. J. F. immediately sent for Assey for the purpose of sending him to Yule to call him out, but Assey very wisely told him that nothing could be more absurd than resenting an affront he had received for what he had done in his public capacity, that he was amenable only to the Supreme Government and not to any individual, especially to one inferior in rank and who had been guilty of the gravest breach of subordination. J. F. was not at all convinced by what Assey said to him but was at length prevailed upon to let Assey call on his friend Mr Palmer who immediately saw the impropriety of J. F. going out with Yule and they both went together to Mr Edmonston who went with them to Mr Dowdeswell, both being members of Council and Edmonston being Lt Governor. They reported the case to Lord Hastings[1] who immediately wrote to J. F. and ordered him by no means to think of meeting Yule and ordered a

[1] Governor-General of Bengal.

prosecution against Yule in the Civil Court for the assault and likewise a Court Martial to try him for insolence to his superior authorities, and told him that nothing but the most unqualified apology to J. F. and to the Government should stay the proceedings of both courts against him and that it must depend on J. F. after all whether he would accept the apology as unless J. F. consented to accept it proceedings should be carried on in both courts against him. Yule offered to make any apology which J. F. agreed to accept very readily as he had no malice against him and the Marquis of Hastings dictating the apology which Yule made both to J. F. and the Government the affair ended. Lord Hastings and the public in general at Calcutta thought it an aggravation of Yule's conduct that J. F. was not recovered at the time of the insult from a severe illness and that he took no precaution not to disturb J. F.'s family when he made his preposterous visit. Assey said he thought the affair very much delayed J. F.'s recovery.

29th. Meeting at the Oak Tree. Received the Chief Constable's report of the deficiency of Weights and Measures. The two greatest defaulters were two Methodist preachers, both grocers, one at Leeming and one at Tanfield. The Leeming man fined in the full penalty. Col Serjeantson and Mr Morley were both present, Morley came from Harrowgate and told us all the Costabadies except Miss C and Fanny were there and that they returned Tuesday next and were going to Scarboro' after their return. Mr Milnes was with them. I thought the black mare would have died of a violent fever occasioned by a kick given her as we suspect by the black poney as it was evidently done by a horse that had

LOUISA, MARY AND HARRIET

daughters of John Fendall of Bengal

shoes on. The tendon and nerves were cut through of the hind leg and another wound under her tail. However she is in a fair way as the fever is abated. She was twice bled. Henry Howard came to dinner and Dr Whaley came to invite us to dine with him on Monday and go to the horsemanship which is now exhibiting every night at Ripon. Finished my sermon last night for the repair of Chester Cathedral. Finished carrying the Soulmas field of barley.

30th.   Preached this morning according to the direction of the Bishop of Chester for the repair of the Chester Cathedral and obtained by my eloquence thirty shillings and as soon as the sermon was over I sent the Churchwardens round after the example of Lancaster and as soon as they had collected gave the Blessing. Did duty in the evening also. S. A. Commeline dined here. Almost all the farmers contributed something and the collection was quite as much as could have been expected considering that our own tower is not yet paid for; if my parishioners were not edified I think it was not my fault but the Bishop's, I am however inclined to think they were informed. I wrote to Mr Claridge and sent to Mr E. Carter and Mr Newsam to meet us tomorrow at Ripon. I think the collection today would have been greater had the last instalment for our tower, which was built at the sole expence of the parish and cost £500, been paid and I cannot help thinking that this would be the best mode of repairing all ecclesiastical buildings by a Church Rate to be paid by instalments. The parish of Wath which cannot be considered as particularly opulent has borne the burden of paying off the principal and interest of £500 in five years with very little inconvenience and what a light

burden would the £7000 at which the repairs of Chester
Cathedral are estimated have been borne in the same period
by the whole diocese! And I am of opinion that the new
Churches will be more easily built by some such plan as this
than by any other mode.

31st. Went with my wife and the girls, the two Miss
Howards, Mr Newsam and our man John in and about the
barouche to dine at Dr Whaley's who was gone to Burton,
taking E. Carter's in the way. We met at dinner Dr Thorpe
(who was also going to Burton to meet Dr Whaley in a
consultation) and Henry Howard, his sisters not dining but
coming to join the party after dinner to proceed together
with a Miss Broud to the Circus of Horsemanship to the
benefit of Miss Bannister a famous equestrian heroine who
did all the sword exercise standing on a horse at full speed
and afterwards danced on the tight wire with great elegance
and grace, did the platoon exercise on the wire and fired a
gun which first misfired and afterwards hung fire which was
more than enough to have thrown her off her guard and
consequently off the wire if her nerves had not been uncommonly strong. She was a pretty girl and very neatly
grown excepting that her legs and ancles were rather large
possibly made so by constant exertion in riding and dancing.
The horsemanship by Mr Bridges was truly astonishing and
also the agility of the clown who threw a Somerset over five
horses. Bridges' most extraordinary feats were leaping over
a table at least three feet wide from the back of a galloping
horse and alighting on his back again and afterwards leaping
head first through a balloon (a hoop covered with paper)
from the horse and alighting again on his feet on the horse's

back. We got home about twelve. I sent Henry in the morning to Thirsk for my certificate and his own. A party of servants, etc, to the number of fourteen went to the horsemanship from Wath and Melmerby.

September 1st. This morning was ushered in by a thunder clap at six and a pretty good sprinkling of rain upon our thirsty land which continued at intervals great part of the day so much as prevented me going out to shoot till after dinner, when I was driven home by a clearing shower that wetted my wife through. I went into Cass's which saved me and I saw her recovering from a salivation. Read Marco Polo's Travels which are amusing enough tho' containing a pretty large collection of absurdities and wonderful tales of enchantments and sorceries and miracles. He insists upon the descendants of Alexander by the daughter of Darius being in possession of the throne of Balashan a district of Persia in the year 1270. His account of the nations who always accommodated strangers with the females of their families as a means of making a visit pleasant to them is the only one I have met with where mothers, wives, sisters or daughters are all at the service of the visitor and the more the women are attended to the more they think themselves honoured.

2nd. Went shooting but could hardly find any birds, got only a shot or two and missed. Met Mr Askwith, also complained much of the scarcity of game, had killed three birds. I hear F. Alman had been shooting in the rain Tuesday on Middleton. Heard Tommy Proctor was gone to gaol for a debt to late Mr I'Anson. As soon as I awoke Betsy Mills came into the room and told me the black mare had broken the leg that had been kicked short off and requested to know whether she must not be killed for which I gave orders immediately. I apprehend the bone had been broken at the first. My wife had a letter yesterday from M. N. junior and I had one today and also a long one from Mr Howard about the Bullo Pill and J. F.'s selling the Hereford estate. Mrs N had a letter from Miss Williams giving her account of the moderation and forbearance with which Col Wood's party bore their victory over the Morgans.

3rd.   Went out again shooting, beat all Middleton without finding a bird till I came on Hind's farm at York Gate. Met Hind who said there were both hares and partridges on his farm. Henry killed a hare yesterday with the greyhounds. It rained hard this evening from 9, began about 7 to rain a little. Vegetation does not show itself much improved by the rain. Carried three loads of barley from Middleton field. My boy Tom went to Ripon to see the horsemanship without leave but I found that old Clarkson had gone with him, that the house being but a very thin one they performed scarcely half as many feats as they performed Monday evening.

4th.   Went shooting with Mr Newsam who dined here, had no sport, at least killed only one hare at 14 shots, eight per Newsam and six per me. Received a letter from M. N. junior who is quizzed constantly as she says about James Martin and they say Handford and his wife both want him to make her an offer. By her mentioning J. M. yesterday to her mother and again today to me, I suspect that she suspects there is some truth in her uncle's folly. Qu'en pense't elle? As my wife's maxim is pretty true that no woman knows very well what answer she shall give before the question is asked, I suspect she thinks there is a chance the question will be asked. Quel réponse fera't elle? I think if they were to marry there would be fire and tow. I should think the gentleman exactly cut out to play Petruchio before any man that I know and the only chance for a quiet life would be her not attempting the character of Catherine. I should not like for her to marry him if he is either an unbeliever or a Deist, as to his eccentricities they concern merely her taste and humour and I care little about them. I record now that if we should come to a discussion, I may have proof of maintaining an uniform if not a correct opinion.

5th. Went out and marked trees for posts and rails. Went shooting, met Mr Askwith, killed a leveret, engaged to go with him Monday, engaged ourselves to dine with Mrs Hardcastle. Finished Marco Polo, a very curious book for the time in which it was written, wonderfully accurate in the account of the people, bating his miracles and sorceries, which was the fault of his age rather than himself, contemporary with our Edward the first. Received a letter from Mr Church about Canal shares, also from Lees to say the hurdles were shipped for York and the freight paid. Henry killed a hare with the greyhounds, sent four pigeons to Mrs Fall and a hare to Mr Hattersley. Mrs N rode yesterday to Morley's. Finished cutting all the corn yesterday, began to plow the fallow.

6th. Did duty morning and evening. A woman who has lain in of a bastard child at Nunwick at Jacky Cook's came to be churched, I refused to church her as not belonging to this parish for I think it an impropriety to return thanks and pronounce a man happy who has a quiver full of bastards, this ceremony is not used in the South when women are brought to bed of illegitimate children and I think it very clear that our Church never intended this form of prayer to be used for them. Proceeded with Denham's Physico-Theology. Read Hurd's sermon on "Every soul shall be salted with fire", an odd mode of preaching, he seems to give two guesses at the meaning of the passage and tells his audience they may take which they like. I think that where a preacher gives his audience such a latitude as to tell them that either may be right they will assume another position, that both may be wrong. Wrote to Church about dividend on B and A canal shares, and M. N. junior.

7th. Went shooting and killed two brace of partridges. Read Fellowes' Visit to the Monks of La Trappe. Finished my harvest entirely with the barley in Middleton field. Heard from M. N. junior's letter to Caroline that James Commeline had accepted the living of Norton St Philip to my very great surprise as I offered to ask the Bishop of Bath and Wells to let me resign it to him after I had made the same offer to J. F. N. and he had refused it. Got a thorn into my arm or at least scratched it so as to feel considerable inconvenience from it. Bad account of the Queen in today's St James' Chronicle.[1]

8th. Went shooting and killed nothing. Had Anthony Guyll repairing the wall round the shrubbery which he began yesterday and Clarkson felling trees and putting stoops and rails round the ricks. Mr J. Dalton called here and Miss Smith. Began a sermon of Christ's feeding the multitude.

[1] Queen Charlotte, consort of George III, died in the following November.

Mrs Newton went to Ripon and got thirty pounds at Coates and got an indifferent account of my chance of getting Proctor's money.

9th. Inchboard brought a complaint against Hodgson of Braithwaite for a violent assault upon his apprentice. Received a letter from W. Fendall to consult me on the propriety of purchasing a troop of which he expects to have the offer, to which I replied that I thought the chance of the reduction was too great for him to venture. Rode with Mrs N to Col Serjeantson, saw Morley and Mr Wilson shooting. In the evening had our Mell or Harvest Home which as my corn was all cut by Smith and his wife and Wells' wife was to my astonishment replenished with amateurs to the amount of 70 men, women and children as reported to us by Henry. Just had a glimpse of Mr Claridge's carriage passing through Wath as we returned from Camp Hill and I find Miss Claridge and her brother were with Mr C in the carriage. Saw Mr Hattersley in Richard Broadwith's stack yard go and hide himself behind a stack whilst we passed. Heard yesterday by Dr Whaley of the death of Mrs Monson who would scarcely be prevailed upon when he visited her to allow that she was ill and the dropsical symptoms were so far advanced that Theakstone immediately saw her danger and sent for Whaley who immediately pronounced it a gone case. She had been lately to Redcar and returned much improved in general health tho' her complaint which was an internal one was of 20 years standing. Saw a very bad account of the Queen today in the Courier at Camp Hill. Finished Denham's Physico Theology and read Campbell's narrative of a Voyage round the World.

10th. Went shooting, had ten shots and killed nothing, found on my return Lord Henry Kerr and James Fendall arrived. Dined at Mr Morley's with Capt Comby, Mr Wilson of Jesus College, Col Serjeantson and Mr Hartley from Harrowgate who lives in the neighbourhood of Egremont and who recognised us as having seen Caroline driving our carriage in that neighbourhood, he appeared a very gentlemanly and agreeable man.

11th. Went shooting with James Fendall who killed a hare and a brace of partridges. Went to dine at Masham where we met Mr and Mrs Lawson of Kirkby Malzeard, she younger than her husband at least thirty years, her sister Miss Burrow plump fresh looking wench, Mr Burrell, Mr Baines, Capt Porter from Mr Danby's. He is an oddish sort of man and I did not much like him, perhaps because he told me Mr Claridge had been proposed as a member of the News Room at York by Tweedy and had been blackballed as well as Atkinson the surgeon, as they admitted no professional men or servants as he reckoned Mr Claridge. He said he had lived two years in Newfoundland and on my saying that they used their dogs in that island for draught and various purposes he said he had never seen one so used in his life. Heard from Mr Claridge that my venison will come by the Glasgow mail tomorrow night and the girls had divers letters from India. Heard from Eliza that she and the boy were set out for France as from yesterday. Sent to invite old Mr and Mrs Carter and Mr and Mrs J. Dalton to dine on Thursday who accepted the invitation. J. Fendall got wet in going to Masham, returned at 11.

12th. Went out shooting and killed one bird, J. Fendall

killed one and Salt a hare. Mr Morley and Capt Comby at dinner.

13th. Did duty morning and evening. Mr Hattersley at dinner. In the evening received a basket of game, four partridges and a hare from Mr Claridge and a packet of correspondence on the subject of Costabadie having gone shooting on Lord Ailesbury's land near Jerveaux. I am very sorry for it as Costabadie will be very much annoyed and a forbidding to shoot is always a closing of intercourse between the forbidder and the forbidden and I am pretty sure this case will not prove an exception. I was very sorry also on Mr Claridge's account as it is a confirmation of what I have heard urged against Mr C whenever almost his name has been brought up, viz: there is no certainty in an agent, he is Mr Claridge as long as suits his purpose to associate with the gentlemen of the country but when it suits his purpose he then is only Lord A's agent or steward. No one believes that Lord A would refuse anyone liberty to shoot that Mr Claridge would approve, and everyone believes that when any person is referred for leave by Mr Claridge to Lord A or by Lord A to Mr Claridge that the answer he will receive has been prearranged between them; and if it were not so there could not exist that excellent understanding between them which does exist. Powlett's saying he would not sit down with C because he was a steward was one of the greatest pieces of impudence that ever came out of the mouth of the son of a country attorney. Sent hares to Wriggleworth, Burnell, Mrs Mason and Mrs I'Anson, partridges to Law Daniel. Requested Howard to prepare a security for Bellerby tenants. No Bedale Club today in consequence of Mrs Monson's death. Received a haunch of venison from Lord A, invited a party who all come but the Claridges who sent word they will come Friday. Letters from India request the girls not to write double letters on account of postage. Took Dr Whaley a brace of birds and a hare to Howards and a basket of Carlisle codlins. No rain here though the river was bank high as we went to Ripon and Col Serjeantson was wet through in returning to Camp Hill from Craven. Nothing can exceed the abundance of mushrooms with which the country abounds at present. I should think 40 parcels have been brought in by different persons to this house within the last week. The blacksmith's boy alone having brought nine, fourpence a basket. N.B. On my asking Capt Comby whether he had ever been at Newfoundland he told me he had been there upwards of a year and had been Judge or a Judge in the Island. On my asking him whether it was usual to harness dogs in the Island, as Capt Porter had told me he had been there two years without seeing it, he assured me that not only was the harvest brought in by them but that all the wood burnt in St John's was brought to the town by harnessed dogs. Now who can account for Capt Porter's assertion that they are never harnessed or that he was two years in the Island without seeing it? Promised Morley some Carlisle codlins who promised me some strawberry runners. The Recorder of Ripon and Dr Harrison at Church at Wath.

14th. Rode with J. Fendall and Caroline to Capt Dalton's and Tanfield Hall Gardens. Began to set my Cape wheat. Received a note from Mr Askwith to shoot tomorrow at Middleton. I shall go if it is dry to Ripon but we have now prospect of abundance of rain. Received a leash of partridges from Mr E. Carter and Henry killed a hare.

15th. Went to Ripon to call on Howard to get Coates to pay Lees for hurdles and get a £5 bill to send the Bishop of Chester. Dined at Howard's, bought gloves and gaiters, saw Miss A. Compson and Mr Berry at Howard's. Left Anne to remain till Thursday. Sowed wheat white and red above the turnips in the far field.

16th. Granted a summons to Capt Barton against a woman for rioting at Asenby, also to Col Serjeantson's keeper against Isaac Hollowell of Sinderby for shooting. Went out with J. Fendall and killed two hares and three partridges between us. Received a letter from Mr Meade and one from Mr Claridge on the subject of Costabadie. I find by his letter that Mr Scrope has the deputation of the manor where C was shooting. This in my present idea makes Mr Claridge's inter-ference more improper as to the forbidding. The first note was all that ought to have been sent and especially until it was certain it had been received. Mr Claridge's reply to me is shifting his ground. His first letter to me was not, as I apprehended, to ask me whether Costabadie had done wrong but whether he himself had done right. Costabadie admits that he had not done right and Mr Claridge makes no reply to my argument about the main point which was C's veracity.

17th. Mr and Mrs Carter, Mr and Mrs Askwith, Capt and Mrs Dalton, Mrs, Dr and Mrs Harrison at dinner on Lord A's haunch of venison. Gave Burnell and Mrs Mason and Broad-with a hare each. The blacksmith's boy was paid 10/- for twenty dishes of mushrooms. Col Serjeantson's keeper laid an information against Isaac Hollowell for shooting without being qualified. James Fendall told a story of a woman coming to his tutor Mr Villers to request permission for her son to ride nine times round his pear tree with his face towards the tail of the jackass in order to cure the whooping cough.

18th. Mr, Miss and H. Claridge, Mr, Mrs and two Miss Howards and Miss Compson at dinner. Mr Claridge said that I invited him Friday to eat the venison which I denied, but on his producing my letter I was obliged to knock under and apologize for asking him to eat the venison when we ate it the day before. Went shooting with Mr Askwith who killed a brace of birds and I killed one.

19th. Meeting at York Gate, convicted Isaac Hollowell of Sinderby in £5 penalty, committed Hannah Cass to gaol for want of sureties to keep the peace, sent Brathwaite and Inchboard's apprentice to settle their dispute of the assault on the apprentice. Licensing day. Received a letter from J. Commeline still at Rome, containing among other things the following translation of a French Song which he says contained sixteen lines in the original which he without losing any idea has comprised in eight.

> Usque sit in manibus vel nympha vel amphora nostris
> Queis grata dederim basia lenta vice.
> Te laetus, Cytherea, et laetus te, Liber, adoro;
> Vino caldus amo, caldus amore bibo.
> Hoc tamen intererit nymphae vinoque, puella
> Grata magis juvenis, testa vetusta magis.
> Sic fuero potor felix, sic faustus amator,
> Cui vetus est Bacchus cui juvenisque Venus.

Before the two last I inserted the following:

> Si tamen annorum numerus par detur ubique
> Octodecim nymphae sint totidemque mero.

And in return I sent him these lines

> Canino's grot is famed in story
> For Paula's love and Petrarch's glory,
> A Mary and a Charles[1] that we know
> Frequent a grot, but not Canino,
> Where Charles his Mary's praise rehearses
> And breathes his soul in Petrarch's verses,
> While Mary tremblingly alive
> Smiles and forgets he's sixty-five.

I alter the two first of J. C.'s verses thus

> In gremio deter mihi nympha vel amphora, labris
> Utraque cum vellem non prohibenda meis.

20th. Prayed with Kitson's daughter, did duty in the morning. Administered the Sacrament to Kitson's daughter and five others. Prayed with Mrs Waters, did duty in the evening. Wrote to Lord Ailesbury about William's troop. Sarah Anne Commeline dined here. Henry killed a hare yesterday. James Fendall played at cricket and dined with Mr Morley. Mrs N rode same day to Kirklington. John Harrison at Church. Sent the hare to Houldrich.

> How sublime are the lovers, how wise they appear,
> While Petrarch and Laura resound in the ear!
> But Petrarch and Laura discover their folly
> When he is her Charley and she is his Molly.
> The name sure of Bragge is far worse than Jim,
> And then Cousin Jimmy's far younger than him.
> When tired then of Petrarch and all such fine names
> She at last may contrive to be called Mrs James.

[1] Mary Newton and a certain Charles Bragge.

If James should be cruel she then would be silly
In refusing the title of sweet Mrs Willie.
Should they fail in making an impression her heart in
At last she'll put up with her poor little Martin.

21st.   A considerable deal of rain has fallen today. Letter
from M. N. junior, also from Costabadie who takes no notice
of what has passed between him and Mr Claridge. Sent for
the carriage from Jerveaux. Killed a hare. The Bellerby
tenant came with the remainder of the Lady Day rent,
£5. 1. 0. Part of the large apple tree blown down with a
large basketful of apples. Read the 13th Satyr of Juvenal
with J. Fendall as he is to be lectured on it the first term at
Trinity Hall.

As soon as Little Bit is what they call *passée*
I think it very likely she'll marry Mr Assey.

22nd.   Dined at Mr Askwith's with Mr and Mrs Howard,
Miss Compson, Mr Morley, Mr and Mrs Walker and Recorder
Harrison. J. F. killed two brace of partridges.

23rd.   Drove to Boro'bridge with Jas Fendall, took my
two guns, found the stock was crooked so much that it was
absolutely impossible I should have killed with it, had the
gun straitened, the screw that fastens on the lock filed shorter
and the lock made easier to fire, left the Wogdon to have
the lock mended. It rained very hard at night. Gathered in
the barberries. J. F. N.'s birthday.

24th.   Went shooting, blank day.

25th.   Killed a partridge and J. F. a brace of hares. A letter
from J. F. N., his wife obliged to go to Calais instead of
Boulogne. The keeper of the Thornbrough Turnpike came

about the man's passing through with water, I told him as
I told Mr Baines, the water was his own, on which he replied
"Yes, but he sold it". That, said I, is exactly the reason I
determine he is not to pay. The water was his own and the
act excuses all the persons of Thornbrough who carry their
own property thro' the Bar. If they hire out their cart to
carry what belongs to other people they are liable. Received
invitations to dine at Mr Howard's tomorrow and at Col
Serjeantson's Tuesday and Mr E. Carter's on Wednesday.
Mr Barstow called. Began to plow Middleton field for wheat.
Received a note from Mr Newsam with bad accounts of his
mother.

26th. Had a thorn taken out of the middle of that part of
the body which Derham calls a large cushion of flesh by my
wife last night. I can't imagine a much better subject for
a caricature than this would furnish as one of the effects of
partridge shooting. It having rained the greater part of the
night it continued so to do. Mr Howard's friend did not
come shooting to Wath till 2 o'clock. Meeting at York Gate
in order to fine the persons whose weights in the Wapentake
were deficient. Received the Statutes bound from Langdale's.
Dined at Mr Howard's with Mr Kendall who has a place in
the Barrack Office and I apprehend lives at Knightsbridge.
The Regent's name being mentioned he took up the cudgels
so much in his defence, called him a good fellow, that I
would have laid my life that he had a place and was paid for
preaching. He was however a sensible, gentlemanly and
agreeable man but bored a little by our friend to sing with a
hoarseness and a sore throat, he sings with considerable taste,
apes Braham a little. Mr Walker and John Harrison dined

at Howard's and we did not get home till this morning by our Wath clocks, being full ½ past 12.

27th. My bill drawn by T. Proctor on Mr T. Wyche of Ripon came back dishonoured yesterday and noted "no effects". I sent a note from Mr Howard to Mr Wyche to apprize him of it and to desire he would immediately provide for it. Mr Howard's friend Kendall killed two brace of partridges and H a hare. A letter from Eliza at Boulogne and one from Lord A. Eliza says she was very much pestered by the police and passport fellows. Sent a goose to Mrs Howard. Did duty morning and evening and churched M. Dalton's wife. Caroline received a letter from Mary containing a secret which though shown to my wife was not to be shown to me because I say I hate secrets but I am certain that the secrets everyone detests the most are those they are told of without being told what they are and I should like to know who is the author of my not being in the secret, Mary, Caroline, or my wife. As this secret would reveal who has the highest opinion of my discretion, I have some curiosity to know it. Received a letter from Java saying the long lost fossils were shipped at Batavia on the 9th May, 1818, on board the Chapman, Capt Drake, and sent consigned to Joshua. Gave Wells £10 to go to Collings' sale to buy a tup lamb. A good deal of rain fell last night.

28th. Went shooting and killed a partridge. Called on Mr Barstow at Skipton Bridge with Mrs N.

29th. Went shooting with Mr Barstow, killed a partridge. Dined with Mrs N, Anne, and J. Fendall at Col Serjeantson's on a haunch of venison, no one there but ourselves.

30th. Dined at Mr E. Carter's with Mrs N, Caroline, Anne, and Jas Fendall, Major Elsley, Mr, Mrs and Miss Anne Gale. Received letters from Mr Wyche to say he could not take up the bill, from David Morgan about his interest, and from J. F. N. saying he could not get the house at Cross he expected. Went shooting and killed a partridge. Miss Ridsdale brought home my prints and begged me to put into her raffle. Mrs Commeline forgot I lent her £5 tho' we all remember it and it is down in my book with £15 lent H. Fendall. Wrote to Joshua for tea, and about the fossils and the Bibles not arriving.

> Had Little Bit with Assey wed
> And by that spouse some children bred,
> There would have been, as John supposes,
> A great improvement in the noses.
> But as his legs were not a pair
> I praise the judgment of the fair,
> Who, being very fond of dancing,
> Thinks nought about the nose enhancing,
> But wants a spouse she hopes may tend
> The figure of the legs to mend.

The Serjeantsons were full of the grand ball given at Woolley Park on young Wentworth coming of age, but Major Elsley says the party were made up of inferior persons from Leeds, York, and Sheffield and was by no means select. Physicked the young mare, all the horses in and out of the house have bad colds.

October 1st. Wells returned from Mr Collings' sale without buying anything but bringing with him a marked catalogue of the cattle which averaged £127 a head. One bull 621 guineas, one tup 156 guineas. Four bull calves as follows:

Diamond 102 guineas bought by Donaldson, Albion 140 guineas bought by Shaw, Harold 201 guineas bought by Whitaker, Pilot 270 guineas bought by Booth. Lord Althorp gave the highest price for a cow, 370 guineas for Nonpareil, three-year-old. Mr Robson gave the highest price for a two-year-old, Ruby, 331 guineas. Mr Maynard gave the highest price for a yearling heifer 145 guineas, Sweetbriar. Messrs Simpson and Smith were the purchasers of Lancaster by Wellington at 621 guineas. Sent to Boro'bridge for a cask of wine and 60 iron hurdles from London. Put the two-year-old colt in the traces between Miller and Grey for the first time and he went quite quietly.

2nd. Went to Ripon, saw John Fall who told me that old Proctor had thirty pounds of good money put in his hands purposely to pay me by his son when he sold his cattle at Topcliffe Fair but that he kept that in his pocket and paid me with the bill upon Wyche. Put the tups to the ewes, one of the lambs got by Rob's tup to Wright's ewes and the other with one of my own lambs to the other 12. Rob's tup lamb marked with blue on the breast and the other with red. Killed a sheep, weight 65 lb. Sent the first two bushels of the new wheat to mill. Mrs N received a letter from M. N. junior telling her of her applying to Mr R. Raikes for his opinion and advice about an application to the Bishop of Gloucester for leave to resign Biddisham but that he would neither give opinion or advice or interfere in the least in the business, how often have I mistaken an acquaintance for a friend! It is however a happy delusion while it lasts and not to be given up after many disappointments. Carried a brace of partridges to Mrs R. Allanson. Could not meet with either Mr Howard or Coates at home to speak about the bill but I shewed the letter from Wyche to the clerk in the Bank, Mr Waite. Sowed beans in the garden.

3rd. Sowed peas in the garden. Went shooting with Mr E. Carter who killed 4½ brace of birds, I killed 1 bird and 1 hare and James F 1½ brace. Finished sowing Middleton field. Rained the greater part of last night. Called yesterday at Mrs Howard's who told us that both at their own house and at Throxenby Robert Howard and his wife made them constantly wait near two hours for their breakfast and four hours often for their dinner, giving thus a very concise description of four fools. Sent Mrs Prince and Mrs Hattersley each a brace of partridges. Hear that young Proctor had been promised Mrs Prince's farm by Sir B. Graham and that Askwith had applied for Proctor's. Askwith told me that Sir B. G. had sent him a general deputation of his manors dated by himself but he forgot to sign it. N.B. Mr Carter's two dogs were very good but puzzled a little when they got slack after three hours hunting. Put on my new velvet shooting jacket first time.

4th. Wrote to M. N. junior and sent her a £5 Bank of England bill No 15810 to Mr Weller's, Gloucester. Did duty morning and evening. Churched Smith of Melmerby's wife and christened his child. The bride, Mrs Walker of Melmerby, walked to Church in the dirt in a pair of white kid shoes and had on a white satin pelisse. Askwith said that young Proctor was only promised the first refusal of Mrs Prince's farm. Preached a new sermon on the Syrophoenician woman.

5th. Began plowing Soulmas field for wheat. Bought three Quey calves at Prince's sale, a plow and cart bridles.

6th. Received a letter from Mr Allanson announcing that
he had sent a haunch of venison to be at Ripon on Monday.
On sending to Ripon it had not arrived. Gathered the apples
for the cyder off the tree in the seed field. J. Fendall went to
breakfast, shoot and dine with the Serjeantsons. Gathered
near a bushel of bullaces. Took Mrs I'Anson a brace of
partridges. Made the first bread of the new wheat. Winnowed
16 bushels of white wheat to sow Soulmas with. A letter
from Mr Howard about Wyche and Proctor's bill, calls
Coates an infatuated man for making his banking concerns
public, whereas it is only a proof to me that his demand on
his late partner's effects is right and that he is not afraid of
having his bank's concerns inspected.

7th. Went with Jas Fendall to Catterick in the gig, thence
on horseback to Richmond races where we saw the Comus
that was third for the St Leger beat easily by a colt of Mr
Riddell's called King Corney. We then saw King Corney
beat easily by Blacklock, supposed to be the best horse in
England at the time he was running and not to have been
equalled since the days of Eclipse. We then saw Blacklock,
the Duchess, Dr Syntax and a young one of Mr Powlett's
called The Juggler start for the Cup. Blacklock got the start
ten or twelve yards and continued it for three miles though
pressed very hard for the whole way by the other three
between whom there seemed but little difference, in the last
mile Blacklock was completely blown and when he came to
the hill gave it up and just got within the distance Post.
Dr Syntax won but did not beat the Duchess or the Colt by
a length on the four miles. Saw Major Hall, D'Arcy Hutton,
Major Elsley, Morley, Mr Bourne, H. Costabadie, the hand-

some man from Reeth, Mr Booth, Mr R. Booth, Mr and Mrs Askwith, Mr Jacques, Powlett with Fall, Whitwell, etc. John Waters was knocked down by two men but very little hurt. Called and drank tea with E. Carter after stopping to eat a pigeon pye we carried with us to Catterick and get home before ½ after 11. N.B. I had done my pye before James Fendall arrived. Met poor Newsam, who gave a very bad account of his mother, and Hunton, going coursing.

8th. The overseer of Marton-le-Moor after being summoned came and absolutely refused to pay the pauper who had been obliged to keep his bed a month and two days and left the house declaring they would not do it. Mr Barstow came here to shoot, he and I and J. Fendall each killed a bird. Mrs Prince's man applied to know if she could be compelled to keep him till his year was out or paying him his whole year's wages. I advised him to take what they offered which was £13. 10. 0. out of £15, and as he wanted six weeks of completing his service it amounted to something less than the administrators offered. I assured the overseers of Marton-le-Moor I would indite them and I mean to keep my word. Mr and Mrs Barstow and Mr Gilpin and his brother sent word they would dine here on Saturday. The venison arrived yesterday but not without having a few maggots from having been so long delayed on the road.

9th. Robert Newby who had been ordered relief by me from the overseers of Marton-le-Moor swore that since the 15th of January last he had received no relief whatever, and that he had been confined to his bed for 26 days for which time they allowed him nothing. The overseer denied the charge and said he was paid up to last Saturday night.

I insisted on the pauper being paid and that if the overseer could shew that he had been relieved the money should be refunded. The overseer positively refused but returned with the books next day and having deposited the money with me proved that Robert Newby was perjured for that he had often during the time specified received relief and there did not appear to be anything due to him. We dined at Azenby with the Howards and Miss Hodges and did not get back till near 12 o'clock. I went to Proctor's sale where the things seemed to sell extremely well, especially the shearlings some of which fetched £2. 17. 6.

10th. J. Fendall went hunting with Mr Bell and the mare fell with him into a ditch. Mrs N went to Ripon. I went shooting and we all got wet through. Col, Mrs, Miss E. and Miss G. Serjeantson, Mr Gilpin, Mr B. Gilpin, Mr and Mrs Barstow and Miss Catherine Jones dined here on Mr Allanson's haunch of venison which turned out very well and was trimmed by 12 of the party out of 14. Miss Claridge called on her way to Hexby and said Mr C was very much hurt that we would not go to Jerveaux when we were last invited, but as he absolutely refused to fix any time when Miss C pressed him and as he always has his prospective diary in his pocket, I thought he knew our coming there would be in-convenient and I was glad to be excused, as I did not wish to be prevented wheat sowing which must have been delayed while we were at Jerveaux. Miss C says our not going pre-vented her coming to Wath. Whose fault was that?

11th. Did duty morning and evening, administered the Sacraments and christened Gregg's child in the evening. S. A. Commeline dined here and told us one of Mr Askwith's little boys thought that Mrs Allanson's trumpet grew on to her ear.

12th. Went shooting and killed one partridge and J. Fendall another. Three men from Melmerby came to complain of being taken for and called poachers and accused Priestly, Auton, young Blyth and Terry. Found letters from Mrs Commeline, Joshua, Mr Claridge and Mrs Vilet, the last full of abuse of Lord A for his conduct at Burderop races. Winnowed 12½ bushels of wheat and began taking up my potatoes that the pigs might have something to eat. Mr Askwith told me that Mr Hunton had been coursing at Melmerby and killed six hares out of seven and asked me if I had given him leave and told me he had sent notices to Frank Alman and two or three others for shooting at Pick-hill. The masons laying on the coping and pitching a footpath across the road to Church.

13th. Coursed five hares and killed none. Ripon Ball, 90 persons there, played whist with very bad luck, lost 8 rubbers out of 10. Charlotte Costabadie came to Wath from Theak-ston to go with us to the ball. Put the colt in the old carriage to try if he would go well. He went very steadily. Finished the coping and pitching. Came back from the ball with Mr Morley.

14th. Went to the Bedale Club, drove Charlotte Costa-badie and deposited her at Theakston and took up Mr Morley and carried him on to Bedale where we met Mr Monson, who directed us to go to the Royal Oak, not thinking it safe to go to the Black Swan as Mr Bedford had been very ill and also his wife, tho' Mr Campbell said there was nothing in-fectious in Bedford's complaint and that his wife's illness proceeded entirely from her uneasiness on her husband's account. Two Mr Monsons and two Mr Elsleys and Mr Morley and I made the whole party. Paid my subscription and for my books, Francklin's Correspondence, Sir Joshua Reynolds, three volumes, Mme Laroche Jacquelin, Life of Raphael, Vaundencourt's Ionian Isles, Mr Monson requested me to go to Ripon to put some questions to the clerk and trustees of the Savings Bank.

15th.   Which I did this day and found only the Dean and Mr Oxley, the former instead of giving all the information and assistance in his power seemed to look upon us Bedale trustees as rivals, as spies, who came to see the nakedness of their land and as interrupters of their clerk in his business of taking deposits. Called at Coates' Bank and signed the deed accepting Proctor's assignment, Coates said we should receive 20 shillings in the pound. Called at Howard's and get the bond for the Bellerby tenant to sign and carried the books I bought yesterday to Langdale's to be bound, the girls went with me in the gig, lent the barouche to the Howards to go to a grand ball to be given tonight at Newby. Bought a cod and oysters, and Mrs Howard promised to return and spend a few days at Wath by the barouche to-morrow. Agreed to go coursing with Morley on Saturday. Received an invitation to Mrs Askwith's christening dinner on Tuesday and to a ball there on Wednesday next. The Agriculture meeting were afraid to dine at Bedford's and dined about thirty or forty in the Town Hall at Bedale on Tuesday.

16th.   J. Fendall rode Mrs Fall hunting and had two falls, which may teach a youngster to ride steady. Visited Mrs

Waters and Kitson. Went shooting, killed nothing. Mrs Howard and Miss A. Compson returned in the barouche with Miller and the colt, being the first time the latter ever had a female carcase behind him. Chest of tea arrived. A long letter from James Commeline to Anne. George Serjeantson called to lay two informations but I was not at home. Capt Dalton's man requested me to let ten gimmers[1] stay here tonight as they were unable to get home. Sent the account of Collings' sale to Commeline.

17th. Mrs Howard and Miss Compson went home. I went coursing with Mr Morley and Mr Askwith to Norton, saw plenty of hares and killed a leash. Executed the sale of the Canal shares and sent it to Church at Brecon and wrote thereon to Canon Williams. Was much pleased to hear that Mrs Askwith with her husband's permission invited Mr and Mrs Dawson to their ball which is to be given on Wednesday and felt very severe pleasure in the idea that what I glided into my last Sunday's sermon purposely to touch Mr A had some effect. I was well aware it was a very delicate and difficult point to handle. Anything direct or abrupt would have defeated its own purpose and it was no easy matter to touch him without being apparently personal or appearing so either to him or to others. The text however was such as could not alarm him or give suspicion and I rejoice he made the application which I fully intended he should to himself of that which was conveyed in the most general terms I could avail myself of. I was again gratified by the way in which Mrs Harrison said to me at Ripon when speaking of Mr Askwith's intended ball "And the Dawsons are to be there".

---

[1] Two-year-old ewes.

18th. Did duty morning and evening. Mr Hattersley at dinner. We ate upon Saturday half a dozen pigeons which were sent to Blacksmith for the parson, of course we thought ourselves entitled to them.

19th. Wrote to Mrs Commeline about the living of P. Norton. Rode to Ripon with Mrs N, went to the Book Club, present Dr Whaley, Dr Harrison, Mr Berry, Mr Oxley and B. N., ordered Woman or *Pour et Contre*, Hogg's Brownie, Birkbeck's Notes on America, Jones' History of the Peninsular War, Rosive's Life of Lorenzo de Medici, Richards' Sermon on the Poor Laws. James Fendall went shooting and killed a brace of birds. Letter from Mrs Fendall[1] to consult us on the propriety of taking Mrs N. Hobhouse and her son to live at Nass and on the salary she ought to have for them to live two months in the winter at Cheltenham. Winnowed 27½ bushels of oats on Friday last. Answered Mrs Fendall's letter and told her she ought to have £500 per annum at least. Heard Mr Walker was out of danger and Mrs Whaley better. Bought a new coat and a pair of riding breeches. Read Eustace's Tour and think he is the best dissenter I have met with, rather prolix about the Churches, especially such as have nothing at all extraordinary about them. Finished the last Tales of my Landlord of which the fourth volume is the worst. I think Walter Scott has the peculiar art of growing worse and worse and yet preserving his popularity. One poem after another was worse than the former, just so his Tales and every volume of every tale continues in a similar climax of deterioration.

20th. Dined at Mr Askwith's after having christened two

---

[1] Widow of William Fendall.

of his children, the party consisted of 19 and we had plenty of turtle. The party was Mr and Mrs Askwith, Mr and Mrs Trigg, a merchant of Hull, a maker of linseed cake and oil, a converter of lead into paint, Mr and Mrs Jacques of Easley, Dr, Mr, Mrs and Miss Harrison, two Miss Baines, Mr and Mrs Newton, Miss Commeline, Mrs and Miss Askwith, Mr A's mother and sister, Mr Grimstone. I visited poor Kitson after the christening and she died before night. Went shooting with J. Fendall.

21st.   Today Charlotte Costabadie arrived to dinner. Went in the evening to a ball at Mr Askwith's and the company was as under: Mr and Mrs Askwith, Mr and Mrs Trigg, Mr and Mrs Dawson, Mrs, Miss and Mr Harrison, two Miss Hebensons, Mrs Graythorne and her two sisters, Mr Stewart and Miss Dowling, Mr Berry, Mr T. Humphreys, Mr and Mrs Jacques, four Miss Elliots, Mr Rowcliffe, Mr Booth, Mr Dennison, Mr Hunywhill, the Recorder, Mr Clough Taylor, Mr Morley, Mrs Henry and Miss Howard, Mr Fenton, Miss A. Compson, Miss Hodges, two Miss Baines, Miss Askwith, Major Hall, Mr Nicholson, Miss Commeline, Mrs Thomas Harrison, Mr, Mrs, Miss A. and Miss C. Newton, Miss C. Costabadie, Mr J. Fendall. Heard today from M. N. junior that Mary Fendall was shortly to be married to Mr Charles Bathurst which gives us all great pleasure. The ball at Norton went off extremely well, every one seemed pleased and in good spirits, there was a great deal of dancing with some quadrilles and we got home by 4 o'clock in the morning. Morley told me he had paid the three guineas, the Justices' subscription for wine at Northallerton. I won about 35 shillings at Norton having lost as much or more at Ripon Ball.

22nd.   C. Costabadie amused us by comparing her own
neck with that of Mr Richard Booth, she returned today to
Theakston. Mrs Newton rode along with her and invited
Mr and Mrs E. Carter to come here on the 30th to meet the
Dawsons who engaged themselves to come here last night
and the Askwiths will also come here to meet them. Finished
plowing the Moor for wheat. Gathered mushrooms. Paid
Burnell the taxes. I omitted in my list, Miss Hodgson, Mr
Bruce, Mr Stewart, Mr Fetherston, Miss Cook and a man
like Mr Assey. Received a letter today from Mr Claridge to
request my attendance on Tuesday at the Bedale Savings
Bank in his place as it is his turn, which I shall promise to do.

23rd.   Dined at Mr Gilpin's, Hollin Hall, with Mr and Mrs
Howard, Miss Compson, Miss Preston, Miss Silvester, the
Dean of Chichester (Bethell) and Major Walker of the Fifth
Dragoon Guards, this last was a very agreeable man and told
good stories about the dandies, said there were poodle
dandies and bear dandies, that one of his acquaintance cut
his ear with the corner of his shirt collar, it was starched so
stiff, when he attempted to turn his head, another burnt his
chin by ironing the bows of his neckcloth after it was tyed.
Said a book with plates was coming out to instruct the un-
initiated in the art, to be called Cravatiana. That Brummell
had a large dressing room and kept two valets who each laid
hold of one end of his neckcloth and walked round his chair
while they wound it round his neck. Said young Gulston
of whom we heard as being at Harrowgate could neither
turn his head to the right or the left but when he wanted to
speak to his footman bent his head back till his face became
horizontal and then said, "John, go to Miss S" (who was

sitting within three of him on the same side of the table) "and say I will drink wine with her". John goes, returns and says she will be very happy. "Fill her glass then, John, and tell me when she bows." John did so. "Now, sir", quoth John. Gulston bowed his head over his plate but was not able to turn his head or even his eyes to see whether the lady bowed as John told him. I could not alter the opinion I first formed of the Dean of Chichester when I saw him at Richmond, that he is a stiff and a stupid fellow. Mr Gilpin grows in my liking as does Bernard Gilpin who was of the party and said he had seen four woodcocks the day before. We took up the Howards and brought them back from Hollin Hall.

24th. Mr Hattersley came to say that Mr Jones the curate of Pickhill had gone away without giving notice, that the Church had in consequence gone unserved for two Sundays and that the churchwardens had requested him to do the duty tomorrow and as he supposed till a new curate should be appointed. I wrote to tell Morley of it as he said he wanted Hattersley while he went into Cumberland. James Fendall, who tried to get a place in the mail last night and failed, went tonight to Cambridge. Sent Wells to sell two tups at Boro'bridge but he sold neither. Finished the Moor. Saw a brace of pheasants and 20 hares in Melmerby Winn. Killed two hares and two partridges.

25th. The clerk looked out the Lessons and Psalms for the King's Accession but I thought considering the state of the King the whole was better omitted and I read as for the 23rd Sunday after Trinity. Mr Hattersley had a fit returning from Pickhill. I desired him to let me send for some medical aid but he refused and they sent word he was much better. Christened Auton's girl and churched his wife. Transcribed a worn-out sermon and began another for next Sunday.

26th.   Anne went to Theakston in the gig and I lent Miller to Mr E. Carter. Mrs N went to Ripon, I went shooting and killed one partridge. Received an invitation from Mr Redfern to dine there on Wednesday. Called on Mr Hattersley and found him as well as usual. Received a letter from J. F. N. at Dover. Took up potatoes. I observed today an appearance on a new sown wheat field on which the wheat was not up which I never saw before. The whole field was spun over with lines of cobweb from one to two feet long and they were so close together that as the sun shone upon them they had a sheam of light as if the sun had shone on the water. They seemed to be almost parallel to each other and to be drawn across the ridges, the whole surface of the field which was more than two acres was covered with them. Morley sent Mr Redfern's note down by a boy of the name of Oliver and, as the boy says, bid him ask for sixpence, tho' I think he sent another note besides mine to ask Hattersley to do his duty as there is no chance of his being engaged at Pickhill as they say the vicar has resigned as well as the curate gone away. Sent a brace of partridges to Mr Walker and a hare to Mr Howard.

27th.   Went to Bedale to attend the Savings Bank for Mr Claridge, took there £20 of Mary Waters'. Just as I was going to Bedale Mr Hattersley came to me to say he was very sorry he had undertaken Mr Morley's duty instead of doing duty at Pickhill and on my saying "Why sorry?" he said,

"Because I have never received a farthing for doing 14 Sundays twice and going nearly as many times to do occasional duty on week days and as they pay me at Pickhill I think it would be very absurd to go to Kirklington where I am not paid". I said, "Surely he did not mean that he had never received anything", and Mr H declared he had only had a dozen of wine and a few pigeons. I therefore said I thought if that was the case he ought for his own sake to serve Pickhill but that he should let Morley know but that there might be some mistake as I could not believe Mr M did not mean to pay anything. I called at E. Carter's and found Costabadie expected and when I returned from Bedale I found Costabadie with his son and his daughter Charlotte and that the two former intended going to dine and sleep at Wath. I therefore trotted on lest there should be no dinner except just sufficient for my wife, Caroline and me. I called however to apprize Morley that Hattersley would not do his duty and not finding him at home I left word to that effect with Robert, and said that Mr Hattersley gave for a reason that he had not been paid. I found on my return that Morley had been at Wath while I was at Bedale and had seen Mrs Newton and Mrs Hattersley (Mr H not being in the way) and that Mrs H had not encouraged to expect that her husband would do Morley's duty or Morley given any reason to expect that he would pay Hattersley for the past. Morley walked on to dine at Mr Howard's at Ripon and I troubled myself no more about the business. The Costabadies, father and son, dined and slept here and I went out to shoot with them (28th) in the morning, we shot 11 times at hares and killed nothing. Set out about 2 for Theakston and picked up Anne in our way to Langton Lodge where we arrived exactly as their clock struck five and found Mr Redfern very thin but better than I expected to see him, Mr and Mrs Fombelle, Mr and Mrs Robertson, a very beautiful woman, and a Miss Buchanan of uncertain age, spent a pleasant afternoon and got up (29th) soon after nine, walked about the premises, heard an excellent account of Mrs Hobhouse, the lady whom Mrs Fendall writes me word she has consented to take to live with her during her husband's absence in India for £600 per annum, with her little boy and two maids, and having invited Mr and Mrs Fombelle if they were travelling South to spend a day or two with us on the road, they agreed to come to us on Tuesday, Mrs N having told them we were engaged to go out on Thursday to Mr Claridge's, we left Langton and the ladies ordering the carriage to be opened we set out for Theakston where we found the Costabadies, dined with them at E. Carter's on a very bad haunch of Lord Darlington's venison, returned at night with the Costabadies to Wath, where I found a note from Mr Morley the contents of which were as follows. "Dear Sir, Understanding from you some time ago that an airing in an easy gig for a couple of hours, a comfortable dinner for himself and his wife and his daughter and an occasional present of wine, game, etc, were a satisfactory return to Mr Hattersley for his services, I confess I was much surprised by the extraordinary message left at my house when you did me the favour to call. I should be sorry that Mr Hattersley should suffer any loss by his services at Kirklington. I have therefore engaged a clergyman from Ripon to do my duty in my absence, who has undertaken it without any wish for remuneration. Amongst my many faults a want of liberality I trust is not one. I beg compts, etc, and remain yours truly."

Answer: "Dear sir, As Mr Hattersley declined doing your duty I thought it right you should know as early as might be. I therefore called at your house and not finding you at home left the message with your servant. As I was merely the instrument of bearing the message, I think your answer would have been more properly addressed to Mr Hattersley than to me, and I should not have replied to your note but for the sake of protesting against ever having given you the least reason to think that Mr Hattersley would not expect a pecuniary remuneration for his services. I do not mean to set a value on Mr Hattersley's services to you or to estimate your liberality to him nor is it necessary I should, as I have no doubt that point will be effectually settled before your return in a letter from the Bishop of Chester to you". I must comment on the wicked falsehood which this note of Morley's is intended to convey that I should be instrumental in preventing Morley paying Hattersley. Is it likely that I who pay Hattersley without employing him should wish Morley to employ him without paying him? Again would not anyone believe that Morley, from his note, had engaged the clergyman from Ripon in consequence of the message delivered by me to the servant? The fact is Morley was at Ripon when I delivered the message and had engaged the clergyman before he received it. Again, is not the note intended to convey to me that the Ripon clergyman is to do the duty for nothing? I can only say I don't believe it and if I did I should only say it was of a piece with the rest of Morley's meanness to expect it.

30th.   Mr and Mrs Askwith, Mrs Trigg, two Miss Baines, Mr and Mrs Dawson, Mr and H. Costabadie and Charlotte,

Mr and Mrs E. Carter at dinner. Shooting with Costabadie, killed four hares, one rabbit, one partridge.

31st. Meeting at York Gate, sent a woman to Northallerton for failing in sureties to keep the peace towards another woman of Azenby. Of all the brutes I ever yet saw in a female form this woman, who was an Irish woman and a soldier's widow, appeared the most abandoned incorrigible. Morley began the subject of Hattersley and behaved in a most brow-beating style. The Howards and Miss Compson came to dinner and to stay at Wath.

November 1st. Did duty morning and evening, churched Siddall of Melmerby's wife and baptized his son. Mrs N received a letter from her sister.

2nd. Went shooting with Mr Howard who killed a leash and I a brace of partridges. Miss Compson rode my young mare, was highly delighted with her but became so exhausted after dinner by the fatigue of riding her that she was near fainting and had to go to bed.

3rd. Letter very satisfactory from James Fendall at Cambridge. Mr and Mrs Fombelle came to dine and sleep, very agreeable, the Howards here.

4th. The Fombelles left us for York and the Howards went home at night.

5th. Letters from R. Paul and W. Fendall, the first enclosing money for tea, the other requiring authority to act for his father in settling the accounts with Mr Davies and the Bullo Pill. Gave Mr Hattersley a copy of a letter to the Bishop of Chester. Saw the death of Sir S. Romilly[1] by his own hand

---

[1] See note on p. 101.

in a feverish frenzy in the St James' Chronicle this morning, in consequence of the loss of his wife. Went to Jerveaux, was overtaken at Ellington Scrubs by Mr Menzies on his way thither and Mr J. Tweedy arrived in five minutes after us, the latter we left there, the former set out home directly before us. I could not have supposed there could have been such a brazen effrontery in any one who had ever talked politics on one side the question to have so entirely turned tail and to have the impudence to call the opposition my side when the last time I saw him it was his own side and he was entirely a Bardertite, a reformer, an universal suffrage man and what not. We were very kindly received and found Miss Hopper there, a very nice unaffected girl, eyes, figure, hair, mouth, skin, very much *à mon gout*, her nose alone I should like to smooth, whiten and polish. Miss C looks very thin, thinner perhaps for her friend who is rather plumpish and as Madame Roland has it *bien meublée*.

7th. Went to Middleham Moor to the Fair through a hard rain and found Scotch sheep so dear that I bought not. Found on my return that Mr Morley had sent a note and a hamper of wine to Mr Hattersley, who returned it, and I also received a note from him detailing a long conversation between himself and my wife and me which never existed but in his own invention, to which I replied it was very painful to me to be obliged again to protest against his statements and to deny the truth of the whole of it. I told Tweedy of what Capt Porter said of C being blackballed at York and he was much nettled and said Miss C felt it most extremely and told me that game was the cause of it. I was exceedingly pleased to meet Costabadie and his eldest daughter, the first on account of its being proof that what had passed about shooting had not interrupted the intercourse, the day passed off remarkably well and my friend behaved most admirably. I could not have had such command over myself. Menzies gave Mr C one or two very hard rebuffs without being conscious of it. We brought Mrs Hardcastle with us back from Masham. I paid my rent and my expences of bringing down the carriage and packing the carving and the deputation. Found a letter from J. Commeline from Geneva, who seems to think I was influenced in what I said to him by wanting it[1] for John, a greater mistake than I ever knew him make before. A letter too from Eliza who seems delighted at finding herself again in Old England. She mentions having brought over Harriet Whitelocke and John having had a fall and hurt his arm in hunting. Costabadie told me he had not the least doubt C. Milnes would have had his son Henry if he would have had her and I dare say I have some young friends whom she would not refuse to escape from the clutches of her unfeeling, sottish father.

8th.   Did duty morning and evening, churched two women. Wrote to Lord A, to James and William Fendall. Mrs J. N. complains she can't tye her husband's neckcloth to please him now he has hurt his arm by the fall, so I send her this advice.

> Next time your dandy spouse abuses
> For neckcloth tied not as he chuses,
> Throw by that rag of starch and sope
> And hang him soundly with a rope.

My pluviameter, which is only a quart bottle and a funnel of larger diameter than the bottle, has been from the 1st September to the 6th November in filling and it was on that day

[1] I.e. the living of Philip St Norton.

after excessive rain that the stream which generally runs under Soulmas bridge had any water in it since June.

9th.   Sent for Charlotte Costabadie who rode the poney from Theakston, went shooting with Mr Robert Howard and had no sport, saw snipes, wild ducks, hares and partridges. Have not yet seen the thermometer below 45. Received a letter from Mr Thompson and answered it. The death of Sir S. Romilly was one of the most awful lessons that it was possible to convey by the case of one individual on the subject of taking care lest we fall while we think we stand. Here was a man of the most amiable character in private life and the highest public reputation both as a lawyer and a politician, who had seven children religiously educated and for whose provision his well earned reputation and great abilities procured an income as the papers of the day tell of between £16,000 and £17,000 per annum, that is exclusive of Sundays more than an average fifty guineas per diem, depending on that life which his own hand in a moment destroyed, not in the agony of an unexpected calamity but for the loss of his wife whose death he had for some months at least been taught to expect and for which he declared himself prepared. Can anyone think of this without reflecting on the nothingness of man and all his possessions and attainment in this world or not compare them again with the treasure laid up where neither moth nor rust doth corrupt? Can any man say what he shall not do when such a man as Romilly has done what he has done, and what can we think of Mr Menzies and his reflection that only eminent Whigs like Whitbread[1] and Romilly do these things? Is not

---

[1] Samuel Whitbread, member for Bedford, died by his own hand in 1815.

this in the true liberality of his party and in a pharisaical spirit, declaring "God, I thank thee I am not a Whig, I support the Regent and Lord Castlereagh and I shall never cut my throat".

10th.   Ripon Ball, a very good one, I won near three pounds winning seven rubbers out of ten, played with Col Dalbiac, Askwith, Charnock, Dawson, Dennison, Robert Howard, returned very late, my wife later as I went to the ball and returned with the Askwiths. Tweedy was very magnificent, I should suppose there were 120 there.

11th.   Bedale Club and the Committee of the Savings Bank, Serjeantson, Clarke, J. Monson; attended the latter but did not dine. I took C. Costabadie back to Theakston and called to offer to take Col Serjeantson to Bedale but he was to return to dine at Thorpe. At dinner were Mr Monson, Dr Scott, Mr Elsley, Mr Robson, Col Pulleine, Mr Carter (whom I took and brought back in the barouche) and myself. Dr Scott gave a long account of his curate in Essex who kept the commission for licensing him in his pocket for the purpose of bringing an action against the Dr for employing an unlicensed curate and a great deal more. Heard of despatches arriving from Sir Hudson Lowe at St Helena with an account of a plot for Buonaparte's escape. Caroline went to dine at Theakston and I returned to drink tea and bring her home. Charlotte Costabadie was at school with Sir Robert Wilmot's daughter, said to be run away with by the Banditti and her father killed in J. Commeline's letter from Geneva.

12th.   Called on Mr Askwith to go coursing but he was gone to Ripon, killed one hare. Mrs N took Mrs Hardcastle to Masham in the barouche. I met Mr Hattersley who showed me a letter he received from Bishop of Chester who seems to decline interfering as he can not enforce payment but where a curate is licensed. Dr Scott was brilliant.

13th. Dined at Howards with Major and Mrs Brooke, Mr Robert Howard, etc, Major and Mrs Bowen at tea and whist. At Groves' sale in the morning bought four stot calves for £11.7.0.

14th. Hunting with Lord Darlington at Sleningford, Lord D, Capt O'Callaghan, Mr Maude, Strangeways, Major Hall, G. Serjeantson, Milbanke, Harrison, Clarke, Hall, killed one fox, ran one to earth, lost one. Wrote to Mrs Wilmot, to Mary Newton, to little Jack. Heavy rain after dinner till 10. Saw Dr Scott at Sleningford and Col and Mrs Dalbiac, who came with Col and Capt Dalton to see the find just below the house.

15th. Thermometer at 8 a.m. 43, for the first time this winter it has been below 46. Did duty morning and evening. Christened M. Dalton's girl. Mr Barstow came to church and told us Mrs Barstow was brought to bed on Tuesday of a boy christened Thomas. Mr Hattersley and Sarah Anne dined here.

16th. Went hunting to Snape, never got to the hounds till they had killed near Carthorpe a fox found at Lew wood. Found another at Haskett, same party as Saturday with addition of Sir J. Beresford, Col Lee, J. Monson, Mr Scroope and Clough. Mrs N and the girls to Ripon in the barouche. Thermometer above 45.

17th. Dined at Azerley with Mr and Mrs Askwith, Mrs Lucas, and Miss Hodges. Received a letter from one Ady telling me he could inform me of something to my advantage and requiring a quarter of what I should recover for his intelligence. Wrote to little Jack.

18th. Wrote to Joshua and made him plenipotentiary to treat with Ady who is a hatter in Houndsditch. Killed a whistling snipe yesterday. Walker of Melmerby came about a pew in the church, having had a dispute with Pearson about sitting there. Found a fox yesterday in Wrigglesworth's turnips. Mr and Mrs Howard and Mr and Mrs J. Howard, Henry and Miss Howard and Miss Compson, Mr and Mrs Askwith, Mr Newsam dined here. Received the money for my Canal shares from Canon Williams by a draft on Sir P. Pole and Co and remitted it to Joshua, desiring him to acknowledge the receipt of it. Went shooting with two Howards, killed two hares. Newsam told us that Morley gave a guinea a Sunday to serve his church which is served by Charnock, Plews' usher, and paid the same for occasional duty, as F. Ellerton told Newsam.

19th. Went to Camp Hill to remove a man from Burniston to Pickhill. Col S told me G. Britain had been to serve two notices on his two sons and told him he was obliged to do it as Mr Morley had prevailed on Lord Bridgewater's steward to give him the order to do it at his very great regret. Called on J. Beck to reprove him for not receiving the S.S. Called on Mr Pearson and Mr Watson about a dispute between them of sitting in the gallery. Mrs N went to Ripon. Heard of the death of the Queen who died Tuesday evening. Received a remittance of a thousand pounds from J. Fendall in India by a bill on Paxton's, payable at six months' sight, together with a memorial to be presented to the Court of

Directors, how I can get it presented I know not but will do my utmost to get it done in the most likely mode to be effectual. Visited Mrs Waters, gradually sinking. Wrote to the Bishop of Chester, enclosing five pounds as the amount of subscriptions and donations of the Parish.

20th. Went shooting, killed a partridge, returned before 2 to attend the vestry about Walker of Melmerby's having a pew and it was determined that he should build a new pew for the churchwardens and take to theirs and take out a faculty to attach it to his house. Went to Mr Askwith's to tea and whist with Robert Howard and won.

21st. Went hunting on Mrs Fall and mounted Mr Newsam on the young mare, found a fox at Kirklington which ran under Carthorpe, Theakston, Leeming, to Holtby Tunston and Brough where the fox was lost and I had little less than twenty miles home. There was one of the largest and most gentlemanly fields I ever saw, Lord Darlington, Lord Tweedale, Mr Lambton, Mr Milbanke, Sir J. Beresford, Mr Barrett, Mr R. Pierse, Mr Barstow, Major Elsley, Major Healey, Mr de Lisle, Mr Harrison, Mr J. Monson, Lady D and a young Lady Vane and a young Vane, Mr Newsam, G. Serjeantson, Mr Clough, Mr Hutton, Mr Addison. Wrote a long letter to J. Fendall in India. Remitted five pounds to the Bishop of Chester and John Fendall's bill on Paxton to Joshua. Mr Newsam dined and slept here. Mrs N and girls in the carriage to Ripon. The hounds ran an hour and five minutes without a check and ran 45 minutes more. Barrett told us that J. Commeline was near being married to an English lady at Florence and would not believe that Lord Byron had written manuscript notes in the Fourth Canto of

Childe Harold lent him by Smith or that he vowed not to cut his hair till his wife was dead.

22nd.   Thermometer at 9 was 36½, the lowest this autumn as yet. Did duty morning and evening. Told Hattersley the Bishop of Chester had written about his affair with Morley to the Dean of Ripon. Read Tuckey's Voyage to the Congo or Zaire, seems to have brought on the mortality that prevailed in his crew by sleeping too much in the open air, by the quantity of women everywhere offered them and too great fatigue. The thermometer never being above 80 or under 69 and the St James' Chronicle says today that while British troops were storming a fort in the E. Indies the thermometer was 145. There is a letter of J. Hobhouse's in the St James' Chronicle addressed to the Editor which does him more credit than all his other writings, there is no affected display of learning, no acrimony, no pedantry, no dogmatising, no Jacobinism. I could have liked one only expression changed which does not sufficiently express the abatement of pleasure which he felt at having his father's name brought forward. I mean to collect a few philological questions respecting the meaning of compound words, for instance how came a word which in English probably means to stand under and a word which in Latin means to read between, to signify the same thing, *Intelligo* and understand. Young mare very lame from a stub outside the thigh above the hough a little, done Saturday.

23rd.   Wrote to Eliza and William Fendall.

24th.   Dined at Mr Walker's with two Howards, their wives and Miss Compson, Dr Whaley, Mr Bruce, and Mr Nicholson, three sisters of Walkers, Mrs Walker ill in bed.

25th. Dined at Mr Howard's with Mr Cayley, a most agreeable entertaining man, tho' perfectly deaf and dumb, has great curiosity, writes very quickly and speaks in a sort of growl which has such a tendency to articulation that people who are used to him understand what he says, he is a widower with a son and two daughters. The daughter who came to tea with Mrs R. Allanson and with whom they are staying is not dumb but perfectly deaf without her trumpet, his boy is neither deaf nor dumb, is at Rugby School and remarkably intelligent, the mother was also deaf and dumb, the youngest daughter is not either deaf or dumb. There was a lady of the same name at Mrs Allanson's lately deaf and dumb also. He played at cards but denounced whist as too trying to the temper and told a story of his father's scolding Miss Cayley, the grand-daughter, so much that she would never play again.

26th. Went to visit a poor man in the last stage of consumption at Pamaby's in Leeming Lane and went coursing with Mr Newsam afterwards.

27th. Went hunting to Lord Grantham's, Newby, found a fox which was lost at Devonshire Winn, found another between Macfarlane's and Hutton which went to earth at Norton close to Jeffrey Houseman's farm. Dined at Mrs Lucas' with the Howards, the Harrisons and Mr Newsam. J. Harrison told us he had given a hundred for Sam Parker's horse and that he should be much better pleased with having given it to G. Serjeantson for Lady Sarah.

28th. Meeting at the Oak Tree, I'Anson in London, Mr Newsam officiated as clerk. About 1 Morley drove up in his carriage by himself with post horses as coming from the North, no conversation passed and no notice was taken of him either by Col Serjeantson or me more than a nod, and we spoke of nothing but the judicial matters before us, he left us and we talked of him afterwards. Col S expressed a wish to know whether Morley had influenced G. Britain in forbidding his sons to shoot at Howgrave and as I was returning I met G. Britain at the gate of his field and asked him whether he had done it at Mr Morley's instigation, he said he had not, he had done it on his own account. How this can be reconciled with his going to Camp Hill to forbid the two young men by order of Lord Bridgewater's agent and apologising for being obliged to do it, does not appear but it was not worth my while to enquire. Mr Cayley and his daughter called at Wath while I was at the Oak Tree, expressed a desire to shoot and was very curious and entertaining to the girls, Mrs N being at Ripon and having met him in his way to Wath. Letters from India with a duplicate of the bill for £1000, from Mr Warner and from M. N. junior. Heard Jim Commeline was to be at home very soon, in London by the 10th of next month. Mare still very lame. J. Newsam went. Saw E. Carter at Oak Tree, borrowed coach horse to break in his own. I forgot to mention that as I was going to Newby yesterday a farmer at Copt Hewick picked and gave me some young gooseberries as a proof of the mildness of the season which I brought home in my pocket, being the second crop the tree has born in 1818.

29th. Did duty morning and evening, administered the S.S. to Mr Squire and Mrs Waters, christened two children in the afternoon. Wrote to C. Loder and Mr Gauntlett.

30th. Went shooting with Mr Cayley who shot two hares. Mrs N told us that Sarah Anne was to leave Mrs Askwith who had told her she expected a governess to do the office of an upper nursery maid. Miss Claridge and Miss Hopper came to Wath.

December 1st.   Went in the gig to Camp Hill by appointment with Col Serjeantson, from thence to Mr E. Carter's where I left Miller to break in his two horses to the carriage, from thence to Bedale to the Savings Bank where I had the interest adjusted for Eliza and Mary Waters, H. Barnett, Anthony Guyll, Bendiloe, and E. Mills, from thence to Wensley where I found a Miss Grey whom I thought much plainer than any person there thought her.

2nd.   Went to Bellerby with the Costabadies, found neither Thistlethwaite nor Allanson at home, left the bond and desired they would execute it and bring it down to Wensley,

3rd.   which they did this morning, found Mr C very intent on inditing the roads Powlett had obstructed and shut up in the neighbourhood of Bolton Hall unless the prohibition of C's shooting was withdrawn. Left Wensley a little after 12 and drove to Jerveaux to see Mr Knight who was not at home and then continued my journey home where I arrived at 4. Found Mr and Mrs E. Carter had been at Wath in their carriage with Miller and his chestnut horse.

4th.   Waited at home till 1 for Mr Cayley but the weather was too wet for him to come to shoot, called to enquire after John Beck who has a very serious attack of typhus fever and visited Mary Waters' mother. Today we had 16 at dinner, four of us, Misses Claridge and Hopper, Howard, Hodges, Allanson, Cayley, Mr and H. Howard, Messrs Cayley, Harrison and Fenton, S. A. Commeline, Miss Compson being too ill to come; in the evening they danced quadrilles.

Heard from S. A. Commeline that her father was going to be married to a Miss Washbourne who lives near Constitution Walk in Gloucester. Bought six scots wethers of Mr Blyth. Miss Claridge and Miss Hopper left Wath. I went hunting with J. Harrison to Butcher House Bar, found a fox at Howe and ran him through Pickhill Wynn across the Swale but no one followed and Lord D tried towards Gatenby and Newton House. Called on Newsam and found him cooking a new horse. Received surcharge of a labourer and a horse. J. Beck rather mending but Whaley says the fever is contagious. Saw two men riding in their carts, Lumley's of Ripon and James Appleton's of Howgrave, both in Howgrave.

6th. Did duty morning and evening. Dr Whaley called. As yet we have had no ice at Wath. Gave notice in the churchyard of my being to receive my tithes on the 15th.

7th. Went hunting to Cundall, Newby, Baldersby and Norton Conyers without finding a fox. Field very large not fewer than 70. Sold my young mare for 25 guineas to Mr Dent who tried to buy her for 22 at Topcliffe Fair. Wrote to William Fendall.

8th. Called on Mr Askwith about J. F.'s memorial and went on to Ripon to call on Major Bowen, meantime Mr Dent came and paid for the mare and took her away. Heard one of those Miss Baines who dined here with the Askwiths about three weeks ago was dead. Ripon Ball, only three single men there. Played seven rubbers and won six, three tables.

9th. Called at Col Serjeantson and J. Beck's and desired Dr Whaley to call on my wife who coughed all night, meant to have gone to the Bedale Club but turned about at Camp Hill when I heard that the Col had gone to York. Dr Whaley came and prescribed for my wife. Letter from M. N. junior.

10th. Cut a cauliflower. Miss Hattersley came and showed me a letter from Mr Morley enclosing a draft for £6 and a long rigmarole saying many respectable clergymen told him that was sufficient and mentioned only Mr Headlam, his brother-in-law, which Hattersley noticed in his reply. I guess the Bishop had written to Mr Headlam to tell Morley he had better settle it. Mr Dawson junior called to pay Sir B. Graham's tithe rent. Went shooting, killed nothing. Sold 12 bushels of wheat and 12 of barley and a pig to J. Humphries. Received a note from Major Bowen (who was to have dined here Wednesday) to decline it. Bottled a hogshead of Vidonia between Mr Howard and me, ran 23 dozen and 3 bottles.

11th. Dined at Mr Allanson's with the Howards, Drs Whaley and Harrison, my wife not well enough to go, Mrs Lucas and Miss Hodges, Mrs and Miss Harrison and Fenton in the evening. Deputy Lieutenants' meeting at the Oak Tree, a mutiny among the constables who refused to pay a shilling for the oath required of them as to the truth of their lists. Beetham of Gatenby the ringleader, all but two complied at last but Morley of Dishforth says he shall take an opinion. The Act gives a power to two Deputy Lieutenants to imprison all constables resisting their orders for a month without bail or mainprize. I was not a Deputy Lieutenant and so only one was present. Query. What is the custom in other districts?

12th.   Went hunting, called on J. Harrison, had a very good run for more than an hour from Studley and brought the fox back there; having lost a shoe and broken the mare's foot very much I could not see the end but the fox appeared quite run down. A small field, only Milbanke, young Dundas, J. Harrison, G. Serjeantson of the red coats.

13th.   Did duty morning and evening. Received a note from Miss Claridge to say she would be with us tomorrow. Burnell called last night to pay his tithe saying he should not be at home Tuesday. A note from Col Serjeantson concerning Whitling of the Oak Tree being out coursing.

14th.   Mr and Miss Claridge called, she remained. Went out and killed a hare and a partridge. Dined at the Harrisons' with Mrs Lucas and the Howards, Mrs Allanson, Mr and Miss Cayley, the girls danced quadrilles. Mr Richardson of Thirsk came over with a warrant against J. F. N. for £40. 6. 6. for his last taxes and behaved extremely handsomely leaving the warrant with me.

15th.   Tithe day, dined at Dalton's. The Costabadies came and Mr Newsam who went shooting and killed nothing and slept at the cottage. Received my tithe all but the £124. Col Serjeantson's keeper came and laid an information against Whitling.

16th.   Mr Newsam went. Miss Claridge and Anne went in Mr Costabadie's carriage to Ripon and brought back Hugh, Ackroyd and George.[1] The Askwiths and Dalton, Mrs Lucas and Agnes at dinner. Went shooting in the morning with Costabadie and killed nothing, heard Walker's wife of

---

[1] Sons of Mr Costabadie.

Melmerby was dangerously ill. Mr Claridge went in the morning.

17th. The Costabadies went, Mr C told me that he and Mr Orde Powlett had had a meeting and reconciliation, that they dined first at Anderson's and that Mr Powlett insisted on their dining with him the next day when he gave them the most splendid dinner that can be conceived and that the reconciliation seemed very cordial. G. Serjeantson swore that he saw Whitling ranging for game with a greyhound and he was convicted accordingly in the penalty of £5, half to the keeper and half to the poor of Carthorpe. Called on Mr Barstow and saw Mrs B and her boy and Miss Jones, he was gone to a Militia meeting at Thirsk. G. Serjeantson wanted to know of Mr Barstow whether Mr Bell's horns were to be sold. Called on my return at Walker's, found Mrs Walker still not relieved and Dr Whaley who called to see Mrs Newton seemed to think her case desperate as the obstruction was still unremoved. I administered the Sacrament to her, her husband, her mother and Mrs Nelson. Mr White came and paid Mrs Prince's tithe. Frank Alman brought me £30 from Trinity College for the poor of Wath and agreed to take his tithe yesterday which he had refused to do to Mr Knight and I sent Wells with a note to Law Daniel who had also refused to set out his tithe turnips which he is now drawing for his cattle. My wife seems to mend a little but looks very thin. Remitted by post four bills to Joshua, value £196. 19. 6. Broke the glass of the barouche the day we dined at the Harrisons'. Sent £41 more to Joshua, being a bill I received from Mr Priestly.

18th.   Went to the Oak Tree, found that the shilling had
not been demanded either at Bedale or Thirsk of the constables for the oath required to be taken by them on giving
in their lists. Found that Lumley's cart had not been out
on the 4th inst. and that it was Britain's, as Appleton's man
who was fined for the same offence knows both the man and
the cart and met him on the 4th both going and returning
from Kirklington. The Howards dined here and Miss
Compson. Went hunting, had no sport but a grand luncheon
at Mr Tim Hutton's at Clifton Castle, as there was a great
field I should imagine forty at least lunched there. Letter
from J. F. N. touching his surcharge which has determined
me to bring an action against Mr Wastell of Beaconsfield and
take the sense of the jury whether a person removing from
a place with an establishment too large for his means is
obliged to keep up the same establishment merely because
he has moved.

20th.   Did duty morning and evening. Called on Walker,
Chief Constable's, wife with whom I prayed yesterday and
administered Sacrament yesterday. Paid J. Waters his wages
by £10 cash and directing Joshua to lay out £7 in the funds
for him. Received the rent for the land at Sharow, £3 for
half a year due Michaelmas last. Received a box of fossils
from Java which had been thrown overboard at Java and
the box cut asunder in the middle at the Custom House and
entirely spoilt, all the labels off, etc. Mr Hattersley at dinner.
Law Daniel agreed to take his tithe on the old terms for
four years.

21st.   Went to Ripon with Caroline, found Mrs Walker
had died in the morning. Called and administered the

Sacraments to old Wilton of Melmerby and sent Appleby to him, who thought he had an inflammation in the bladder and was not likely to live. Got £20 in silver at the bank and £100 in Bank of England bill at Harrison's, called on Howard and mentioned J. F. N.'s tax affair. Saw Mr Rowcliffe who came this

22nd. morning to lodge an information against a man of Dishforth for snaring hares, to whom I mentioned the tax affair and he recommended a case being sent from the Commissioners here of whom he is one. I went to Camp Hill to commit Britain's man for giving a false name when riding in his cart and mentioned Rowcliffe's idea to Col S who coincided. I returned to shoot with Howard and try a new dog he had got from the Moors, the dog promised well though we had no sport, at least killed nothing. Miss Claridge returned to Jerveaux, having received a rebuff from her father for not going yesterday. We dined at Camp Hill with Edward Carter and J. Newsam, who dined here yesterday. A great rhime and such a fog as to make it difficult for Henry to find his way over Kirklington Green, he being obliged to drive us in consequence of John's mother dying this morning while I was at Camp Hill.

23rd. Buried Mrs Walker. Dined at Howard's with Mr Bury and his son, Mrs Lucas, Miss Hodges, J. Harrison and Major Bowen.

24th. Wrote to W. Fendall and Dr Geldart[1] who had written a very gratifying account of Jas Fendall. Wrote to Joshua, sent him a hare, turkey, pig and goose. Wrote to

[1] J. W. Geldart, tutor of Trinity Hall and brother of T. C. Geldart, Master from 1852 to 1877.

C. Loder and Mrs Vilet. Buried John Waters' mother. Went over to Ripon to rectify a mistake with Coates who had given a sovereign in mistake among the silver and I have not been able to make my accounts come right by £20. Settled with Wells up to 28th inst. Received of him £35 for barley. Drew a memorial or case for J. F. N. to the tax office. Paid Farrer £33 for a year's letters. Hear H. Fendall was ordained last Sunday and received a letter from Mr Claridge offering the Bishop of Chester's mare for £20 to winter to which I shall reply in the negative. Also a letter from Canon Williams to request me to ask my bishop to ordain a Welchman at Brecon I know nothing about.

25th.   Christmas day. Did duty morning and evening. The thermometer yesterday at 9 a.m. was only 20, today 24. Administered the S.S. to 25 Communicants. S. A. Commeline at dinner. Wrote to Canon Williams, Mr Claridge, Mr Villers, Waite, Farrer, Richardson of Thirsk. Frost seems going, thermometer 35 at 11 pm.

26th.   Spent the whole morning in paying bills, received Appleby's for the poor, remonstrated with him, paid him my own. The Howards came to dinner and slept at Wath. Sent J. F. N. warrant and statement to Col Serjeantson and Mr Carter and the boy with a letter to Mr Richardson's.

27th.   Did duty morning and evening, read a citation for Tristram Walker's faculty in the morning, addressed the overseers on Appleby's bill and promised them ten pounds towards it. Gave away the Poor and Sacrament money amounting to £37 and added about two guineas, which with the blankets bought at Home's makes up about five pounds and with ten for the doctoring, ten for the schooling at

Heldridge, ten for Bibles and puddings at home, makes up the principal parts of my donation to the poor of Wath. Told Smith he should have the bit of land in Tanfield now in Whitwell's possession. Wrote to Mr Claridge and offered £15 for the Bishop of Chester's mare. Heard my venison was to be at Leeming Lane Wednesday next. The frost and rhime went off without rain. Beans and peas look well, gathered roses and July flowers. Dr Whaley called, brought back the Voyage to the Congo. Sold the old carriage to Williamson for five guineas. Paid Henry his wages up to July last. Paid J. Humphries all but £10.

INDEX

For EU product safety concerns, contact us at Calle de José Abascal, 56–1°,
28003 Madrid, Spain or eugpsr@cambridge.org.

www.ingramcontent.com/pod-product-compliance
Ingram Content Group UK Ltd.
Pitfield, Milton Keynes, MK11 3LW, UK
UKHW040619240426
470322UK00010B/213